Religion and Human Rights

Volume 2

This series investigates how religion can both challenge and contribute to a vibrant human rights culture in different national contexts, as well as in cross-national contexts. It offers empirical and theoretical perspectives on the different generations of human rights, and generates new knowledge on the connection between religion and human rights.

All religions claim that their ethical aspirations and moral duties contribute to the well-being and welfare of individual human beings, groups, and communities. This applies particularly to the golden rule which plays an important role in the ethical groundwork of all religious traditions, and which is also foundational for human rights. However, to what extent is this universal principle actually observed within and between different religions, within and between nations, and within the secular world? To what extent (if at all) do religions contribute to the realisation of human rights or to the prevention of violations of human rights? This series addresses these questions by means of an empirical and comparative approach. Each volume focuses on specific human rights. This second volume offers an empirical perspective on the first generation of civil human rights.

More information about this series at http://www.springer.com/series/15597

Hans-Georg Ziebertz • Carl Sterkens
Editors

Religion and Civil Human Rights in Empirical Perspective

Springer

Editors
Hans-Georg Ziebertz
Faculty of Theology
University of Würzburg
Würzburg, Germany

Carl Sterkens
Faculty of Philosophy, Theology and Religious Studies
Radboud University
Nijmegen, The Netherlands

ISSN 2510-4306 ISSN 2510-4314 (electronic)
Religion and Human Rights
ISBN 978-3-319-59284-8 ISBN 978-3-319-59285-5 (eBook)
DOI 10.1007/978-3-319-59285-5

Library of Congress Control Number: 2017954352

Printed on acid-free paper

This Springer imprint is published by Springer Nature
The registered company is Springer International Publishing AG
The registered company address is: Gewerbestrasse 11, 6330 Cham, Switzerland

Contents

Introduction vii
Hans-Georg Ziebertz and Carl Sterkens

1 **Religious and Humanist Perspectives on Human Rights** 1
Raymond J. Webb

2 **Predictors of Attitudes Towards Human Dignity: An Empirical Analysis Among Youth in Germany** 17
Hans-Georg Ziebertz, Susanne Döhnert, and Alexander Unser

3 **Understanding Human Dignity. Theoretical Groundings and Empirical Findings Among the Youth in Belarus** 61
Olga Breskaya and Susanne Döhnert

4 **Religion and Civil Rights in Italy: An Empirical Exploration Among Secondary School Students** 91
Francesco Zaccaria, Francis-Vincent Anthony, and Carl Sterkens

5 **The Role of Religion in Society, and Its Relation to the Attitudes Towards Human Rights in Chile** 121
Joaquín Silva and Jorge Manzi

6 **Social Capital and Religion in the Public Sphere: Attitudes to Visible Forms of Religion Among Norwegian High-School Students** 141
Pål Ketil Botvar

7 **Freedom of Religion and Freedom of Religious Clothing and Symbols in School: Exploring the Impact of Church Schools in a Religiously Diverse Society** 157
Leslie J. Francis, Andrew Village, Ursula McKenna, and Gemma Penny

8 **Attitudes Towards Freedom of Religion Among Nigerian Students** 177
Modestus Adimekwe and Hans-Georg Ziebertz

9 **Advancing Civil Human Rights Culture in Tanzania** 215
Clement Fumbo and Carl Sterkens

Index 231

Introduction

Human rights are one of the basic foundations of liberal democracy. However, human rights are rights that need to be constantly maintained and improved upon – by politicians and political parties and, ultimately, by everyone. This situation makes both human rights and democracy fragile entities. A wide societal support of human rights is an essential requirement for the understanding, development and protection of values that can be regarded as binding across cultural boundaries. Also, public support is crucial for the growth of a human rights culture and the creation of social conditions that respect and protect these rights.

This volume offers an empirical, and not merely legal, perspective on the so-called first generation of human rights. It explores the legitimisation of these human rights by individual people, both because of their religion and because of their vision of what constitutes human dignity. This empirical approach provides an important complementary perspective for legal, political and public debates. Empirical research can ascertain the extent of agreement that human rights law has with human rights and can clarify the factors that induce or reduce people's support of human rights. The key question in this volume is to what extent do adolescents in different countries support civil human rights and what influences their attitudes towards these rights?

In this volume, religion is chosen as the key concept that might influence attitudes towards human rights. The relationship between religion and human rights is very complex. Historically, when human rights were integrated in democratic constitutions, most religious communities regarded them as dangerous. Among other issues surrounding the concept of human rights was that of freedom of religion and the separation of religion and state; religious communities showed little enthusiasm for either of these notions and, in some cases, displayed barely concealed animosity. Until today, religious institutions and their representatives, as well as individual believers, may have doubts about or even fundamental objections to specific human rights on religious grounds. In this regard, one thinks of concerns relating to personal and family law, gender equality and the whole issue of religious truth claims. Notwithstanding all this, today, the majority of religious institutions and communities generally embrace human rights. Religions are, in many respects, powerful political, social and cultural institutions that contribute to human rights awareness, and the core of most, if not all, religious traditions hold up the dignity of the person; indeed, many religious beliefs support the respectful treatment of others. Nonetheless, the dual role of religion with regard to human rights warrants continuous and serious consideration.

This volume is thematically focused on the ambiguous relationship that exists between religion and the first generation of human rights. These civil rights and liberties include, amongst others, the right to life, equality before the law, the freedom of religion, the freedom of speech, the freedom of assembly, the right to privacy, the protection from discrimination and the prohibition of inhuman treatment. Although the separation between religion and state is not explicitly part of the codified lists of human rights, it offers important conditions for it. Separation of religion and state is therefore implicitly related to this first generation of human rights. In this volume, we will shortly refer to the totality of first-generation human rights as 'civil rights' for the following reasons. The French *Déclaration des Droits de l'Homme et du Citoyen* (1789), generally considered as the highlight in the genesis of human rights in continental Europe, already carries in its title explicit reference to civilians as the bearers of rights. And the two classic United Nations Covenants of 16 December 1966 make a distinction between the first generation of 'civil and political rights' and the second generation of 'economic, social and cultural rights'. But there is also a more substantial reason why these first-generation human rights are called 'civil'. Although these rights developed in an environment characterised by a strong mistrust of government in general, it relatively soon came to be realised that human rights need the protection of institutions. Not more than 16 months after the fall of the Bastille, Edmund Burke argued, in his *Reflections on the Revolution in France* (1790), that a gradual, constitutional reform was the best protector of human rights, rather than a revolution that overthrows any form of governance. Burke seemed to realise that human rights would remain merely speculative ideas if there were no institutions to protect them. In reaction to his reflections, which were increasingly interpreted as anti-revolutionary, Thomas Paine (*Rights of Man,* 1791) defended the position that political revolution is perfectly legitimate when a government does not safeguard the natural rights of its people. Nevertheless, Burke's views paved the way for ongoing reflections on 'citizenship' as conditional for the full realisation of human rights. Referring to the Second World War, Hannah Arendt (*On Revolution*, 1963) observed the phenomenon of individuals' tragic loss of rights when these individuals are denied full citizenship. In short, the notion of the rights of individual human beings is an empty one if these rights are not protected and upheld by independent jurisdiction in democratic environments. While a revolution could satisfy the need for the primary rights of 'life, liberty and property', at least in the limited meaning of freedom from unjustified restraint, it is only when people share in government that human rights can develop to their full potential. In this sense, the first generation of human rights are 'civil' and 'political'. To repeat the opening sentences of this book: human rights are not only the foundations of democracy; in turn, they need a democratic political community to maintain and improve them.

The papers in this volume offer a broad-ranging description of youths' attitudes towards civil human rights and the factors underlying these views. The national studies in this volume represent the discussion of this issue during the annual conference of the international research group Religion and Human Rights (www.rhr.theologie.uni-wuerzburg.de); this conference was held in Würzburg, Germany, from 10 to 13 December 2014. The research group was made up of scholars from about 20 countries. A distinctive feature of the research group is that the participating scholars have used the same measuring instruments in different countries. In all instances, respondents are students, either those at the end of secondary school or those in the first year of college. This means that it is possible to validly compare empirical outcomes across national borders. Although the participating scholars share the same general research question, the selection of empirical measurements and the formulation of specific hypotheses may differ according to the specific interest.

In the first chapter, Raymond J. Webb offers a theoretical reflection on human rights from the perspective of the world religions and humanist world views. Webb underpins the necessity of a broader conversation about human rights. He calls to mind the fact that there are several approaches to justifying human rights. These approaches are present in the contemporary world, and any reflection on the foundation of human rights has to take them seriously. Webb bases his views on the Roman Catholic tradition of natural law, the Protestant covenant approach, the Muslim *umma* point of view, the Orthodox focus on sinless behaviour and the humanist-humanitarian activist approach. Webb compares the different traditions in regard to foundations, group versus individual approaches, relationship and influence on and from the state and current developments. He is convinced that all these perspectives can be profitable for the implementation of human rights.

The next two chapters deal with the foundation of human rights. Most declarations state that human rights are based on the dignity of man. Historically, the understanding of human dignity was regarded as a reflection of a person's social position and his or her behaviour. Dignity could therefore be lost as a result of losing one's social rank or because of one's indulgence in immoral behaviour. In contrast, the contemporary dominant understanding of human dignity relates human dignity to all people in an equal way: dignity is inherent to humanity and is independent of people's individual social position or moral quality. Religious traditions offer distinctive conceptions and foundations of human dignity. In the Christian tradition, for instance, dignity derives from the belief that humankind is created in the image and likeness of God. In philosophy and law, there is an ongoing controversy about the concept of dignity. While some consider this term to be meaningless and superfluous, others try to formulate operational definitions which are specific enough to evaluate their implications. What can empirically be said about the relevance of the concept of dignity?

Hans-Georg Ziebertz, Susanne Döhnert and Alexander Unser examine in their paper how German adolescents evaluate different understandings of dignity. They also test to what extent these understandings influence youths' attitudes towards human rights. Their findings show that youths' understanding of human dignity is relevant in terms of their level of support for civil human rights. More specifically, among German youth, it was found that the conviction that dignity is an inherent quality of human beings is a predictor for attitudes towards human rights.

Olga Breskaya and Susanne Döhnert examine which understanding of human dignity is represented and preferred by students in Belarus, where the Orthodox Christian tradition is dominant. These authors not only reflect, therefore, on the theoretical concept of dignity as used in academic literature but also pay attention to the understanding of human dignity articulated in the official documents of the Russian Orthodox Church. This study tests for the hypothesis that youths who are more strongly committed to the Russian Orthodox Church are in stronger agreement with the Church's convictions concerning human dignity. The authors also determine how and to what extent attitudes towards human dignity depend on the cultural, social and religious identity of the respondents. The concept of inherent dignity is significantly predicted by the degree of empathy of young Belarusians and by the father's degree of religious commitment.

Francesco Zaccaria, Francis-Vincent Anthony and Carl Sterkens present findings from their research in Italy. The authors first investigate what role religion has played in developing a civil rights culture in Italy. They present an historical overview of the interaction between the Catholic Church and civil rights issues with a focus on Italy and provide a sociological assessment of the current situation. They also describe the theological foundation of the Catholic Church's involvement in civil rights in contemporary Italian society. In order to clarify the relationship between religion and civil rights among young Italians, these authors have collected data among secondary school students. Because of the dominant position of Roman Catholicism in Italy, the sample consists mainly of Catholic students. The authors explore, empirically, how Italian youth value civil rights, whether different degrees of religious commitment influence their attitudes towards human rights and to what extent personal characteristics, religious socialisation and psychological traits relate to the support of civil human rights. These authors describe the partial and differential influence of personal and contextual religious attitudes on civil human rights. In general, the data reveal that religion has a pivotal role in the debate about and the support of civil rights but also that the influence of religious identity on the support for or rejection of civil rights differs, depending on the type of rights under discussion.

Joaquín Silva and Jorge Manzi analyse students' opinions about the role of religion in Chile and the potential influence of religious attitudes on attitudes towards human rights. First, the authors develop a theory about the relationship between religion and the public sphere in the Chilean context. The relatively new democratic regimes in Chile encourage religions to play a renewed role in the protection of human rights. The authors then investigate Chilean youth's perception of the role of religion in the public sphere, as well as the varied relationships between this perception and attitudes towards and practices related to human rights. Empirically, the paper shows that the perception of the role of religion in public life varies between members of different denominations. This can be explained in terms of the self-conception of every religion and the role and function religion plays in society. At the same time, this relationship between religion and human rights is also shaped by the historical context and the way the public sphere is organised. The paper shows that young people mainly expect religion to focus on spirituality and that religions should adapt to society rather than seek to change it. The authors interpret this finding from the perspective of individualisation as one of the phenomena related to secularisation. The younger generation no longer recognises the important role religion once had in Chilean society, especially in the promotion of social justice and the protection of human rights. This corresponds with the finding that (with the exception of freedom of religion) other civil human rights bear little relation to religion.

The primary focus of the next group of articles is on aspects of freedom of religion. Pål Ketil Botvar closely observes the public debate in Norway about the use of religious symbols as part of personal attire and the use of prayer rooms in public schools. Botvar asks if attitudes to public forms of religion can be interpreted according to the theory of social capital. Botvar concludes that social trust is an essential component in social capital and the strategies accompanying social capital. How Norwegians cope with religious symbols and prayer at school mirrors the degree of trust there is in freedom of religion. The hypothesis thus implies that trust, generated in face-to-face settings, develops into a more generalised social trust that has profound effects on large-scale modern societies. The analysis of the Norwegian data shows the explanatory power of social-capital indicators on attitudes to freedom of religion in the public sphere.

Leslie Francis, Andrew Village, Ursula McKenna and Gemma Penny focus on religious clothing and symbols in schools as an issue of religious freedom. The authors analyse data collected among young students in England, Wales and London; these student respondents were either educated in state-maintained church schools or in schools without a religious foundation. This research analyses whether or not religious, personal and psychological factors relate significantly to attitudes towards freedom of religion. Especially with regard to the 'mission' of the school, the authors conclude that students attending church schools hold neither a more nor less positive attitude towards freedom of religious clothing and symbols in school compared with students attending schools without a religious foundation.

The last part of the book offers empirical insights in the attitudes of youth in two African countries. Modestus Adimekwe, Hans-Georg Ziebertz and Susanne Döhnert present findings from research among youth in Nigeria. The paper takes three indicators for freedom of religion in the Nigerian context into consideration: government's interference in religion, prayer practice at school and the wearing of a *hijab* at school. In some Nigerian federal states, there are open conflicts about these issues. The empirical questions of the paper are as follows: what are the attitudes of school students towards the three dimensions of freedom of religion? To what extent do demographic characteristics, religious belonging, individual beliefs, trust in religion and the perception of religion and conflicts in society predict attitudes towards human rights? The assumption is that, given the lack of a precise definition of the freedom of religion in Nigeria's Constitution, the youth would display negative attitudes towards religious freedom. But the results reveal that the respondents of this study hold, in fact, rather positive attitudes towards the concept of freedom of religion.

Clement Fumbo and Carl Sterkens investigate the traditional difficulties faced in advancing a human rights culture in Tanzania. They describe the problems, causes and deeper reasons that hinder the advancement and application of human rights in Tanzania. Despite the fact that, in theory, Tanzania fully embraces human rights, the country falls short when it comes to applying them. The authors argue that specific cultural traditions and customs are to blame for human rights abuses. Strict and conservative beliefs and practices in Tanzania do not align with human rights. More specifically, traditional family values and gender-role stereotypes, arranged (child) marriages, belief in witchcraft and extrajudicial killings and unjust law enforcement are all implicated in causing harm to a culture of human rights.

As the diversity of the contributions in this volume shows, the relationship between religion and civil human rights is complex and multifaceted. Studying this complicated relationship calls for a variety of theoretical perspectives and rigorous empirical testing in different national contexts. We hope this volume offers a challenging example of the benefits of adopting an international and multidisciplinary approach to this subject.

Hans-Georg Ziebertz
Carl Sterkens

Chapter 1
Religious and Humanist Perspectives on Human Rights

Raymond J. Webb

Abstract The United Nations' 1948 Universal Declaration of Human Rights is the best known comprehensive statement on human rights. The foundations of these human rights, however, can be manifold. There are several approaches to founding principles of human rights. This paper considers some of these perspectives: (1) a Roman Catholic natural law perspective; (2) a Protestant covenant approach; (3) a Muslim "umma" point of view; (4) an Orthodox understanding; and (5) a "humanist-humanitarian activist" approach. While discussing the various perspectives on "first generation" civil and political human rights, this paper makes some comparisons in regard to foundations, group versus individual approaches, relationship and influence on/from the State, and current developments. It is argued that each of these voices is needed in the ongoing development of the human rights discussion and implementation.

Introduction

Jacques Maritain has famously noted that, at a 1947 meeting of a UNESCO commission on human rights, someone said that people strongly ideologically opposed could agree on a list of rights, "but on condition that no one asks us why" (Maritain 1949, 9). Maritain (1949, 10) asserts that it is important to agree on common statements for guidance of action, even if it is not possible to agree on the theory behind the common beliefs. The "why" is where the argument begins. Maritain has argued that moral consciousness, human awareness of natural law, is developing. So human awareness of human rights is similarly growing slowly. This would be a justification for the diverse foundational perspectives behind the acceptance of human rights.

David Hollenbach (2003, 242–3) notes that lists of human rights can be the result of common practical reason. Common answers can be discovered through different particular foundational reasoning. He asserts that moral consensus on human rights

R.J. Webb (✉)
University of Saint Mary of the Lake, Mundelein, IL, USA
e-mail: rwebb@usml.edu

H.-G. Ziebertz, C. Sterkens (eds.), *Religion and Civil Human Rights in Empirical Perspective*, Religion and Human Rights 2, DOI 10.1007/978-3-319-59285-5_1

ethics will require designating (1) to whom are the requirements of the ethos owed, (2) what good do people have claim to, (3) who is responsible to provide for the good, and (4) what social and institutional arrangements are necessary to realize the good life (Hollenbach 2003, 243).

But Michael Ignatieff (2001, 81–90) asserts that universal human rights must be argued for on the basis of a practical and political consensus. Arguments from religious or metaphysical foundations must be avoided. Ignatieff contends that the reason for human rights is empathy based on the common human experience of fear and the conviction that humans should not have to live in fear. A non-foundationalist, Ignatieff wants us to look at what rights do for people: protecting their agency and ability to resist harmful forces and objecting to what people agree is insufferably wrong (Hollenbach 2003, 239). Of course, it can be argued that Ignatieff's position is itself foundational.

While the United Nations' 1948 Universal Declaration of Human Rights (UDHR) is the best known comprehensive statement on human rights, there are several other broad perspectives on human rights, these approaches have tried to describe human rights and to substantiate these rights based on foundational and non-foundational approaches. The problematic here is to continue to develop support for human rights in theory and practice, while supporting the inclusion of a variety of approaches – foundational and non-foundational – in the conversation. One does not want the broadly agreed-to rights declarations to be dependent on the foundational positions, such that if the foundation changes the rights declaration must change without consultation with other participants. But people's rights positions have often developed seemingly out of foundations, and these interlocutors probably have much to continue to contribute, even though not always through the portal of UDHR.

Universal Declaration of Human Rights (UDHR)

Jacques Maritain (1949, 10) wondered at the preliminary UNESCO meeting referred to above, whether the universal declaration is "[…] an agreement conceivable among men assembled for the purpose of jointly accomplishing a task dealing with the future of the mind, who come from the four corners of the earth and who belong not only to different cultures and civilizations, but to different spiritual families and antagonistic schools of thought?" Nevertheless, the Universal Declaration of Human Rights (UDHR) was adopted by the General Assembly of the United Nations in 1948. It was developed by members of the Human Rights Committee, chaired by Eleanor Roosevelt, with the help of international experts such as Canadian John Humphrey and French Rene Cassin. Civil and political rights as well as economic, social, and cultural rights were included. One can see a position that rights are linked and indivisible, although this position has been challenged and changed. The UDHR was in large part the culmination of a growing body of human rights advocacy and specifically in reaction to the horrors of two World Wars. Centuries before, John Locke discussed natural rights, the notion that humans created by God were by nature free and equal. Jean-Jacque Rousseau popularized this position in his writings. Thomas Hobbes contributed to the modern liberal view of morality by emphasizing the purpose of government as protecting the limited goods of life, personal liberty, and property (Kraynak 2014).

Maritain (1949, 11) asserts:

> [My] way of justifying the belief in the rights of man and the ideal of freedom, equality, and fraternity is the only belief solidly based on truth. This does not prevent me from agreeing on these practical tenets with those who are convinced their way of justifying them, entirely different from mine or even opposed to mine in its theoretical dynamism, is likewise the only one based on truth.

Despite the claims of natural law theorists, Munro (2003, 120) agrees that that any version of "natural law" is only accessed through our own particular categories, either culturally, linguistically or religiously. But he sees that we can make social contracts – following Hobbes and Locke – in which people agree to be subject to certain ordering principles through very broad discussion and then hold others accountable to them. These norms, principles, values, laws, and codes have been discussed, debated, written down, and agreed to by representatives of states, cultures, religions, and linguistic traditions and can serve as the basis for trying individuals for violations or even crimes against humanity. The goal of the UNESCO conference and subsequent drafting of the UDHR was practical not theoretical. So, the conveners came to agree on practical conclusions while disagreeing on the theoretical means for justifying those conclusions.

It should be noted that there are other formal declarations on human rights, including: European Convention for the Protection of Human Rights and Fundamental Freedoms (1950); International Covenant on Civil and Political Rights (1966); International Covenant on Economic, Social, and Cultural Rights (1966); United Nations Declaration on the Elimination of All Forms of Intolerance and Discrimination Based on Religion or Belief (1981); The African Charter on Human and People's Rights (1981) and The Declaration on the Rights of Persons Belonging to National or Ethnic, Religious, and Linguistic Minorities (1992) among others.

Five Perspectives on Human Rights

In this section, I will present five perspectives on human rights: Christian (Catholic and Protestant), Orthodox, Muslim, and humanist-humanitarian. The focus is on "first generation" civil and political human rights. Drawing on the UDHR, these rights can be described as emphasizing the protection of and non-interference with liberty. Included are the rights to life, property, equality before the law, public hearings which presume innocence, privacy at home, travel and residence in one's country, asylum seeking, marriage and family, educational choice, intellectual property, and freedom of belief, religion, speech, opinion, assembly, association, participation in government, elections, choice of employment, protection from compulsion, slavery, torture and cruel punishment, arbitrary arrest and exile. [Second generation rights relate to economics, society, and culture; third generation to development, health, sharing of resources, environment, etc.] I will discuss whether each of the five perspectives is foundational or non-foundational, the complexities of its relationship to the State, the dynamic of the relationship of the individual and the group, and current developments.

Catholic Perspectives

Though drawing from origins in Aristotle and St. Paul, the development of Catholic positions on human rights – rooted in the notion of natural law, which is accessible to all persons, regardless of their beliefs – was strengthened by Thomas Aquinas and continued through Pope Leo XIII's *Rerum Novarum* in the late nineteenth century up to the present.

Maritain is a Catholic exponent of natural law theory. Human nature has specific ends and natural law is "the ideal formula of development of a given being" (Maritain 1951, 86). Maritain's notion of natural law is an empirical rather than rationalistic one (Munro 2003, 115). It is discovered by humanity over time through experience (Munro, 114–115). For Maritain, "only when the Gospel has penetrated to the depth of human substance will natural law appear in its flower and its perfection" (Maritain 1951, 90).

Theologically, human rights are grounded in God's action as creator and as redeemer through Jesus Christ (Joseph Allen 1988, 347). Because of being created as an *imago dei*, each person has a dignity or worth, which is not to be subjected to the group. Human reason can discern the demands of human morality. Upon this basis, John XXIII (1963) wrote *Pacem in Terris*, which presents a human rights charter supporting the full range of human rights proclaimed by the UDHR. In the area of civil-political rights, this included free speech and self-governance, marriage, family, right to life, bodily integrity, religion, and participation in government (11,14,14 48, 52), *Gaudium et Spes* (Pastoral Constitution on the Church in the Modern World) of the Second Vatican Council interestingly bases its position on a theological interpretation of the experience of many cultures. The Council proclaimed that "the right to religious freedom has its foundation in the very dignity of the human person, as this dignity is known through the revealed word of God and by reason itself" (Vatican Council II 1965, #2). It linked the full scope of human rights with very core of Christian faith. Also mentioned are the first generation rights to choice in marriage partner, education of children (52), ownership of private property (71), participation in juridical-political structures and governance (75). It is noted that the Church is not to be "confused" with the political community, not bound to any political system (76).

Since the Second Vatican Council, the Catholic Church has become an active supporter of human rights around the world (Hollenbach 2011, 340). The recent *Compendium of the Social Doctrine of the Church* (Pontifical Council for Justice and

Peace 2004) affirms the Catholic Church's commitment to human rights as moral standards to which all nations and cultures should be held accountable. Like earlier church documents, the compendium grounds the link between Christian faith and human rights (Hollenbach 2005, 16–17). Hollenbach would say that the church's support of human rights is now seen as linked with its mission to proclaim the Gospel. Continuing in this vein of exploratory thinking and advocacy, Robert McElroy (2014, 14) finds that Pope Francis "identifies [economic] inequality as the foundation of a process of exclusion that cuts immense segments of society off from meaningful participation in social, political and economic life." Hence, there is an interrelationship of generations of rights, with first generation political rights being impinged upon by violations of second generation economic rights. John Allen (2009, 363) contends that besides using the biblical image of the human as an imago Dei, Catholicism will continue to draw more and more on human rights language, as the best path toward "cross cultural consensus and the requirements for justice". For Allen, "the rights have to be rooted in a common human nature that makes them universal, inalienable, and eternal" (363). He recognized the difficulty of developing a universal "human rights architecture" in a multi-polar world (442).

One can describe a "Catholic perspective" as foundational; having moved from group to individual focus with concern for humanitarian group values; not involved with most States, except perhaps in Spain, Italy, the Philippines, and to a diminishing degree, Poland. Each of these countries has passed or is considering legislation which the Catholic Church has opposed. A current trend that bodes well for continuing and increasing support of human rights are the initiatives of Pope Francis. He has called for a focus on the poor and persons at the margins, a broader discussion involving many voices rather than pre-scripted pronouncements (e.g. the Synod on the Family), possible decentralization (a revival of the importance of national hierarchical groups and national decision-making), and attention to survey data (e.g. collection of worshipper questionnaires in preparation for both sessions of the Synod on the Family). The head of the Congregation for the Doctrine of the Faith, Cardinal Gerhard Muller, has declared the "end of the war on liberation theology" (Valente 2013). Liberation theology sought to empower persons in small groups to read the Scripture and seek greater control of their own lives. This empowerment in the public sphere has first generation implications of participation in government and other political-civil aspects of life. In another area of focus, the Orthodox Ecumenical Patriarch, Bartholomew I, attended Jorge Bergoglio's inaugural Mass as Pope. This precedent setting event and subsequent meetings indicate serious efforts toward rapprochement and reunion. The religious dimensions of support for human rights – freedom of religion, association, and participation in civil government by believers – would seem to be strengthened.

Protestant Perspectives

The characteristic, but not only, focus of Protestant groups has been on the covenanted relationship of individuals with God. John Witte notes that that the theory and law of human rights is "neither new nor secular." They are the result of "ancient Jewish constructions of covenant and mitzvoth, ancient Qu'ranic texts on peace and the common good, Roman Catholic canon law concepts of *ius* and *libertas*, classic Protestant ideals of freedom and conscience […]" (Witte 1998, 258). The Reformation itself was a human rights movement, resulting in freedom of individual conscience, freedom of political officials from church power, freedom of local clergy from popes and princes. The human person is created in the image of God, justified by faith, *simul justus et peccator* (righteous and at the same time a sinner), called to a distinct vocation, standing in equal dignity with all others. People are all equal before God and neighbour, "vested with a natural liberty to live, to believe, to serve God and neighbours" (Witte 1998, 260). But as sinners prone to evil, the restraint of law is needed to deter them from evil and force them to repentance. Association with others brings a rule of law and love to us in a communal way. Witte (262) believes that Protestant teachings and practice have shaped the development of Western democracies and constitutional reform and can lead the human rights movement away from libertarianism, from sacrificing the individual to the community, and from limitless expansion.

J Robert Nelson (1982, 1) argues that Protestantism has been the major force for securing, extending, and enhancing human freedom, specifically freedom of conscience, freedom from unjust exploitation or oppression, and freedom to live a properly human life. Like Witte, Nelson sees Protestant history as a series of successes in emancipating people for the enjoyment of greater freedom. The focus on the individual is seen by many as a characteristic of Protestantism (e.g. private interpretation of Scripture, a man and his God, the rugged individualist). The 1948 UDHR can seem to read like a "Protestant" document, with its singular subjects and verbs throughout the 30 articles. Protestantism enhances the eminence, value, and integrity of the individual person. It is concerned for the individual, but not individualistic. Personal responsibility is important. God created each person and Jesus saves each. Private judgment in matters of faith is equated with freedom of conscience. Personal responsibility in morals and ethics may not be evaded. Nelson (1982, 4) asserts that the claim of one person, however, to require satisfaction of a given human right cannot in all cases be held to be absolute. The right of one member of the community must not be used to override the well-being of the whole, any more than the whole community may annul the right of any one member. One Protestant concept of church is as a given social entity – the Body of Christ. In a second notion of Protestant communion, the church is a covenanted entity into which all persons are brought, a free, voluntary association. The individual precedes and the polity is congregational. The right and autonomy of each person is prior to society's right. Nelson (1982, 5) therefore claims that Protestants are more willing co-operators in secular movements for civil rights and justice than others, including Catholic and Orthodox.

A current Protestant trend which may affect human rights is the "decline" in mainstream, social Gospel, human rights-supporting denominations and a rise in fundamentalist, Pentecostal, and Evangelical currents, which may have different emphases. The historical Protestant contribution to the development of human rights in theory, advocacy, and practice is manifest. This thinking and force for practice cannot be marginalized without some peril to the movement forward. Despite some movement, Evangelical embrace of human rights language, save religious rights, has been slow in the Evangelical context. Critique of government in regard to first generation rights has seemed weak (Nichols 2009). Pentecostals in Central America sometimes engage in "rescuing" gang members for the sake of conversion. Usually, membership in a gang is a "life sentence." It is human rights work, although there is reluctance to use that term, the comfortable language being biblical or theological, rather than political. In fact, the first generation rights to life, freedom of association, and protection from cruel punishment are involved. Governments are reluctant to protect former gang members, who fall victim to their former gangs as well as unrestrained vigilante groups. Drawing on history, including apartheid South Africa, Horn (2007) concludes that the Bible, nationalism, contemporary political movements, and acceptance are strong forces driving Pentecostals, at the expense of human rights language, cooperation, and activism.. Efrain Rios Mott enjoyed specific Evangelical support during his time as president of Guatemala. Catholics, with a strong advocacy of human rights, were then under severe pressure from the Rios Mott government (Scott 2008). This may possibly, but not necessarily, indicate a priority for Biblical belief over humanitarian stances. Evangelicals like Rick Warren and programs like that of the Pepperdine Law School do use human rights language and work for human rights. Nichols says that such positive movement is often unnoticed, Theological obstacles do remain (Nichols 2009, 661–662). In any event, whatever Pentecostal or Evangelical voices will say in regard to human rights must be engaged.

The traditional mainline Protestant perspective has been foundational, focused on the individual, related to some states but only symbolically, not generally influential with the state, but unclear in regard to the aspirations of fundamentalist groups. Evangelical Protestantism tends more toward theological, rather than human rights language. Political groups which are "anti-communist" or supportive of the coming of the end times enjoy support, with little concern about human rights. Bringing the individual into the community is important, for the sake of his salvation (and implicitly in support of his first generation rights).

Orthodox Perspectives

One notes that the Ecumenical Patriarchate, with residence in Turkey, is in a delicate position with regard to its relationship to the government there and its own exercise of various aspects of human rights, especially freedom of religion. However, the primary focus in this section is the Russian Orthodox Church. The principal Russian Orthodox Church document on human rights is The Russian Orthodox Church's Basic Teaching on Human Society, Freedom and Rights (*Osnovy*), adopted by the Bishops' Council in 2008 (Russian Orthodox Church, Department for External Church Relations 2008); it is a modification of an earlier document. Inna Naletova (2012, 232–233) describes the Orthodox conception of human rights, as "emphasizing the importance of faith, moral responsibilities, and love of the fatherland, [and resonating] with religious authoritarian value-outlook" (cf. *Osnovy* III.5). Kristina Stoeckl (2014) notes that there are no juridical rights in the document. She claims that *Osnovy* "looks at human rights as a set of rules that frame the individual's relationship with the community and with itself (its moral and inner conduct), and not, as is the case of the secular human rights instruments, as a set of regulations and protections that regulate the interaction of institutions of power with individuals" (Stoeckl 2014, 85). So *Osnovy* fits human rights principles into this frame of reference of responsibility, morality and individual duties related to God-given dignity. Little attention is paid to protective rights. In human rights, the Church does not defend the individual against arbitrary interference by the state, but any religious intervention is in view of a bettering of the "sinful individual" (*Osnovy* I. 5). What the Church might do is to attempt to "intercede" and "appeal" to the state (*Osnovy* IV.2). The Russian Orthodox Church wants a comfortable relationship to the state. *Osnovy* does emphasize the rights of the Church and of society as a whole rather than the rights of the individual (*Osnovy* IV. 9). Stoeckl (2014, 86) sees internal church human rights conversation as dealing with strategies to defend the Orthodox religion with a particular human rights strategy against other human rights perspectives. Siskova (2008) quotes one of the drafters of *Osnovy* (Aleksandr Dugin) describing the document as a "powerful philosophical institution designed to influence the legal model of the Russian state."

Interestingly, survey data show that the ethic of an Orthodox religious authoritarianism is not equally strong in all countries in Eastern Europe, and it excludes neither a possibility of co-existence with different values, nor a consensus on practical matters (Naletova 2012, 233). She notes that persons surveyed in Eastern countries who indicated a preference for an ethic of moral responsibility, rather than authoritarianism, valued personal freedom, social responsibility, and a perspective more in line with Western liberal concepts of human rights.

The Orthodox perspective is foundational, group related, involved with the state, in a relationship of mutual influence with the state. A positive Orthodox movement is the advancing conversation between Rome and the Ecumenical Patriarchate of Constantinople. Given the autocephalous (national) arrangement of Orthodox churches, their situations in relationship to states which were formerly part of the Soviet Union will be varied and hence, their human rights positions may be varied (Cf. Preda 2012). How much their human rights stances will need to be self-protective in regard to the state is not clear. Orthodoxy shares concern about secularism with Islam and Catholicism (a pressing concern more under Pope Benedict XVI than under Pope Francis). As the Russian Orthodox Church looks at and alters its relationship to the state, to authority, and to human rights, it seems important that access to the wider human rights conversation be available to it, in a way that resources further discussion. Orthodoxy's hesitation that human rights discourse is basically "Western" always deserves serious and sensitive consideration.

Islamic Perspectives

Saudi Arabia was one of the eight nations that abstained from voting in support of the UDHR in 1948, the others being South Africa and communist bloc countries. These nations did, however, issue the Universal Islamic Declaration of Human

Rights in 1981, arguing for both human rights and traditionalism in religion. In a second document, the Cairo Declaration on Human Rights in Islam, issued by the Organization of the Islamic Conference (OIC, now the Organization of Islamic Cooperation) on August 5, 1990, is found in Article 1(a):

> All human beings form one family whose members are united by their subordination to Allah and descent from Adam. All men are equal in terms of basic human dignity and basic obligations and responsibilities, without any discrimination on the basis of race, colour, language, belief sex, religion, political affiliation, social status or other considerations. The true religion is the guarantee for enhancing such dignity along the path of human integrity.

Articles 24 and 25 of the Cairo Declaration on Human Rights in Islam add that "All the rights and freedoms stipulated in this Declaration are subject to the Islamic Shari'a" and that "The Islamic Shari'a is the only source of reference for the explanations or clarification of any of the articles of this Declaration."

For Muslims, the imprint of God is in every human being. Humans are created with intuitive reason and an innate capacity to know right from wrong. Individuals can be recognized as a persons with dignity and as members of a civil association founded upon equality of rights and responsibilities within the framework of the modern nation-state (Sachedina 2009, 23). But they need God's continual guidance to fulfil their true roles in society (12). Vertical obligations to God are linked with horizontal obligations to human beings, and vertical reverence to God calls for horizontal reverence for humans. The worldwide community of Muslims – the *umma* – becomes the horizontal connection (Oh 2007, 27–28). "Political commitments are not separated from religious beliefs" (Oh 2007, 25). Islam may be more comfortable with duties than rights, but they go together (cf. Soroush 2000, 129). For every right, there are three duties: that the right not be eliminated, that the state protects people from its deprivation, and that the state protect the right for those unable to protect it for themselves (Oh 2007, 34).

Abdulaziz Sachedina (17) says that Islam can support a common moral position founded upon "a universally recognizable" description of individual autonomy, common good, and cultural differences. He claims that in the theological and legal traditions of Islam are found the antecedents of the modern concepts of liberty, pluralism, and human rights (44). He also asserts that Islam, of all of the world's religions, with its comprehensive doctrine about the moral duty to institute good and prevent evil, is the most identified with attempts to govern human life in all its manifestations in this world and the next (45).

Abdolkarim Soroush claims that Islam provides an awareness of the issues of material and social equality that other belief systems do not provide (Oh 2007, 23). Islamic thinkers promote effective government and the creation of supporting institutions to this end. Sachedina (2009, 145) argues for the immediate attention to the actual human rights of women in Islamic countries as well as in scholarly understanding. He calls for conversation with "other claimants of comprehensive doctrines," lest the "relativism" of the Eurocentric sources of the UDHR make it functionally irrelevant in Muslim contexts. He is concerned about the relationship of society and the individual (145). "The ultimate goal of this conversation is to reach a consensus about human agency linked to human dignity as a special mark of humanness that is entitled to inalienable human rights" (Sachedina 2009, 13). So discourse is an opportunity for Muslim traditionalists to consider the Islamic heritage in relationship to the notion of the "autonomous self," as well as the basic notions of human dignity and human agency.

Soroush distinguishes between Islam as a repository of truths and Islam as an identity (which the Prophet Muhammed never intended) (Soroush 2000, 22). Sachedina (2009, 182–183) notes, "An exclusive particular communal system that forged the group's identity as the bearer of the religious truth in a different social-political order is in direct conflict with the universal human rights discourse". Where a society has become religious, Soroush contends that it would be undemocratic to form a purely secular government, but for a religious government to be democratic it must partake of collective wisdom and respect human rights (126). Extra-religious debates should be respected by religious government and their outcomes "heeded" (128). "Observing human rights (such as justice, freedom, and so on) guarantees not only the democratic character of a government, but also its religious character" (129).

Islam is foundational, focused on the group, involved and influential with the state. Current events illustrate very different connections with the state, much different in Saudi Arabia and Egypt, for example. A much destabilized Middle East has led to Sunni-Shi'a war and, at times, unclear or negative relations with non-Muslim minorities. A question that is continually raised is about what can genuinely be called "Muslim" and what is an illegitimate, exploitive use of the word. There are several conversations within Islam about the "one" Islam in the modern-postmodern world. A positive development of the past 25 years is that dialogues between Muslims and Protestants and Catholics exist in several locations, with strong support in the United States.

Humanist and Humanitarian Perspectives

The humanist and humanitarian perspectives considered here dynamically relate first generation rights theory, situations "on the ground", and the effect on other generations of rights. Noted here are William Easterly, economist and philosopher Amartya Sen, and theoretician-medical practitioner Paul Farmer. Their work is consistent with Maritain's belief that a list of human rights actions can be formulated, even while there is disagreement on principles. The concerns of the activist community have implications for first generation rights. The contexts from which they speak cannot be neglected. Oh (2007, 3) notes that, unlike the conversation between Islamic scholars from previously colonized countries and Western thinkers, human rights scholars do not often feature the colonial experience in their writings. When colonial effects are ignored, they linger as an unresolved distraction from fruitful progress in support of all generations of human rights.

William Easterly argues that if the first generation rights of the individual are not upheld and respected, immediate aid schemes will only have short term effects, if that. The broad outline of his argument is that sustainable development, after so much failure, requires learning from history rather than acting as if all is a blank slate; not shorting individual judicial and political rights for the sake of the nation/people/group; and favouring the spontaneous solutions of the local people involved rather than the grand design by outsiders (Easterly 2013). So, one could contend that the development plans of Jeffery Sachs and the United Nations Millennium Development goals for 2015 struggle because of under-emphasis on human rights and local input at the expense of material aid expediency.

Farmer (2005, 20) is sensitive to cultural contexts. Nevertheless, he decries a cultural relativism which would seem to excuse human rights violations within groups. Sen (1999, 150) notes that a fine reading of the data does not support the notion that a certain denial of first generation rights assists economic development: "In fact, there is rather little general evidence that authoritarian governance and the suppression of political and civil rights are really beneficial in encouraging economic development…Systematic empirical studies give no real support to the claim that there is a general conflict between political freedoms and economic performance". Where a cultural overlay is used to defend questionable practices, several cautions may help. In regard to those outside of the particular culture, colonial or neo-colonial or seemingly Western dominant stances may distract from an unbiased consideration of the human rights issue. Ad intra, where power is shared in a culture, there seems to be more possibility of arriving at a more generally agreed upon human rights position when there is democracy (rather than dictatorship, etc.) or the informed freedom of individuals to decline a practice which is widely abhorred (e.g. female genital mutilation).

Sen rejects Jeremy Bentham's claim that human rights are nonsense, simply being another name for what is already a matter of law, "children of the law" – no law, no human right. For Sen, proclamations of human rights are "strong ethical pronouncements as to what should be done" (2009, 357). Human rights must meet tests of content and viability (358). They must be critically important and must merit the acceptance of social responsibility to promote or safeguard them (358). The underlying ethical claims about such rights must survive open, impartial, critical scrutiny, open to arguments coming from others and to relevant information (358–359). The legislated right comes from prior ethical assertion (359). Besides fostering legislation, human rights discourse can foster social monitoring by non-governmental organizations, promote awareness, education, and advocacy through communications media. Sufficient, but non total, social consensus as to the importance of a particular right for many people can include a particular right in the "canon" of human rights, with corresponding obligations on the part of others to work for the fulfilment of the freedom contained in the right (366–367). Sympathy promotes the awareness of others' concerns, but an additional factor is the possibility that one can actually aid in the prevention of the violation of a right (374). Rights claims from this humanist perspective rest on the ability of the ethical claims underlying them to survive rigorous public, impartial scrutiny that the right is essential to human well-being (386).

A significant theoretician-practitioner with great involvement in Haiti, Rwanda, Russia, and Peru, the physician-anthropologist Paul Farmer focuses on health care and the interconnecting types of rights related to it. The health thriving of the poor will also be determined by the level of fulfilment of their social and economic rights (equity), which in turn affects their civil and political ones (Farmer 2005, 9,75). Farmer is in agreement with Sen (1999, 3), who contends, "Development requires the removal of major sources of un-freedom: poverty as well as tyranny, poor economic opportunities as well as systematic social deprivation, neglect of public facilities as well as intolerance or over-activity of repressive states". For both Farmer and Sen, when people are powerless or have no real social or economic rights, this indicates that they have no substantial political rights also (Farmer 2005, 17). Excessive periods of detention before trial in Russia as well as the cruel punishment of severe overcrowding in jail, both violations of first generation rights, led to high risk of normal-protocol resistant tuberculosis, affecting both prisoners and those they would come in contact with, including family members and even guards. Refugee Haitians run afoul of a two-tiered United States refugee system that requires them to be repatriated without inquiry into their actual danger upon returning to Haiti (67). This is in part the product of U.S. laws, based on confidence in a pro-U.S. Haitian government which in fact repressed first generation human rights. Dubiously legal confiscation of land for a dam in Haiti (first generation issue) led to former farmers having no means of employment, leading to men and women going to Port au Prince for employment, increasing the risk of HIV-AIDS and loss of life in a health resources deprived country. Another two-tiered immigration stance barred HIV-positive applicants from entrance into the U.S. Ironically, appeals against human rights violations are often to powerful states, which themselves may have caused the violations (242). This experiential evidence approach moves toward first generation rights. What appear as violations of second and third generation rights, in fact are or lead to first generation rights violations.

In the above examples we can see de facto deprivation of liberty, equality before the law, the right to family, choice of employment (sadly in the case of prostitution), freedom from cruel punishment (minor offenses leading to overlong incarceration and high likelihood of tuberculosis). Though intertwined with second and third generation rights violation causes, these are violations of first generation rights.

The humanists and activist humanitarians considered above are non-foundational. Humanists argue from philosophical grounds. Humanitarians bring specific evidence and cases to the discussion. I believe they demonstrate how violations of individual rights affect the community. The state is the guarantor of human rights. It must be noted that non-governmental organizations (NGOs) do not and cannot sustain positions as governmental substitutes, however powerful they may be, unless they become neo-colonizers. First generation participation in governance rights affect well-being at all levels. NGOs are most valuable in pointing to the evidence. Often focused on persons at the margins, NGOs can demonstrate that, for example, health care without social and economic rights does only short term good. Detention without speedy trial can spread disease from the prison to the outside world. The interrelationship of judicial rights and health rights is an example of discoveries from the activist humanitarian perspective. The various findings of non-governmental organizations should influence the human rights conversation toward effective actions or framing the theoretical conversations toward nuances of real world problems and relationships.

Conclusion

Although there is some disagreement about this, the development of the UDHR was in part driven by the historical events of World Wars I and II, as well as the Armenian Genocide, the Holocaust and Stalinism. New historical experiences and new awareness of slavery, torture, summary executions, even in the name of religion, have led to new perspectives on human rights or greater urgency in their implementation. The seemingly universal condemnation of these latter as violations of first generation human rights grew over a long – too long – time.

A deeper rationale for human rights is still developing, so practical lists of generally agreed upon rights are necessary. The argument that non-foundationalism is possible is not sufficiently developed. It is not clear that the human empathy, sympathy and universal fear of abuses – this emotional valence – will serve as a universal criterion for what is to be included on lists of both positive and negative human rights. One may be in accord with the position of Maritain that a theoretical universal perspective, for him understanding of natural law (a basis for human rights), is evolving as consciousness evolves. In fact, Maritain contends that "no definition of human rights will ever be exhaustive and final" (1949, 74).

There may be at the core of humanity a core set of human rights. The appreciation of these rights is growing as well have seen above. Arguments about content may well focus on discussions of second and third generation rights. I would contend that the core is discoverable over time, through the processes of philosophical human reasoning and reflection on experience – individual and global-historical. Twentieth century events have been illuminating and catalytic.

While no group should be privileged in the development of human rights, not to include a broad range of voices leaves the conversation incomplete. Neither religion nor secularism should be privileged. Religion (or ultimate value and life systems) is a substantive aspect of culture; we cannot see without cultural eyes. Exclusion of religious or cultural perspectives from the conversation about human rights may deprive us of fonts of insight as the appreciation of human rights and their practices grows. We then may be distracted by (often valid) charges of pro-Western bias, covert colonialism, and new hegemonies. For the sake of universality, we may be moving away from foundations, but that is a long road to a common theoretical source. From foundational perspectives have come much of the content of our core list of human rights. The "discovery" process being experienced in Christian Orthodoxy as well as in Islam may unearth new areas of focus. Foundational positions are very important for many person in their lives. However, as mentioned above, a common foundation for human rights is not in sight.

Drawing from the earlier arguments, I do not find support for the position that cultural considerations can justify diminishing individual rights. However, individuals do have responsibilities to the community, obligations for the sake of the common good, a sine qua non for living together. In any event, cultural relativism must not protect actions which would permit or shield de facto rights violations, e.g. mutilation.

We can briefly review questions related to the relationship of the perspectives considered above to the State. Certainly Orthodoxy and Islam influence relevant states. It is not illegitimate for persons and institutions to try to influence the state. However, first generation rights have expectations of equal treatment for all persons, with citizenship carrying additional privileges and responsibilities. For a "religious state," this charge is quite complex. In addition, the undoubted good work and insights in support of human rights and necessities by the Non-Governmental Organizations community must be accompanied by a positive "evolution" of governments and nations in real support of human rights progress for long term effects. NGOs are not a substitute for the national governmental responsibilities. Individualism, libertarianism, and "pure" Marxism are not shown to ultimately safeguard human rights.

Human rights support will come from the prior ethical convictions of individuals, from group consensus ideally for the common good of all (as in the UDHR and various laws with accompanying sanctions), and from making known situations which appear to violate or promote first generation human rights. It will also come from appreciation of the fact that the newest human generation has a different historical and cultural experience than the framers of the UDHR. If growing perceptions are practically influenced by historical events, then the experience of the current generation of 15–20 year olds may affect human rights consciousness. The effect of higher education levels, awareness of women's rights, information technology, regional conflicts without world war, new focus on the rich-poor gap, the foreseen and unforeseen consequences of globalization, and a re-focus on the effects of and current vestiges of colonialism will affect the awareness and practice of judicial and political rights and perhaps open up to exploration new vistas of human rights. The larger conversation is cumbersome, inefficient, unruly, and very necessary.

References

Allen, J. L. (1988, October). Catholic and protestant theories of human rights. *Religious Studies Review, 14* (4), 347–353.

Allen, J. L. (2009). *The future church: How ten trends are revolutionizing the Catholic Church*. New York: Doubleday.

Easterly, W. (2013). *The tyranny of experts: Economists, dictators, and the forgotten rights of the poor*. New York: Basic Books.

Farmer, P. (2005). *Pathologies of power: Health, human rights, and the new war on the poor*. Berkeley: University of California Press.

Hollenbach, D. S. J. (2003). *The global face of public faith: Politics, human rights, and Christian ethics*. Washington, DC: Georgetown University Press.

Hollenbach, D. S. J. (2005, October 31). Human rights in Catholic thought: A new synthesis. *America, 193*(13), 16–18.
Hollenbach, D. S. J. (2011, March). Human rights in a pluralist, unequal globe: Contributions of Jesuit universities. *Catholic Education*, 338–345.
Horn, Nico. (2007). *The influence of state ideology on Pentecostal thinking after world war ii, with special reference to white Pentecostals in South Africa*. http://www.iclrs.org/content/events/28/765.pdf
Ignatieff, M. (2001). *Human rights as politics and idolatry*. Princeton: Princeton University Press.
John XXIII. (1963). *Pacem in Terris (Peace on Earth)*. Chicago: Claretian Publications.
Kraynak, R. P. (2014, November 13). *Thomas Hobbes: From classical natural law to modern natural rights*. www.nlnrac.org/earlymodern/hobbes
Maritain, J. (1949). Introduction. In: UNESCO (Ed.), *Human rights: Comments and interpretations* (pp. 9–17). New York: Columbia University Press.
Maritain, J. (1951). *Man and the state*. Chicago: University of Chicago Press.
McElroy, R. (2014, November 13). Market assumptions. *America, 211*(13), 14–18. http://americamagazine.org/issue/market-assumptions. Accessed 21 Dec 2014.
Munro, B. R. (2003). The Universal Declaration of Human Rights, Maritain, and the Universality of Human Rights. In W. Sweet (Ed.), *Philosophical theory and the Universal Declaration of Human Rights* (pp. 109–126). Ottawa: University of Ottawa Press.
Naletova, I. (2012). Human rights – The Russian Orthodox Churches' Teaching and survey data. In A. Brunig & E. van der Zweerde (Eds.), *Orthodox Christianity and human rights* (pp. 214–235). Leuven: Peeters.
Nelson, J. R. (1982). Human rights in creation and redemption: A Protestant view. In A. Swidler (Ed.), *Human rights in religious traditions (1982) Journal of Ecumenical studies* (pp. 1–13). New York: Pilgrim Press.
Nichols, J. A. (2009). Evangelicals and human rights: The continuing Ambivalence of Evangelical Christians' support of human rights. *Journal of Law and Religion, 7,* 629–662. University of St, Thomas Legal Studies Research Paper No. 09–02. http://ssrn.com/abstract=1334338. Accessed 18 Mar 2015.
Oh, I. (2007). *The rights of god: Islam, human rights, and comparative ethics*. Washington, DC: Georgetown University Press.
Pontifical Council for Justice and Peace. (2004). *Compendium of the social doctrine of the Catholic Church*. Libreria Editrice Vaticana [Washington, DC: USCCB Publishing].
Preda, R. (2012). Human rights and their reception in Orthodoxy – A Romanian perspective. In A. Brunig & E. van der Zweerde (Eds.), *Orthodox Christianity and human rights* (pp. 293–313). Peeters: Leuven.
Russian Orthodox Church, Department for External Church Relations. (2008). *The Russian Orthodox Church's basic teaching on human society, freedom and rights*. https://mospat.ru/en/documents/dignity-freedom-rights. Accessed 17 Mar 2015.
Sachedina, A. (2009). *Islam and the challenge of human rights*. Oxford: Oxford University Press.
Scott, B. C. (2008). *The crossroads of religion and development: The Ixil region, Evangelical religion, and Rios Montt*. Monograph. Athens: University of Georgia. http://www.scribd.com/doc/236454912/Religion-y-Rios-Montt
Sen, A. (1999). *Development as freedom*. New York: Knopf.
Sen, A. (2009). *The idea of justice*. Cambridge, MA: Harvard University Press.
Siskova, A. (2008). *Russian Orthodox church sets tone on human rights*. Radio Free Europe/Radio Liberty. http://www.rferl.org/content/Russian_Orthodox_Church_Sets_Tone_Human_Rights/1181014.html. Accessed 17 Mar 2015.
Soroush, A. (2000). *Reason, freedom, and democracy: Essential writings of Abdolkarim Soroush*. (Ed., intro. Mahmoud Sadri, Ahmad Sadri, Trans.). New York: Oxford University Press.
Stoeckl, K. (2014). *The Russian Orthodox Church and human rights*. Oxford: Routledge.
Vatican Council II. (1965). Gaudium et Spes: Pastoral constitution on the Church in the Modern World.

Valente, G. (2013, June 13). *The war between the Liberation Theology movement and Rome is over*. Vatican Insider, La Stampa. http://vaticaninsider.lastampa.it/en/the-vatican/detail/articolo/teologia-della-liberazione-freedom-theology-teologia-de-la-libertad-vaticano-vatican-25842/. Accessed 20 Mar 2015.
Witte, J. Jr. (1998, Fall). Law, religion, and human rights. *Journal of Religious Ethics, 26*(2), 257–262.

Chapter 2
Predictors of Attitudes Towards Human Dignity: An Empirical Analysis Among Youth in Germany

Hans-Georg Ziebertz, Susanne Döhnert, and Alexander Unser

Abstract Historically, the dominant understanding of human dignity was contingent, by which we mean that, according to this view, dignity was regarded as depending on a person's social position or behaviour. A loss of social rank or immoral behaviour meant that it was possible to lose one's dignity. However, since the time of the enlightenment, an understanding of dignity arose which claimed that dignity should be regarded as something inherent to all human beings; by its very nature, this inherent dignity could not be lost. Although there exists some controversy in both philosophy and law about the content and scope of what is meant by "dignity", various declarations in human rights charters and constitutions refer to human dignity as the foundation of rights. This paper explores three different dimensions of dignity. Empirically, the authors will examine how German adolescents (N = 2,175) evaluate these types of dignity and we will discuss which predictors are significant. The general assumption is that different understandings of dignity exist among German youth and that religious belief, the ability to be empathic and sensitive, social class affiliation and socialization are all predictors of attitudes towards dignity. The analysis shows that empathy and religious belief are the strongest predictors.

The goal of this paper is to explore the views of German youth on human dignity. The paper also seeks to find out if attitudes on dignity can be predicted by religious beliefs, interpersonal awareness and certain socio-demographic characteristics. The paper is organized into four parts: (1) it starts by clarifying the concepts used in this study; (2) it describes the design of the empirical study; (3) it presents the empirical findings; and (4) it ends with a conclusion.

H.-G. Ziebertz (✉) • S. Döhnert • A. Unser
Institute of Practical Theology, University of Würzburg, Würzburg, Germany
e-mail: hg.ziebertz@uni-wuerzburg.de; susanne.doehnert@uni-wuerzburg.de; alexander.unser@uni-wuerzburg.de

H.-G. Ziebertz, C. Sterkens (eds.), *Religion and Civil Human Rights in Empirical Perspective*, Religion and Human Rights 2, DOI 10.1007/978-3-319-59285-5_2

Theoretical Introduction

This first paragraph offers a brief overview of how the concept of human dignity is used in the literature and how this term is connected with human rights. The paper then goes on to focus on possible predictors of attitudes towards human dignity: religious belief, interpersonal sensitivity and social context. This conceptualization provides a theoretical platform for the empirical study that follows.

Human Dignity

Our understanding of the term "human dignity" has changed considerably as a result of the cultural history. According to one tradition, dignity is regarded as contingent upon certain properties. This property may be social, where dignity is related to a person's social role and social function (e.g. someone's dignity depended on whether he was a judge, a bishop or a president). The expressive dimension is connected with a person's behaviour. Here, someone is said to demonstrate dignified behaviour if he or she is able to control his or her desires and emotions (in the case of, for example, conflict). In other words, expressive dignity in behaviour is noble conduct. Aesthetical dignity relates to dignified bodily movement (e.g. a priest conducting the liturgy; those taking part in a funeral); aesthetical dignity also relates to buildings (e.g. cathedrals) and certain places (e.g. cemeteries). When talking about contingent dignity, the observable phenomena are that people project dignity when they perform certain roles, engage in certain behaviour, and when they are connected to numinous objects (cf. Schaber 2012, 20–21).

When Cicero spoke of human dignity (*dignitas*) this term was a Latin translation of the Greek *axioma*. In the Greek tradition, *axioma* was contingent on someone's social origin, social position and behaviour. The Stoics invented the differentiation between *axioma* and *axia*. *Axioma* is a feature of reasonable persons and a type of inner value, while *axia* is a hallmark of everyday objects. Cicero connects *dignitas* with *ratio*: man has reason and intellect, the human person is not fully determined by nature. It is the ability of human beings to act guided by reason which makes them different from the animals (Rosen 2012, 12). Human beings can eschew pleasure, can resist their impulses and can choose to live frugally and abstemiously. A lifestyle that is based on a resistance to natural impulses lends dignity to the person who adopts such a lifestyle. If dignity is an observable and desirable phenomenon of behaviour it is consequently a normative ideal for people to behave in accordance with this ideal. Human beings are obliged to use their abilities to act with dignity – but they may also fail (cf. Schaber 2012, 21–23). If failure is possible, dignity is connected with behavior and this understanding of dignity is contingent. On the other hand, this view includes the notion that human beings can transcend behaviour that is determined by nature. In short, Cicero prepares the ground for a view of dignity that claims dignity as intrinsic to human beings as such (Rosen 2012, 12).

During the Renaissance period, Pico della Mirandola's work was valued as an important contribution to the development of a modern understanding of dignity. In his reflection on human nature, Pico della Mirandola elaborated on the distinctiveness of man which, he claimed, was mainly rooted in the fact that man was free not to fulfil any preordained role. In other words, human beings can make free use of the capacities given to them by the Creator (God), something that is not true of any other creature. Pico della Mirandola took the argument further and went on to state that dignity can be regarded as a characteristic of all human beings, that dignity was not reducible to people's roles or behaviour, but that is was a condition of man based on the will of the Creator. However, what happens if people make an undesirable use of their abilities?

Thomas Aquinas, in the *Commentary on the sentences,* wrote "dignity signifies something's goodness on account of itself" (quotation in Rosen 2012, 16). Aquinas' words could be read as supporting the concept of inherent dignity. Nevertheless, it can be shown that Christianity operates with a dual concept of dignity. One dimension is that the image of God is mirrored in man and that human beings share the dignity of God. The other dimension is that man is part of God's creation and challenged to realize God's plan of creation in his or her life. From this understanding, it follows that dignity is bestowed on someone when that person behaves in accordance with God's plan. A consequence of this view is that dignity can be lost when human beings sin. Behaviour, therefore, is still an important element of dignity. Aquinas can state that, as a result of free will, man can decide right or wrong, for or against God (see Schaber 2012, 23–24). Against this background, dignity is a given gift, but is nevertheless contingent because it depends on behaviour.

In all the cases mentioned above human dignity is something that can be lost, either because someone has failed to live in accordance with God's will, or because he or she has lost a certain social status. Although the elaboration of dignity shows that the term has different aspects, dignity remains dependent on behaviour and status. The term dignity is related to duties, but not to rights. This understanding of human dignity was to remain dominant in European thought until the time of the Enlightenment.

In modern times, the work of the philosopher Immanuel Kant initiated the beginnings of a change in the understanding of what constitutes human dignity. Kant distinguishes between general human needs and something that has an end in itself. What relates to human needs is a question of taste; it has a marked price and a relative value. What constitutes the condition under which something can be an end in itself has an intrinsic value rather than a relative value. That condition is morality and humanity is capable of morality, which means that only morality has dignity (cf. Rosen 2012, 20–21). Morality is based on autonomy, which is the basis of the dignity inherent in human nature. Human beings can make reasonable decisions based on rational considerations, and they can control their desires and impulses; in short, humans are capable of moral behaviour and they carry the moral law within themselves. Indeed, this is what all humans have in common. Dignity is not based on whether and how life is practiced in moral terms, but is grounded on the capacity for moral behaviour. According to Kant, the full meaning of dignity is restricted to human beings only because no other creature is characterized by having autonomy. Rosen reminds us that autonomy, for Kant, is different from the modern understanding of autonomy (freedom of choice, of lifestyle, etc.). According to Kant, the notion of autonomy contains two concepts: the *autos* and the *nomos* (self and law). "What Kant has in mind as autonomy is the idea that the moral law which we must acknowledge as binding upon us is 'self-given'" (Rosen 2012, 25). Kant developed the concept of human dignity as a moral principle. Human dignity is based on morality, and morality is an inherent characteristic of humanity.

It should be stated that, as far as Kant was concerned, there was no direct "line", so to speak, from dignity to rights. (In fact, this connection was only established by the United Nations in 1966, in its International Covenant on Civil and Political Rights; in this Covenant, the individual was recognized as a citizen and equipped with rights (Lohmann 2014, 18–20).)

However, neither did the concept of dignity follow a straight line of development, nor have all scholars been convinced that the term is meaningful. Nietzsche polemicized against dignity as a "conceptual hallucination" and Marx called it an "empty phrase". The question is still raised today: If dignity is replaceable by other concepts, is it in fact a superfluous term?

There are, currently, numerous attempts to define this concept more precisely (see McCrudden 2013 with a multitude of excellent papers). Some authors vote for a substantive operationalization of the term and specify those concrete rights that characterize human dignity (cf. Birnbacher 1995). These authors understand human dignity as a collective term delineating a series of specific rights (fundamental rights) which can be distinguished from others (lesser or non-fundamental rights). However, this attempt creates new problems: Why choose one content rather than another? How realistic is the possibility of consensus when the decision is about substantive definitions?

Furthermore, the concept of human dignity is challenged by naturalism; according to naturalism, human beings are natural beings and humankind is a product of evolution. Ideas of the Enlightenment, that man is a special species, distinguished by reason, self-consciousness and a free will, are incompatible with naturalism (Wagner 1992). In other words, the empirical basis of important preconditions is now subject to heavy criticism. This criticism is even more marked when it comes to religious interpretations of the concept of dignity, especially as these interpretations relate to transcendent claims.

From a religiously committed position, the question is raised if inherent dignity can be defined without a reference to transcendence. For Martin Kriele (1986), the idea of human dignity has its roots in Stoic philosophy and the Christian tradition. For Kriele, the concept of dignity is not something that can be entertained at all without referring to these metaphysical roots. According to Kriele, although the protagonists of the Enlightenment avoided (religious) metaphysics, they did not eliminate transcendent reasoning. Hans Joas has proposed the term "sacralised person" to substantiate the emergence of the term "human dignity" (Joas 2011).

However, in today's pluralist society, there is no common worldview and no unified idea of what constitutes man. At the same time, the lack of any common denominator by which to define the term "man" seems to be very unsatisfactory, both for individuals and for the world community (Kress 1999). To bridge this gap, the term "human dignity" comes into use, a term that fulfils the function of providing a core concept on which to establish basic human rights. There seems to be broad acceptance of the concept of dignity (more precisely, the concept of inherent dignity). Both religious and non-religious parties can agree to such an understanding. Reiter (2004) claims that, if dignity is understood as inherent to all human beings, than it is a secondary matter whether we assume that dignity is "given by God" or even simply "given".

The philosophical debate contains many open questions about the definition of human dignity and its relation to concepts such as respect, grace, honour, equality, etc. This text does not claim to offer a solution of the problems mentioned above or to propose an integration of the divergent understandings.

In this section, the concern is to define the parameters that will enable us to "translate" conceptual ideas into empirical measuring instruments. A fundamental differentiation is the contingent and non-contingent interpretation of human dignity. Because the meaning of inherent dignity is widely shared, we have assumed, empirically, that this understanding is the one most widely accepted. Non-contingent interpretations are not without supporters, but we have assumed that these interpretations are not, generally speaking, regarded as convincing.

Human Dignity and Human Rights

Notwithstanding the philosophical debate about the precision, explicitness and unambiguity of the concept of dignity, there is no doubt that dignity is of fundamental importance for our understanding of human rights. In practical policy, both the United Nations and European Union agree that human dignity legitimizes and justifies individual rights. Human dignity seems to express best the fundamental ethical concern to substantiate all claims for humanity comprehensively. Dignity is therefore recognized as the legal concept that precedes all other rights (Grimm 2013).

Since the Universal Declaration of Human Rights (UDHR) in 1948, declarations of human rights have referred to human dignity as a key concept for human rights or even their very foundation. The UDHR (1948) uses the term "inherent dignity" in its preamble and states that "recognition of the inherent dignity and of the equal and inalienable rights of all members of the human family is the foundation of freedom, justice and peace in the world." All human beings are born free and equal in dignity and rights (art. 1) and everyone has the right to life, liberty and security of person (art. 3). The International Covenant on Civil and Political Rights (1966) speaks very clearly about the foundational character of human dignity. In its preamble, the document says: "Considering that, in accordance with the principles proclaimed in the Charter of the United Nations, recognition of the inherent dignity and of the equal and inalienable rights of all members of the human family is the foundation of freedom, justice and peace in the world. Recognizing that these rights derive from the inherent dignity of the human person … [contracting states] agree upon the following articles ....". This international Covenant argues that every human being has an inherent right to life and that law shall protect this right and that no one shall be arbitrarily deprived of his or her life.

Human dignity is also the subject matter of the preamble and article 1 of the Charter of Fundamental Rights in the European Union (2000). The preamble states that, "conscious of its spiritual and moral heritage, the Union is founded on the indivisible, universal values of human dignity, freedom, equality and solidarity; it is based on the principles of democracy and the rule of law. It places the individual at the heart of its activities, by establishing the citizenship of the Union and by creating an area of freedom, security and justice". Article 1 of this charter adds: "Human dignity is inviolable. It must be respected and protected."

Similar quotations are used by constitutions of nation states, where human dignity is a legitimizing concept for basic rights. That is especially the case in the Federal Republic of Germany. In article 1, the constitution [Grundgesetz] says: "Human dignity is inviolable. To respect it and protect it is the duty of all state power. The German people therefore acknowledge inviolable and inalienable human rights as the basis of every community, of peace and of justice in the world."

These examples show that there exists a strong relationship between human dignity and human rights. Philosophically, one can argue that it is not clear how dignity functions as ground of rights and what rights it grounds. Is there a correspondence with the Kantian formula of universal law "to act only in accordance with that maxim through which you can at the same time will that it becomes universal law"? Finally, is there a direct line from equal dignity to equal rights (see Rosen 2012, 55)? Notwithstanding the ongoing debate about the status of the concept of dignity, in practice the concept of dignity functions as the foundation of rights that people have because they are human beings. For the empirical investigation that forms the subject of this paper, we have used that distinctive interpretation of human dignity as being something that is inherent to all human beings.

Religion, Belief and Human Dignity

Although the discussion of human dignity is not exclusive to Christianity, this concept is reflected in the very beginnings of Christian theology. Indeed, we can state that dignity belongs to the core concepts of Christian belief, because it connects God and humankind by stating that there is an analogy between the two (see papers in McCrudden 2013, 207–288). It is by no means irrelevant for religious people to think in a certain manner about dignity. This is the reason why one can assume that an empirical connection can be found between religion, belief and dignity.

Wetz (2011) shows in his collection of texts from ancient times to today that Church fathers such as Origen, Laktantius, Augustine and Ambrose all developed a concept of dignity. What they have in common is the belief that dignity is the essence of the human self, but at the same time that it refers to a certain order of life. Dignity is primarily based on the fact that human beings are made in the likeness of God. The theological source of this claim is, of course, the book Genesis [1:26–27]: "Then God said, 'Let us make humankind in our image, according to our likeness; and let them have dominion over the fish of the sea, and over the birds of the air, and over the cattle, and over all the wild animals of the earth, and over every creeping thing that creeps upon the earth.' So God created humankind in his image, in the image of God he created them; male and female he created them." Genesis serves as proof that human beings are special creations of God. Also, according to these Church fathers, there is the incarnation of God in Christ – God became human, mirrored in the personal nature of humankind, which is characterized by the free will, and finally underlined by the eminent place of humankind in the natural order of things. Another indirect reference to dignity is seen in Paul's letter to the Romans when he writes: [3:23] "…for all have sinned and fall short of the glory of God, [3:24] being justified as a gift by His grace through the redemption which is in Christ Jesus". These two verses are about justification and justification is promised to all, regardless of their actions – the text can therefore be read as saying that justification is "inherent" to humankind.

In recent history, Vatican II reflected on the dignity of the human person, especially in its declaration *Dignitatis Humanae*. The position taken by the Catholic Church here was further worked out in the Catechism of the Catholic Church (CCC)[1]: [nr 1700] "The dignity of the human person is rooted in his creation in the image and likeness of God (art. 1); it is fulfilled in his vocation to divine beatitude (art. 2). It is essential to a human being freely to direct himself to this fulfilment (art. 3). By his deliberate actions (art. 4), the human person does, or does not, conform to the good promised by God and attested by moral conscience (art. 5). Human beings make their own contribution to their interior growth; they make their whole sentient and spiritual lives into means of this growth (art. 6). With the help of grace they grow in virtue (art. 7), avoid sin, and if they sin they entrust themselves as did the prodigal son to the mercy of our Father in heaven (article 8). In this way they attain to the perfection of charity." In these statements, autonomy and rationality are imbedded, according to the Catholic Church, in a theonomous framework: both are given to man by God Himself.

The CCC continues, in number 1934, to state that dignity is given to everyone: "Created in the image of the one God and equally endowed with rational souls, all men have the same nature and the same origin. Redeemed by the sacrifice of Christ, all are called to participate in the same divine beatitude: all therefore enjoy an equal dignity." The CCC underlines the fact that dignity is foundational and that is must be recognized as prior to other laws in society. In number 1930,[2] the Catechism states thus: "Respect for the human person entails respect for the rights that flow from his dignity as a creature. These rights are prior to society and must be

[1] CCC Part III, sec 1, ch 1: http://www.vatican.va/archive/ccc_css/archive/catechism/p3s1c1.htm

[2] http://www.vatican.va/archive/ENG0015/_INDEX.HTM

recognized by it. They are the basis of the moral legitimacy of every authority: by flouting them, or refusing to recognize them in its positive legislation, a society undermines its own moral legitimacy. If it does not respect them, authority can rely only on force or violence to obtain obedience from its subjects. It is the Church's role to remind men of good will of these rights and to distinguish them from unwarranted or false claims."

For the Catholic Church, dignity derives from natural law, which mirrors divine law. The conceptualization of dignity in Catholic thinking is anchored in the idea of a divine order. In this order dignity is both foundational and challenges people to adopt their life to the divine order.

In Protestant thought, the concept of natural law is clearly rejected (Karl Barth) or virtually absent. We can take the Catechism of the Protestant Church in Germany as an example. This text reflects on human dignity at several places (see Brummer et al. 2010, 313f). The Catechism states that, even if the term "dignity" is not found in the Bible, the idea of dignity is present, especially in the concept that man – according to the first book of Moses (1 Gen 1:26f) – is made in the image of God. This is opposed to a notion of dignity that makes dignity dependent on certain skills, services or characteristics. A consequence would be that such features are present in some people, but for others they are missing. In short, according to this view, dignity is distributed differently throughout humankind. These authors argue that an inherent understanding of dignity must be defended. When scholars of legal law define human dignity, they describe it as a "dowry" which is "given" to man. Such a phrase can be read as a transcendent claim, without naming it transcendent. According to Brunner et al., believers are unembarrassed to identify God as being the foundation of this "dowry". According to believers, dignity is a gift from God and Jesus is the archetype of humanity (Catechism 313ff).

This Protestant Catechism admits the fact that, for a long time, Protestant churches paid more attention to human sin than they did to human dignity. The doctrine of original sin worked to obstruct the view of the law and the dignity of man (Catechism 426). In the period before the Reformation, only believers had a right to dignity: heresy and unbelief allowed people to be persecuted and tortured (because such people were regarded as lacking any form of dignity). However, attitudes changed with the advent of the Reformation and the rise of Humanism. While Humanism justified dignity on the basis of all human beings' ability to reason, a central concept for the Reformers was justification before God. According to Luther, human dignity is exclusively the result of the graciousness of God (Catechism 426).

As far as the Eastern Orthodox Church is concerned, there exists a strong link between dignity and moral behaviour. The Moscow Patriarchate describes dignity as a gift from God and with this gift comes the responsibility to refrain from sin and to align one's life according to the commandments of God - so to become more God-like (theosis). In Christian Orthodoxy, dignity has primarily a moral significance. Orthodoxy is convinced that God's moral commandments are available in every person through the dignity that God gives to all human beings. Human beings can recognize these commandments by their consciences, as Paul writes in the Letter to the Romans (Rom 2:15). According to Orthodoxy, dignity is strongly dependent on human action; in practice, dignity can be unrecognizable. At the same time, Orthodoxy is convinced that man cannot destroy dignity, since dignity has been bestowed upon him ontologically (cf. The Russian Orthodox Church's Basic Teaching on Human Dignity, Freedom and Rights, 2008).[3]

The brief summary of texts of the major Christian denominations in Europe and Central Asia referred to above underlines the importance of the concept of dignity in Christian religious context. For Catholicism, and even more for Orthodoxy, dignity is not reducible to autonomy and freedom of choice, but includes the obligation to align one's life to the divine order. We can therefore assume that believers and religiously sensitive people, for whom religion is important, are particularly supportive of the concept of dignity. These people will all strongly agree with the concept of inherent dignity, although they will also regard moral behaviour as a qualifying element of dignity.

Interpersonal Awareness and Human Dignity

When talking about human dignity, there are theoretical reasons to take the ability of interpersonal awareness – in addition to religion – into account. Here we differentiate between empathy and sensitivity.

There is a strong tradition in philosophy and psychology that emphasizes the importance of rationality for morality. Kant, for example, defines morality as the ability to have insight into moral principles and to act in accordance with these principles. In theory, the function of moral principles is to guide moral judgments and to create a motivational basis for pro-social actions. In the tradition of Piaget's cognitive developmental theory, the dependency of moral judgments on the cognitive development of a person has been the subject of a great deal of research (cf. Kohlberg et al. 1983). However, what these traditions lack is any reference to the importance of emotions in morality. To put it another way: the role of rational reasoning tends to be overestimated, at the expense of the role of emotions.

Research has shown that there is, in fact, a strong relationship between the emotions and moral principles (cf. e.g. Keller and Malti 2008, 411–412). Pro-social motivation is not *per se* a consequence of rational reflection, but is also aroused by emotions (Hoffman 1990b, 48). In social psychology, the concept of empathy, which means the ability to feel with others, is seen as an important link between emotions and morality or moral behaviour. Empathy is defined as "the reactions of one individual to the observed experiences of another" (Davis 1983, 113). Examples are the experience of the other that he or she is sad or happy or that he or she suffers, is discriminated against, etc. Empathy is based on identification, that is, the awareness that the other has the same feelings and needs as myself. Empathy leads to attentiveness and caring.

[3] https://mospat.ru/en/documents/dignity-freedom-rights

Hoffman (1990b, 48) emphasizes the importance of the relationship between empathy and morality. The empathic observation of someone's distress leads to emotions such as guilt or anger. Which emotions are aroused depends on a number of factors, such as causal attribution, accessible information about the situation, (social) concepts of disadvantage, etc. (Hoffman 1990a, 161). What we can say is that the emotions that are aroused are the motivational basis for further pro-social behaviour. The probability of pro-social behaviour increases with the degree of perceived responsibility, on the part of the observer, for the distress of the other. There is no need for the distressed person to be physically present; it is sufficient that the distressed person is present in the observer's mind. Emotions can be aroused by reading media reports, by listening to church sermons, and by attending to lessons in school. That said, it is probable that emotions are more intensive when they are aroused as a result of direct observation (Hoffman 1990a, 162; 1990b, 59).

Empathy can be directed to individuals and to social groups (Hoffman 1990a, 154). In late childhood, children develop the ability to become concerned with the destiny of social groups (f.i. refugees, Sinti and Roma, etc.). Older children have the ability to realize that someone's distress is caused by the very structure of society, a structure that can have very real consequences for an individual's future (Hoffman 1990b, p. 52). For example, when media report about boat people coming from Africa to Europe and reports about Africans who already arrived and who are waiting for asylum in European cities, this can provoke a chain of feelings. Research has shown that people with high empathic skills agree more with those moral principles that emphasize the equality of all human beings than those who support ideas of meritocracy (see e.g. Hoffman 1990a, 164–166; 1990b, 71–72; Montada et al. 1986; McFarland, Matthews 2005, 378–379).

This research was written on the assumption that empathy is a significant predictor for someone accepting the notion that all human beings are endowed with dignity (cf. Hoffman 1990b, 64, 71–72). More specifically, we assume that high empathy skills positively influence the adoption of a non-contingent concept of dignity, whereas contingent concepts (of dignity) will be evaluated negatively by those with a high degree of empathy.

While empathy includes similar emotions with the perceived other, sensitivity is more about "attention for", which does not presuppose, necessarily, that similar emotions are shared. Empathy is more strongly connected to commitment than is sensitivity. The two concepts are related, but are different. Research has shown that the development of moral thinking is connected with certain domains and specific (thematic) experiences. In our research we will explore whether a sensitivity to injustice in society predicts the valuation of human dignity (cf. Doise et al. 1999, 5). Is the perception of tensions between social groups and society relevant for attitudes towards human dignity, f.i. tensions between privileged vs. underprivileged people, between religions, races, etc.?

Generally speaking, sensitivity and empathy seem to be linked to attitudes regarding human dignity. What has been said above about the influence of empathy could be also valid for sensitivity. Nevertheless, an important difference between the two concepts is the degree of interpersonal commitment. Sensitivity is not a trait that necessarily contains a high level of empathy. Empirically, we assume that empathy is more relevant than sensitivity when it comes to attitudes towards group-related tensions in society for positive attitudes towards the non-contingent concept of human dignity.

Social Context and Human Dignity

Up to this point, we have argued that religion and interpersonal awareness are relevant predictors for attitudes towards human dignity. In the following paragraphs, we want to discuss certain socio-demographic characteristics.

Firstly, we introduce the context of students' social class. A longitudinal survey with Icelandic pupils has shown that social class influences people's socio-moral thinking. Adolescents from upper-class families have significant higher skills in socio-moral thinking. The researchers explain these skills by the class-specific socialization process: upper-class families provide their children with advantageous socialization factors (Dravenau 2006, 206–207; Keller et al. 2007). These factors include an intellectual family climate in which children learn to argue and to reflect, parents practice a cooperative and appreciative education style (cf. Baumrind 1971; Tausch and Tausch 1973) and their ideal of education is that their children become autonomous and "moral" persons (Grundmann and Bittlingmayer 2006, 162–170; Dravenau 2006, 208).

In this paper, we have therefore assumed that social class matters, especially as far as the contingent notion of dignity is concerned. Respondents from lower-class families experience the fact that a contingent understanding of dignity is still present in society and that dignity is often linked to reputation and prestige; this, in turn, is often connected with their experiences of an inequality of opportunity in society. Our expectations are that lower-class children tend to accept a more contingent understanding of dignity than do upper-class children. In other words, upper-class respondents will favour the non-contingent concept of dignity more than will the comparison group.

Secondly, we pay attention to the role of parents and peers as agents in the religious socialization processes. Parents are important for their children's moral development; they provide basic orientations by structuring everyday family life, by appreciating and by showing their disapproval of specific behaviour (Krappmann 2001, 156–157; Kramer 2011, 174; Vester et al. 2001, 163, 165; Bittlingmayer 2006, 42; Grundmann 2006, 57–58).

The importance of religious beliefs for the acceptance of human dignity has already been mentioned above. However, religious beliefs do not develop without context, but within religious socialization processes when parents talk about religious issues and when they practice rituals, prayers, etc. (Sherkat 2007, 151; Ziebertz and Riegel 2008, 77). Parents' importance in the process of religious socialization is accepted and the influence of parents does not end with adolescence (Myers 1996, 863). This is in support of the evidence that shows that religious socialization within the family is particularly important if children internalize religious beliefs. Parental religious socialization succeeds when a moderate style of religious devotion is practiced and when both parents agree about religious beliefs and practices (Myers 1996, 863). In this respect, findings show that the mother is often more influential in the religious socialization of children (cf. Klein 1999; Liebold 2005); this is not the case in Muslim families (Ziebertz and Benzing 2012, 50–55). Parents' importance in religious socialization also depends on the national context. Comparisons between fifteen nations show that parental influence on the child's religious socialization increases in less religious societies and decreases in societies that are overtly religious (Kelley and De Graaf 1997, 650–653; cf. Acock and Bengston 1978, 525).

During adolescence, the peer group becomes a significant socialization agent. Particularly during the time the adolescent lives separately from his or her parental home, it is the peer-group that offers security. Indeed, it is sometimes argued that, not only do peers have influence on a youth's religious socialization, but that peers can, in fact, be more important than parents and congregations. Of course, when peers do become more important, parents try to influence the adolescent's selection of friends. Martin shows that peers' influence mediates parents' influence on a youth's religious beliefs and practices (Martin et al. 2003, 179–182).

We have stated that religion and belief influence people's acceptance of the concept of human dignity, but religious socialization will also have an influence. We assume that the mother's influence is stronger than the father's and that peers can have influence. The influence of religious socialization on the acceptance of the concept of human dignity will increase when both parents agree with each other about religious matters, when they practice religion in moderation and when they support a moderate education style. The influence of religious socialization will decrease, when both parents disagree with each other in their religiosity, or when they practice a strict style of religious education (cf. Myers 1996, 863–864).

Finally, in addition to social class and socialization we consider sex (gender) and age to be relevant for attitudes towards human dignity. Because our study is based on a sample of a certain age group, the group chosen is largely homogenous. That makes it difficult to formulate assumptions. As far as gender is concerned, we adhere to the classical opinion that females often demonstrate a higher moral sensitivity than males. Empirically, it is possible that females support more than males the non-contingent concept of dignity, whereas the contingent understanding of the concept of dignity will be independent from gender.

Method

This paragraph discusses the design of the study. We begin with describing how we collected data and our sampling techniques. An important part of the research method is the conceptual model that forms the basis of the research and the way this is operationalized. We shall end this section by presenting our research questions and hypotheses. The research question here is: *What attitude do young Germans have towards the concept of human dignity and what factors influence their attitude?*

Research Procedure and Sample

The frame of this research paper is the international empirical research project *Religion and Human Rights (2012–2019).*[4] The purpose of the project is to explore conceptions of casual relations concerning the relevance of religious affiliation, dimensions of religious convictions, value orientations, worldviews and the socialization context of young people and their attitudes towards human rights.

This article refers to the data collected in the German survey. The basis of the written survey is a standardized questionnaire that was designed by the international research group, and coordinated by one of the authors (Hans-Georg Ziebertz). The final version of the questionnaire was provided in English and translated into the different languages by the national teams.

In Germany, data collection took place from spring 2013 to winter 2013/14. The survey was conducted in 11 of Germany's 16 federal states. A total of 2,157 students were interviewed, and these interviews were conducted in 35 schools in 19 cities. The schools were selected using a three-stage process. First, Germany was divided into five regions (north/northwest; west; southwest; south/southeast and east) in order to consider different attitudes within the population – since several studies have shown that there are significant differences in attitudes within these regions. In the second stage, four, middle-sized cities per region were selected that would adequately represent the different regions (see Fig. 2.1). The schools were then selected on the basis of a random sample. Finally, participants were students in the 10th and 11th grades (about 16 years).

The data collection took place in cooperation with the participating schools. Together with the questionnaires, detailed information and instructions for teachers were sent on how to organize the investigation in the classes. The total number of questionnaires sent to the schools was 3,950, of which 2,243 were returned and 2,157 selected as suitable for evaluation. The final sample included 72.5% Christians, 5.5% Muslims, 17.7% non-religious students and 4.3% belonging to other religious traditions.

North/northwest:	Lingen	Lübeck	Lüneburg	Rostock
West:	Wesel	Düren	Gießen	Trier
Southwest:	Pforzheim	Rottenburg	Ulm	Offenburg
South/southeast:	Freising	Deggendorf	Donauwörth	Schweinfurt
East:	Heiligenstadt	Dresden	Jena	

Fig. 2.1 Cities in which the fieldwork took place

[4] http://www.rhr.theologie.uni-wuerzburg.de

This division corresponds approximately to the data of Western Germany's national census. Of the participating students, 41% were male and 59% female. On average, participating students were 16 years old.

Conceptual Model

In the conceptual model (see Fig. 2.2), the variable we want to explain is human dignity (= dependent variable). We assume that religious belief and interpersonal awareness (= independent variable) are predictors of attitudes towards human dignity. In this research, we were not interested in the causes of belief and awareness; we therefore treat these as independent. A further assumption is that population characteristics will have some importance as predictors of attitudes towards human dignity. We choose the social-class context, socio-demographic features and socialization. In the empirical analysis, we bring in the five predictors using a five-step hierarchical OLS Regression model.

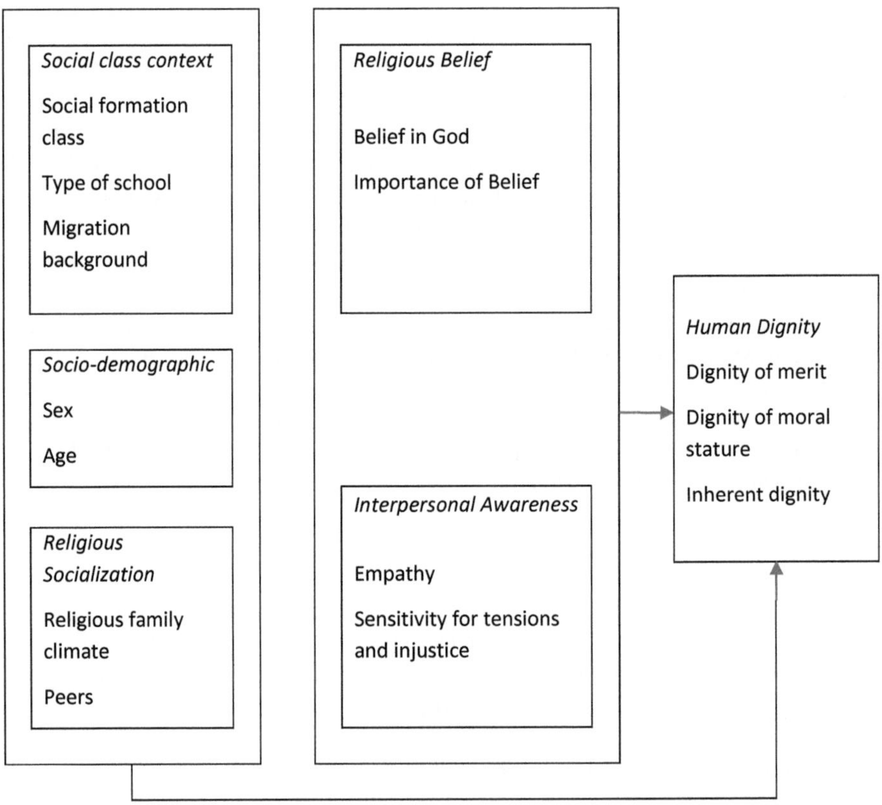

Fig. 2.2 Conceptual model

Conceptualization and Operationalization

In the following paragraphs, these concepts will be described in detail. When instruments are based on scales (instead of single items) we tolerate a Cronbach's alpha of minimum .60.

Human Dignity

Human dignity can be understood as contingent and non-contingent. If human dignity is a differentiating principle, individuals possess human dignity owing to their position within society or owing to personal achievement. This is an example of a contingent meaning of dignity. In contrast, if dignity is an equalizing principle, human beings all possess dignity simply because of their humanity. This is what is meant by a non-contingent understanding of the concept of dignity (cf. Huber 1992, 578; Nordenfelt 2004, 70–78).

In this research, two aspects of a contingent meaning of human dignity are included. According to Nordenfelt (2004), there is, firstly, the *human dignity of merit* – when dignity depends on someone's social position. Secondly, there is the *human dignity of moral stature* – when dignity depends on a person's individual achievements or behaviour. Dignity of merit is operationalized as being dependent on society's appreciation of the person in question; dignity as social stature depends on the person's moral behaviour. The non-contingent meaning of human dignity is defined as *inherent dignity*, which means that dignity is basically connected with humanity (see Fig. 2.3). All three dimensions will be measured by one item (Table 2.3).

(Human dignity of merit)

The value of a person depends on the appreciation given to him or her by others.

(Human dignity of moral stature)

The honour to be given to a person depends on his moral behaviour.

(Inherent human dignity)

Each human being should be recognized just because he is a human being, irrespective of credit or moral behaviour.

Answer scheme: 1=I totally disagree; 2=I disagree; 3=I am not sure; 4=I agree; 5=I fully agree

Fig. 2.3 Dimensions of human dignity

Religious Belief

The concept of human dignity is deeply anchored in the Christian tradition. In this research, belief functions as a possible predictor for attitudes towards human dignity. In order to measure religious belief, three dimensions were selected (see Fig. 2.4). The first dimension concerns personal belief in God and the importance of belief. The Cronbach's alpha for this three-item scale is .81. The second dimension is about trust in religion. The answering scheme runs from 1 (no trust) to 10 (high trust). The third dimension measures religious belonging and lack of religious affiliation.

(Belief in God and importance of belief) → alpha .81

How often do you think about religious issues?
To what extent do you believe that God or something divine exists?
What is your position on the statement: My religion or worldview has great influence on my daily life?
Answer scheme: 1=I totally disagree; 2=I disagree; 3=I am not sure; 4=I agree; 5=I fully agree

(Trust in religion)
If you are committed to a religion, to what degree (low or high) do you generally trust your religion?
Answer scheme: scale 1 (low) – 10 (high)

(Religious affiliation)
Do you belong to one of the religious communities or would you describe yourself as non-religious?
Answer scheme: 16 religions/denominations and the categories ‚other religion' and 'non-religious'

Fig. 2.4 Religious belief

Interpersonal Awareness

As a second non-religious predictor for attitudes towards human dignity–'interpersonal awareness'–was selected. Interpersonal awareness seems to be relevant for the valuation of human dignity because there exists a relationship between empathy, sensitivity and morality. The operationalization of this concept includes 'empathy' and 'sensitivity for tensions and injustice' (see Fig. 2.5).

Empathy is an important concept in social psychology and is defined as "the reactions of one individual to the observed experiences of another" (Davis 1983, 113). A tested scale to measure empathy is the 'Interpersonal Reactivity Index' (IRI) (Davis 1980). From this scale the 'empathic concern subscale' (EC) is used which "measures the tendency to experience feelings of warmth, compassion, and concern of other people" (Davis 1980, p. 117). In this research a scale of three (of previous seven) items of the EC is used with an internal consistency of α=.66.

The second concept measures the sensitivity for tensions and injustice for four different societal conflicts (cf. Doise et al. 1999). These four conflicts are included into the regression model as four single items because the four different conflicts seem to be too different to represent a common dimension of a scale.

(Empathy) →alpha: .66

I often have tender, concerned feelings for people less fortunate than me.
When I see someone being taken advantage of, I feel kind of protective toward them.
Other people's misfortunes do not usually disturb me a great deal. (-)

Answer scheme: 1=strong disagreement; 2=disagreement; 3=uncertain; 4=agreement; 5=strong agreement

(Sensitivity for tensions and injustice)

"In your view…:"
to what degree are there tensions or conflicts in society between rich and poor?
to what degree are there tensions or conflicts in society between citizens and non-citizens?
to what degree are there tensions or conflicts in society between religions?
to what degree are there tensions or conflicts in society between races?

Answer scheme: 1=never; 2=very seldom; 3=occasionally; 4=often; 5=very often

Fig. 2.5 Interpersonal awareness

Social-Class Context

The context of social class is relevant for students' attitudes towards human dignity because research shows that an upper-class family context is a predictor for pupils' skills in socio-moral thinking.

To describe the social-class context four concepts were chosen: the social formation class, migration background of parents, migration background of the student and the type of school the student attends.

The dimension of the social formation class includes the education level of the student's mother and father, calculated as the mean of both levels of education (see Fig. 2.6). This calculation was extended for the following reason: if the education level of the mother and father are different, we assume that the parent with the higher education level will have a stronger influence on the student. We therefore count the higher education background twice and divide the sum by three. When both parents have the same education level, we count this level three times and divide the sum by three.

Further on, we consider whether the parents have a migration background or not. This variable is included into the regression model as a dummy-variable with the following characteristics: "no migration background" (both parents were born in Germany), "partial migration background" (one parent has a migration background), "migration background" (both parents have a migration background). The reference category is "no migration background".

As well as the migration background of the parents we consider the migration background of the student. The categories of this dummy-variable are: "no migration background of the student" and "migration background of the student". Reference is "no migration background of the student". Finally, the type of school the student attends is included as an indicator of the social formation

$$\text{Social formation class} = \frac{\text{MAX(Education (mother), Education (father))+Education (mother) + Education (father)}}{3}$$

Fig. 2.6 Calculation of the social formation class

(Social formation class)
What is the highest level of your mother's education?
What is the highest level of your father's education?

Answer scheme: 1 lower and middle secondary school (Haupt- u. Realschulabschluss); 2 higher secondary education (Abitur); 3 polytechnic degree (Fachhochschulabschluss); 4 university degree (Hochschulabschluss); 5 another degree

(Type of school)
Type of school the student attends

Answer scheme: 1 lower secondary education (Hauptschule); 2 middle secondary education (Realschule); 3 higher secondary education (Gymnasium); 4 comprehensive school (Gesamtschule)

(National background)
Where were you born?
Where was your mother born?
Where was your father born?

Answer scheme: 1 Germany, 2 neighbouring country, 3 another European country; 4 another continent

Fig. 2.7 Social-class context

class. This dummy-variable has the reference-category "higher secondary education" (see Fig. 2.7).

Religious Socialization

Similar to religious belief, religious socialization is a possible predictor for attitudes towards human dignity. Religious socialization means that the students grew up with the values that are relevant in their religion and influence their opinions and attitudes. In contrast to the social-class context, we separate father and mother because other analyses have shown that their influence can be different. In general, the influence of the mother is more relevant for the religious socialization of the children than father the influence of the father. We have no observation data about how religious parents are. The only data we can use is the respondents' perception of their parents' degree of religious devotion. Items are about the belief of the mother and father, how important it is for them to pass on their belief, and to which degree they insist that their children attend religious services (see Fig. 2.8).

(parents´ belief in God)

How would you describe your father's belief and faith in God or a higher reality?
How would you describe your mother's belief and faith in God or a higher reality?

Answer scheme: 1= absolutely unbelieving; 2= rather unbelieving; 3= doubtful; 4= belief; 5= absolute belief

(adopt the belief)

How important is it to your father that you adopt his faith/belief?
How important is it to your mother that you adopt her faith/belief?

Answer scheme: 1= not at all important; 2= not important; 3= fairly important; 4= very important

(worship)

Does your father want you to attend religious services?
Does your mother want you to attend religious services?

Answer scheme: 1= they leave me total free; 2= they appreciate it; 3= they insist on this

(peers)

How would you describe your best friends' belief and faith in God or a higher reality?

Answer scheme: 1= absolutely unbelieving; 2= rather unbelieving; 3= doubtful; 4= belief; 5= absolute belief

Fig. 2.8 Religious socialization concept

The items measuring the parents' belief and the importance of passing on belief will be included as single items in the regression model. The answer scheme is such that the insistence on attending religious services is operationalized as a dummy-variable; the reference is 1: "they leave me total free".

Socio-demographic Characteristics

As socio-demographic characteristics, we include age and sex (gender) into the regression model. The average age is 16 years and the range is form 15–20 years. Sex is included in the regression models as a dummy-variable; the reference is male.

Research Questions and Hypotheses

We can now differentiate the general research questions of this paper:

(1) *How do young people in Germany evaluate the three different understandings of human dignity: dignity of merit, dignity of moral stature and inherent dignity?*
(2) *Are religious belief, personal qualities, social-class context, religious socialization and socio-demographic characters predictors for attitudes towards the three facets of human dignity?*

As far as the predictors are concerned, we will analyse which one explains the attitudes to human dignity best and which predictors are less important. We are also interested in comparing the influence of the five predictors on the different concepts of human dignity with each other. Finally, we want to know if the predictors influence the three understandings of dignity in a similar way, or if they differ in intensity and direction.

In our theoretical reflections, multitudes of reasons were discussed about which assumptions we may have regarding the empirical findings. We have to make a selection and the following hypotheses structure our analysis of the findings:

H1: Human dignity

- 1.1 Respondents support inherent dignity positively.
- 1.2 Dignity of moral stature and dignity of merit are neither positively nor negatively evaluated.

H2: Religious belief (belief in God; trust in religion)

- 2.1 Belief has a strong, positive influence on inherent dignity,
- 2.2 a positive - less strong - influence on dignity as moral stature, and
- 2.3 a negative influence on human dignity as merit.

H3: Interpersonal awareness (empathy; sensitivity for tensions and injustice)

- 3.1 Empathy has a positive influence on inherent dignity and
- 3.2 a negative influence on dignity as merit and dignity as moral stature.
- 3.3 Empathy predicts inherent dignity stronger than sensitivity for tensions in society.

H4: Social class

- 4.1 The higher the social-class context (social formation class; migration background; type of school the student attends), the more positively inherent dignity is valued.
- 4.1 The lower the social-class context (social formation class; migration background; type of school the student attends), the more positively contingent concepts of dignity are valued.

H5: Religious socialization

- 5.1 Parental religious socialization and peers have a positive influence on the valuation of inherent dignity.
- 5.2 Parents have a stronger influence than peers do on the valuation of inherent dignity.

H6: Background characteristics

- 6.1 Women support the inherent concept of human dignity more than men.
- 6.2 Sex has no influence on attitudes towards dignity as merit and as moral stature.

Empirical Findings

This section is divided into two parts. In the first part, we present the frequencies, means and standard deviations of all concepts used in this research paper. In the second part, we run three regression analyses for human dignity as inherent, as merit and as social status. We will test our hypotheses using these analyses and obtain the data required to answer our research questions.

Descriptive Analyses

The order of the following analyses is equal to the previous paragraph in which we described the concepts.

Human Dignity

The students have been asked for their (dis-)agreement on the three concepts of human dignity on a scale from 1 ("I totally disagree) to 5 ("I totally agree"). The means of the three different concepts show that inherent dignity gets the highest acceptance (mean = 3.77), followed by dignity of moral stature (mean = 3.34). Dignity of merit can be found in the negative half of the scale. This understanding of dignity is clearly valuated negatively by the students (mean = 2.26).

Of the respondents, 60.1% totally disagree or disagree with the understanding of human dignity as defined by merit and a quarter are not sure about this concept. However, 14.8% of respondents still agree or fully agree with the understanding of human dignity as defined by merit.

Human dignity as social stature obtains considerably more support: here, only 19.6% totally disagree or disagree with this concept. Half of the students agree or fully agree with human dignity of merit (49.1%). About one third of the respondents (31.1%) are not sure about their position.

The highest support is given to the concept of inherent dignity – with which 65% of all respondents agree or fully agree. Of the respondents, 19.9% have no clear position. What is noteworthy is that 15.3% disagree or disagree totally (Table 2.1).

These results show a preference for a non-contingent understanding of human dignity. But what should not be overlooked is the fact that nearly half of the respondents also support the thinking that dignity is a fruit of moral behaviour. As we mentioned in our theoretical reflection, this understanding of dignity was dominant for centuries and it is still one component (among others) in religious convictions.

Table 2.1 Human dignity (frequencies (%), means and standard deviation)

Items	I totally disagree	I disagree	I'm not sure	I agree	I fully agree	M	SD
MERIT The value of a person depends on the appreciation given to him or her by others.	30.8	29.3	25.0	12.2	2.6	*2.26*	*1.10*
STATURE The honour to be given to a person depends on his moral behaviour.	6.4	13.2	31.1	38.1	11.0	*3.34*	*1.05*
INHERENT Each human being should be recognized just because he is a human being, irrespective of credit or moral behaviour.	5.3	9.9	19.9	32.6	32.4	*3.77*	*1.16*

Religious Belief

One important predictor for attitudes towards human dignity is religion. A scale and one single item represent religious belief.

The scale measures thinking about religious issues, belief in God and importance of religion in daily life. The 5-point answering categories differ slightly but are comparable, and so a scale has been computed. The mean of the scale is 2.73 and the standard deviation 1.01. The mean values of the three items cover a range from 2.49 for the importance of religion in daily life, 2.74 for thinking about religious issues, and 2.99 for belief in God. What is of note here is that none of the items are evaluated positively. It is only the reaction to belief in God that does not obtain a negative score: this item obtains an ambivalent score.

The frequencies show that 42.9% of students express that they never or rarely think about religious issues; 25.4% do this often or very often, 31.7% occasionally. Answers about belief in God are extremely balanced in terms of scores: 35.6% believe and 35.3% do not; 29.2% are uncertain. 49.3% disagree with the statement that religion has a great influence on their lives, while 20.2% agree, and 30.6% are uncertain (Table 2.2).

Table 2.2 Religious belief (frequencies (%), means and standard deviation)

Items	– –	–	+ –	+	+ +	M	SD
How often do you think about religious issues?	14.8	28.1	31.7	18.8	6.6	*2.74*	*1.12*
To what extent do you believe that God or something divine exists?	17.8	17.5	29.2	19.5	16.1	*2.99*	*1.31*
My religion or worldview has great influence on my daily life.	25.6	23.7	30.6	16.8	3.3	*2.49*	*1.14*

As an indicator for the affinity to a religious community, a single item was included to which degree respondents trust in religion. Answers run from 1 (low) to 10 (high). 38.8% of the students vote for the first 3 categories (low trust); 43.7% for the categories 4 to 7 in the middle and only 22.4% indicate high trust in their religion (categories 8 to 10). This result shows clearly a dominance of answers in the negative half of the scale (Table 2.3).

Table 2.3 Trust in religion (frequencies (%), mean and standard deviation)

If you are committed to a religion, to what degree do you generally trust your religion?											
1	2	3	4	5	6	7	8	9	10	*M*	*SD*
14.9	8.4	15.5	9.2	14.3	8.8	11.4	10.8	4.4	7.2	*5.03*	*2.77*

Interpersonal Awareness

This concept is operationalized by the empathy scale and by items about perceived tensions and conflicts in society.

Empathy

The empathy scale includes three items. The scale runs from 1 "strong disagreement" to 5 "strong agreement". The mean of the entire scale is 3.69 and the standard deviation is .78. The mean of all three items is in the positive half of the scale and above the sector of ambivalent answers. The empathy of students is greatest when they see someone being taken advantage of (mean = 3.90), followed by empathic feelings about other people's misfortunes (mean = 3.79). Students show the lowest degree of empathy when they compare the fortune of others and for oneself. That others have less fortune is no reason for strong empathy (mean = 3.38) (Table 2.4).

Table 2.4 Empathy (frequencies (%), means and standard deviation)

Items	Strongly disagree	Dis-agree	Uncer-tain	Agree	Strongly agree	M	SD
I often have tender, concerned feelings for people less fortunate than me.	6.4	16.1	23.9	40.0	13.6	*3.38*	*1.10*
When I see someone being taken advantage of, I feel kind of protective toward them.	2.2	5.4	17.5	49.7	25.2	*3.90*	*.91*
Other people's misfortunes do not usually disturb me a great deal.[a]	25.0	44.4	18.6	8.8	3.3	*3.79*	*1.02*

[a]Recoded in further analyses

Perception of Tensions and Injustice in Society

The second dimension contains students' perceptions concerning whether or not there exist tensions in society with regard to rich and poor, citizens and non-citizens, different religions and races. The scale runs from 1 "never" to 5 "very often". In three of the four cases students observe moderate conflicts. The highest percentage here was 58% – students who perceive tensions between rich and poor often or very often (mean = 3.61), followed by 50.6% who say that tensions between religions are often or very often present (mean = 3.42). Third we find nearly the same percentage of 50.4% who say that conflicts between citizens and non-citizens are often or very often present (mean = 3.45). Students' reactions to potential conflicts between races obtained an ambivalent score. 32.8% say that this conflict happens often or very often, but the biggest group of 44.2% answered "occasionally" (mean = 3.13). If asked which tensions are the most irrelevant (categories never and very seldom), 23% say tension about races, 21.6% tension about different religions, 16.5% mention citizens and non–citizens, and 12.4% think that tensions between rich and poor are not relevant (Table 2.5).

Table 2.5 Perception of injustice (frequencies (%), means and standard deviation)

Items	Never	Very seldom	Occasi-onally	Often	Very often	*M*	*SD*
In your view: to what degree are there tensions or conflicts in society between rich and poor?	1.7	10.7	29.5	41.0	17.0	*3.61*	*.95*
In your view: to what degree are there tensions or conflicts in society between citizens and non-citizens?	2.8	13.6	33.2	36.8	13.6	*3.45*	*.98*
In your view: to what degree are there tensions or conflicts in society between religions?	3.7	17.9	27.8	34.3	16.3	*3.42*	*1.07*
In your view: to what degree are there tensions or conflicts in society between races?	5.2	17.8	44.2	24.7	8.1	*3.13*	*.97*

Empathy and the Perception of Tensions

In the introduction to this paper, we discussed the difference between empathy and sensitivity. At this stage in our analysis, we can provide the assumption that both concepts measure different attitudes with concrete, empirical support. The correlation analysis between three items of the empathy-scale and four items of perceived tensions contain 12 correlations. Nine correlations are not significant; only three are significant. However, even the highest coefficient is just r = .11. We can therefore conclude that empathy and sensitivity are not two sides of the same coin.

Social-class Context

To measure the social-class context, we take into account the social formation class and migration background of the parents and the type of school the student attends. To obtain information about the social formation class, we analyse the parents' highest level of education. The analysis shows that nearly half of the students' parents have lower degrees in education, while a third hold a higher degree. When it comes to university degrees, more fathers than mothers have finished university (Table 2.6).

Table 2.6 Social formation class (frequencies (%))

	Lower secondary education/ second. educ.	Secondary education II	Polytechnic degree	University degree	Another degree
Mother	49.1	17.3	11.0	17.7	4.9
Father	46.5	15.0	11.7	22.2	4.6

As far as the parents' migration background are concerned, the percentages for mothers and fathers are similar. Nearly 80% of the respondents' parents are of German origin, while slightly more than 20% have a migration background (Table 2.7).

Table 2.7 Migration background (%)

	German	Non German
Mother	79.2	20.8
Father	79.3	20.7

The following table shows the different types of schools attended (i.e. in our study). The sample includes 6.6% students attending lower secondary education, 13.5% middle secondary education, 68.8% higher secondary education and 11.1% attending comprehensive school. There are reasons for the dominance of higher education in this study: Teachers of lower secondary schools – and partly also of middle-secondary schools – told us that the questionnaire was too demanding in terms of length, intellectual level, and complexity. Indeed, this was the reason why some schools rejected the invitation to participate in this research study. The number of returned questionnaires from other, lower secondary schools was small. Another reason that higher secondary schools are overrepresented is that this research was done in grades 9–11, and grade 11 only exists in higher secondary education (Table 2.8).

Table 2.8 Student: type of school (frequencies (%))

Lower secondary education (Hauptschule)	Middle secondary education (Realschule)	Higher secondary education (Gymnasium)	Comprehensive school (Gesamtschule)
6.6	13.5	68.8	11.1

Religious Socialization

Religious socialization was measured using three concepts: the belief of the parents, the importance of the parents in passing on their belief to their children, and the parents' intention that their children attend religious services.

The findings concerning the parents' religious beliefs confirm the results obtained in previous research. Mothers are more religious than fathers – at least, according to the perception of children. On a 5-point scale (from absolutely unbelieving, to rather unbelieving, to doubtful, to belief and to strong belief) the mean for mothers was 2.82 and for fathers 2.58. Respondents in this study stated that 50% of their fathers were absolutely unbelieving or unbelieving and that a third of fathers were doubtful. Of all respondents' fathers, 23% had a belief or a strong belief in God. The results for mothers were different. Of all respondents' mothers, 37.9% were absolutely unbelieving or unbelieving, about a third had doubts and 28.3% had a belief or strong belief in God.

We also added an item about the belief of friends because youths often spend their leisure time with friends who have similar worldviews. The results show the mean for students' best friends' belief as being 2.37, what indicates that most respondents' best friends were absolutely or somewhat unbelieving. Altogether, 60.8% of the students' best friends belonged to that category. About a quarter had doubts about religion and 13.4% had a belief or strong belief in God (Table 2.9).

Table 2.9 Religious belief of parents and peers (frequencies (%), means and standard)

Items	Absolutely unbelieving	Rather unbelieving	Doubtful	Belief	Absolutely belief	M	SD
How would you describe your fathers' belief and faith in God or a higher reality?	18.1	31.9	26.9	20.2	2.9	*2.58*	*1.09*
How would you describe your mothers' belief and faith in God or a higher reality?	11.9	26.0	33.8	24.5	3.8	*2.82*	*1.06*
How would you describe your best friends' belief and faith in God or a higher reality?	17.6	43.2	25.7	11.9	1.5	*2.37*	*1.00*

Earlier in this paper, we mentioned the finding that the mother's degree of religious commitment is very important. When the question is raised who takes the initiative when it comes to passing on beliefs, again mothers are more active than fathers are. On a 4-point scale from not important to very important, the mean for mothers is 2.2 and for fathers 2.0. In percentages: respondents answered that 73.4% of their fathers were not interested in passing on their belief, while 26.6% did want to pass on their beliefs to their children. The answers for mothers were, again, very different: for 66.6% of the mothers it was not important to pass on their beliefs, while for 33.3% it was important. Putting aside differences between mothers and fathers, these data have dramatic implications for the future of religious life. The low level of religious socialization will certainly influence religious culture in Germany in general and will have consequences for the curricula of religious education in schools, youth work in churches, etc. (Table 2.10).

Table 2.10 Parents who would like their children to adopt their belief: (frequencies, means and standard deviation (%))

Items	Not at all important	Not important	Fairly important	Very important	M	SD
How important is it to your father that you adopt their faith/belief?	37.3	36.1	17.7	8.9	*2.00*	*.95*
How important is it to your mother that you adopt their faith/belief?	31.5	35.1	21.2	12.1	*2.10*	*1.00*

As a final indicator for religious socialization, we asked respondents to what degree their mother and father wanted their children to attend religious services. Again, the data show that mothers are more insistent than fathers are. According to our respondents' experiences, for 70.1% of their fathers this was not at all important; for 23.7% it was not important and only 6.2% of fathers wanted their children to attend religious services. As far as respondents' mothers are concerned, the results are as follows: 61% do not regard their children's attendance at religious services as important at all, 29.1% regard it as not important, while 9.4% regard their children's attendance at religious services as fairly important (Table 2.11).

Table 2.11 Parents expecting their children to attend religious services ((%)

Items	Not at all important	Not important	Fairly important
Does your father want you to attend religious services?	70.1	23.7	6.2
Does your mother want you to attend religious services?	61.5	29.1	9.4

Regression Models

In this part of the analysis, we treat the three dimensions of human dignity as dependent variables. We research if and to what degree religious belief, interpersonal awareness, social class, socialization, and population characteristics count as predictors for attitudes towards human dignity in the dimensions of merit, social stature and inherent dignity. For the analysis, we use a 5-step hierarchical regression analysis in which we integrate five possible predictors successively. In step 1 we measure the importance of interpersonal awareness, in step 2 religion, in step 3 social class, in step 4 religious socialization and in step 5 socio-demographic characteristics.

Human Dignity as Merit

When human dignity is understood as "merit", the meaning is that a person's value depends on the appreciation given to him or her by others. Table 2.1 has shown how respondents value this concept. The following regression analysis will show if the attitude of Germany's youth towards this understanding of dignity is predicted by interpersonal awareness, religious belief, social-class context, religious socialization, and socio-demographic characteristics. What is the importance of these five different predictors?

Table 2.12 shows that every model explains the variance to a certain proportion (r^2). Each model contributes to the explanation of youth's attitudes towards the concept of human dignity as merit and all five models are significant. The first model, "interpersonal awareness", includes the indicators empathy and sensitivity for tensions regarding injustice. This model explains 1.7% of the variance. When "religious belief" (that is, the student's belief, his or her trust in religion and his or her religious affiliation) is included, the explained variance increases to 3.0%. The third model, "social-class context" (social formation class, migration background and type of school the student attends), explains the dependent concept with 1.6% and the total variance after this step is 4.6%. The fourth model is religious socialization (parents' belief, their desire to pass on their beliefs and their concern that their children attend religious services) explains 1.2%, which give a total of 5.8%. Including the fifth model "socio-demographic characteristics" (sex and age), which only counts 0.2%, we can explain the relationship between dignity of merit and predictors with 6.0%. Altogether, the explained variance is low.

Table 2.12 The influence of personal awareness, religious belief, social-class context, religious socialization, and socio-demographic characteristics on attitudes towards human dignity as merit (hierarchical regression model)

	Model 1	Model 2	Model 3	Model 4	Model 5
Interpersonal awareness					
Empathy	–.121***	–.113***	–.107***	–.101***	–.091**
Sensitivity for tensions and injustice					
Conflicts between rich and poor	.012	.022	.016	.016	.020
Between citizens and non-citizens	.078**	.071*	.071*	.074*	.074*
Between religions	.003	–.008	–.015	–.013	–.009
Between races	–.025	–.020	–.022	–.020	–.026
Religious belief					
Belief of student		–.116**	–.097*	–.120**	–.122**
Trust in religion		.100*	.086*	.057	.059
Religious affiliation					
Muslim		.108	.062	.042	.039
Non-religious		.011	.015	.043	.040
Others		.019	.013	.024	.022
Social class context					
Social formation class			–.074*	–.080**	–.076**
Type of school (student)					
9 years of school			.051	.054*	.058*
10 years of school			.096***	.096***	.095***
Comprehensive school			.035	.042	.041
Migration background (parents)					
Europe/World			–.010	–.007	–.008
World			.030	.031	.031
Migration background (student)					
World			.018	.013	.009
Religious socialization					
Belief in God (father)				.037	.034
Belief in God (mother)				.003	.001
Passing on the belief (father)				.102	.103
Passing on the belief (mother)				.001	.002
Attending rel. Services					
Appreciated (father)				.003	.003
Insistence (father)				–.019	–.019
Appreciated (mother)				.069	.069
Insistence (mother)				.042	.043

(continued)

Table 2.12 (continued)

	Model 1	Model 2	Model 3	Model 4	Model 5
Peers					
Belief in God (best friend)				−.075*	−.071*
Socio-demographic characteristics					
Age					.038
Sex					−.041
adj. R^2 (explained variance)	.017(1.7%)	.030 (3%)	.046 (4.6%)	.058 (5.8%)	.060 (6%)
F	5.339***	4.980***	4.608***	4.034***	3.896***

N = 2,175
*p ≤ .05; **p ≤ .01; ***p ≤ .001
Reference: religious affiliation = Christians; type of school, student: ref. = higher secondary education, migration background, parents = no migration background; migration background, student = no migration background; want student to attend religious services, father/mother = leave me total free; sex = male

In the following paragraphs, we will go into detail. To avoid spurious correlations, we describe the betas of the overall analysis, represented in the right column of Table 2.12 (= model 5).

The concept of interpersonal awareness is constituted by empathy and sensitivity. Table 2.12 shows that empathy has a significant but negative influence on attitudes towards the concept of human dignity as merit (beta = −.091). The interpretation is: if empathy increases, the acceptance of dignity as merit decreases. Empathy is incompatible with the idea that dignity depends on a person being appreciated by others. Such a concept finds no support by empathic youth. The second dimension is 'sensitivity for tensions and injustice in society', which is measured by four items. Only the item about conflicts between citizens and non-citizens is significant (beta = .074). Respondents who experience this conflict show some support of the concept of dignity as merit. Because three items are not significant and the sign is twice negative and twice positive, we do not accept this dimension as a precise indicator for the prediction of human dignity as merit.

The concept of religious belief shows one significant result regarding belief in God (beta = −.122). The negative sign shows that, when belief increases, the refusal to support the concept of dignity as merit decreases. Believers reject this concept of dignity more strongly than do students with low or no faith. The second dimension in this area, trust in religion, is only of low significance until the fourth model is included in the regression model. Model four is religious socialization, which nullifies the influence of trust in religion on attitudes towards human dignity as merit. Finally, religious affiliation was included, but this variable is not significant.

The social-class context includes the social formation class and the type of school respondents attend. Variables include the education background of both the parents and the student. The social formation class is a significant predictor of human dignity as merit (beta = −.076). The influence on dignity of merit is negative.

The higher the social formation class, the greater the tendency to reject this concept of dignity. The type of school the student attends is also significant. If the student attends lower (beta = .058) and middle secondary education (beta = .095), he or she has significantly more sympathy with human dignity as merit than do students with higher secondary education. That indicates the relevance of merit for students with lower education. The second dimension of this concept is the parents' migration background; it was found that migration background is not significant.

The concept of socialization includes various aspects of the religious culture in families and the religious beliefs of best friends (peers). Only peers have a significantly negative influence on attitudes to the concept of dignity as merit (beta = −.071). Students who have believers as best friends are encouraged not to value the concept of dignity as merit. All items regarding parents were found to have no significant influence on respondents' attitudes towards human dignity as merit.

Finally, sex (gender) was not found to significantly influence respondents' attitudes to the concept of dignity as merit.

Human Dignity as Moral Stature

The meaning of dignity as moral stature is that dignity depends on a person's moral behaviour. We work with the same predictor-concepts as before. Although it is unusual to begin with the final conclusion, in this case it makes sense: the complete regression model is not significant (see Table 2.13).

The summary of the complete regression model shows at the bottom of Table 2.13 that only the first model we included (interpersonal awareness) is significant (F = 2.426*). Since the second model (belief) was included, the following F-tests are no longer significant. That means none of the other models predict dignity of moral stature as statistically significant. None of these concepts seems to be precise predictors.

However, it is noticeable that empathy – one of the two concepts of interpersonal awareness – is a predictor in the regression model. From the list of all assumed predictors, empathy is the only concept that explains the students' attitude towards dignity as moral stature. The direction of influence is positive. Empathic students are inclined to accept that moral behaviour and dignity are linked.

Further exploration needs to be done to find more precise predictors that will explain youth's likely attitude towards the concept of human dignity as moral stature.

Table 2.13 The influence of interpersonal awareness, religious belief, social-class context, religious socialization, and socio-demographic characteristics on attitudes towards the concept of human dignity as moral stature (hierarchical regression model)

	Model 1	Model 2	Model 3	Model 4	Model 5
Interpersonal awareness					
Empathy	.090***	.078**	.077**	.081**	.087**
Sensitivity for tensions and injustice					
Conflicts between rich and poor	−.029	−.029	−.028	−.032	−.025
Conflicts between citizens and non-citizens	.018	.021	.019	.017	.020
Conflicts between religions	.014	.011	.011	.013	.012
Conflicts between races	.011	.011	.013	.011	.010
Religious belief					
Belief of student		.063	.058	.065	.071
Trust in religion		−.009	−.012	−.007	−.014
Religious affiliation					
Muslim		−.005	−.023	−.019	−.018
Non-religious		.033	.030	.032	.028
Others		.014	.007	.008	.008
Social class context					
Social formation class			.023	.017	.007
Type of school (student)					
9 years of school			.015	.015	.013
10 years of school			.006	.005	.005
Comprehensive school			−.018	−.020	−.025
Migration background (parents)					
Europe/World			.024	.025	.027
World			.034	.039	.038
Migration background (student)					
World			.032	.033	.036
Religious socialization					
Belief in God (father)				−.021	−.025
Belief in God (mother)				.025	.022
Passing on the belief (father)				−.013	−.009
Passing on the belief (mother)				−.040	−.039
Attending rel. Services					
Appreciated (father)				−.014	−.016
Insistence (father)				−.013	−.016
Appreciated (mother)				.049	.048
Insistence (mother)				.079	.080
Peers					
Belief in God (best friend)				−.023	−.017

(continued)

Table 2.13 (continued)

	Model 1	Model 2	Model 3	Model 4	Model 5
Socio-demographic characteristics					
Age					−.041
Sex					−.036
adj. R^2 (explained variance)	.006(0.6%)	.005 (0.5%)	.004 (0.4%)	.003 (0.3%)	.004 (0.4%)
F	2.426*	1.618	1.324	1.150	1.180

N = 2,175
*p ≤ .05; **p ≤ .01; ***p ≤ .001
Reference: religious affiliation = Christians; type of school, student: ref. = higher secondary education, migration background, parents = no migration background; migration background, student = no migration background; want student to attend religious services, father/mother = leave me total free; sex = male

Inherent Human Dignity

Inherent dignity is the non-contingent concept of human dignity; dignity does not depend on the appreciation of others and behaviour, but is a "given" of someone's humanity. The question is if and how different predictors (see above) explain the attitudes of youth towards the concept of inherent dignity. To answer these questions, a hierarchical regression model was used again. Data were computed by successive inclusion of the five different predictor concepts (see Table 2.14).

The general outcome is that every single model contributes to the explained variance and that all five models are significant.

The first model, interpersonal awareness, which includes empathy and sensitivity for tensions and injustice, explains 4.8% of the variance. With the second model, belief in God and trust in religion, 1.4% are added to the explained variance, which gives a final figure of 6.2%. When the third model, social-class context (social formation class, migration background and the type of school the students attends) is included, the variance remains stable. The fourth model, religious socialization (belief of parents and best friends, parents' desire to pass on faith and for the student to attend religious services), contributes only 0.1% to the explained variance. Finally, socio-demographic characteristics in terms of sex and age explain 1.5% of the variance. In sum, these predictors explain 7.8% of the variance. Compared with the other two regression analyses in this analysis, the chosen predictors are particularly relevant.

In the following section, we shall describe the betas of the overall analysis, represented in the right column of Table 2.14 (= model 5). The influence of the predictor variables on attitudes towards inherent dignity is as follows: empathy has the strongest significant influence on attitudes towards the concept of inherent dignity (beta = .160). The higher the degree of empathy, the more the student agrees with the concept of inherent human dignity. The influence of sensitivity on tensions and injustice is inconsistent – as in the first regression model. Only the item about conflicts between religions has a significant influence (beta = −.068). This item is the only one with a negative sign. The interpretation is that, the less the perception of

Table 2.14 The influence of interpersonal awareness, sensitivity, religious belief, social-class context, religious socialization, and socio-demographic characteristics on attitudes towards the concept of inherent human dignity (hierarchical regression model)

	Model 1	Model 2	Model 3	Model 4	Model 5
Interpersonal awareness					
Empathy	.212***	.192***	.193***	.188***	.160***
Sensitivity for tensions and injustice					
Conflicts between rich and poor	.057*	.062*	.060*	.058*	.041
Conflicts between citizens and non-citizens	.024	.015	.017	.018	.017
Conflicts between religions	−.052	−.061*	−.061*	−.062*	−.068*
Conflicts between races	−.012	.002	−.000	.002	.015
Religious belief					
Belief of student		−.011	−.005	−.036	−.038
Trust in religion		.111**	.112**	.087*	.093*
Religious affiliation					
Muslim		.024	.033	.022	.029
Non-religious		−.049	−.044	−.028	−.017
Others		.000	.004	.007	.010
Social-class context					
Social formation class			−.042	−.045	−.041
Type of school (student)					
9 years of school			−.024	−.026	−.033
10 years of school			−.022	−.015	−.013
Comprehensive school			.006	.013	.022
Migration background (parents)					
Europe/World			−.035	−.033	−.034
World			−.008	−.009	−.008
Migration background (student)					
World			−.009	−.011	−.006
Religious socialization					
Belief in God (father)				.022	.031
Belief in God (mother)				.000	.007
Passing on the belief (father)				.034	.026
Passing on the belief (mother)				.041	.037
Attending religious services					
Appreciated (father)				−.048	−.045
Insistence (father)				−.056	−.051

(continued)

Table 2.14 (continued)

	Model 1	Model 2	Model 3	Model 4	Model 5
Appreciated (mother)				.058	.061
Insistence (mother)				.046	.041
Peers					
Belief in God (best friend)				.036	.020
Socio-demographic characteristics					
Age					−.026
Sex					.128***
adj. R^2 (explained variance)	.048(4.8%)	.062 (6.2%)	.062 (6.2%)	.063 (6.3%)	.078 (7.8%)
F	13.876***	9.450***	5.863***	4.309***	4.817***

N = 2,175
*p ≤ .05; **p ≤ .01; ***p ≤ .001
Reference: religious affiliation = Christians; type of school, student: ref. = higher secondary education, migration background, parents = no migration background; migration background, student = no migration background; wants student to attend religious services, father/mother = leave me total free; sex = male

conflict between religions is, the more the concept of inherent dignity is accepted. However, the four sensitivity items together show no clear tendency, and so we shall not place too much emphasis on these items.

Belief is relevant in one case. Trust in religion has a positive significant influence on a student's acceptance of the notion of inherent dignity (beta = .093). Students who trust their religion support the concept of inherent dignity more than students with little or no trust in religion. Students' beliefs and religious affiliations are not significant in this model.

Neither the context of social class nor religious socialization have any significant influence on respondents' attitudes towards the concept of inherent dignity.

We already mentioned that there is a significant outcome (beta = .128) for sex (gender). This beta means that females are more supportive of the concept of inherent dignity than are males.

Table 2.14 shows that the beta for empathy declines from .212 in model 1 to .160 in model 5. Therefore we conclude: the influence of empathy on the acceptance of inherent dignity can – to some extent – be explained by differences in students' religious belief (trust in religion) and sex.

Conclusions

This final part of our research paper will firstly reflect on the importance of the chosen predictors, secondly it will answer the research questions and comment the hypotheses and, thirdly, it will provide an outlook for future research.

Comparative Reflection About the Importance of Predictors

We have proved the importance of the predictors for the three dimensions of dignity. What can be said about the general importance of the chosen predictors when we compare these? Do these predictors influence respondents' attitudes to the different dimensions of dignity in a similar way or are there any differences in relative weight and/or direction of influence?

The first relevant result in this context is that the five concepts are relevant only for respondents' attitudes towards the concepts of human dignity as merit and inherent dignity. The regression model for dignity of moral stature did not reach the level of significance. Other concepts may predict youth's attitudes towards dignity of moral stature, but not the concepts we have chosen. At least, we can conclude that the predictors we worked with do not explain attitudes to *all* the three concepts of human dignity. As far as dignity as moral stature is concerned, there was one exception. The empirical analysis shows that empathy is a significant predictor in the first model. When other concepts are included, the significance of the complete model disappears. In the following paragraphs, we shall therefore focus on the two dimensions: dignity as merit and inherent dignity.

One of the two most important concepts is empathy. Empathy has a significantly negative influence on respondents' attitudes towards the notion of human dignity as merit and a significantly positive influence on the concept of inherent dignity. With increasing empathy comes increasing support for the concept of inherent dignity. The value of the understanding of dignity as non-contingent and a "given" of someone's humanity seems to be very dependent to the ability "to feel with" people. In contrast, when this emotional ability is developed, respondents reject the concept of dignity that makes dignity dependent on appreciation by others. As we said earlier: the influence of empathy becomes weaker when other concepts are included. As far as the concept of dignity as merit is concerned, students' beliefs and their social-class contexts are of importance; as far as attitudes towards the concept of inherent dignity are concerned, it is trust in religion and sex (gender - female) that are important.

The second important predictor is religious belief, by which we mean belief in God and trust in religion (the religion to which respondents feel most affiliated). The empirical analysis shows that belief in God has no influence on a respondent's attitude towards the concept of inherent dignity, but trust in religion has. This means that respondents who have a positive image of their religion tend to support the concept of inherent dignity. If trust expresses that students are in accordance with the manner, how a religious institution (church) represents doctrines and ethical norms in the past and present, than trust has a broader social scope than doctrinal belief in God. However, belief in God has a significantly negative influence on respondents' attitudes towards the notion of dignity as merit. The more respondents' believe in God, the more they reject the idea that dignity could be interpreted as 'dependent on the appreciation of others'. Trust in religion has no influence on respondents' attitudes towards the notion of human dignity as merit.

The influence of sensitivity (for tensions and injustice) is not clear. One result is that sensitivity to the presence of conflict between citizens and non-citizens has a significantly positive influence on a respondent's attitude towards the concept of human dignity as merit. Those who are aware of a clash between citizens and non-citizens sympathize with an understanding of dignity in which social position and social rank are important.

A reasoning according to Social Identity Theory (Tajfel, Turner 1979) could be that students who perceive conflicts between citizens and non-citizens distinguish between an in-group (citizens) and an out-group (non-citizens), and attribute the non-citizens with lower rank. This distinction could therefore be an indicator for an underlying concept of human dignity as merit. Nevertheless, this is just one possible explanation which has to be examined further. The second result is that sensitivity to the presence of conflict between people with different religions has a significant negative influence on someone's attitude towards the notion of inherent dignity. The awareness of a clash of religions seems to support the view that a respondent is less likely to accept the view that dignity is a "given" of humanity. Again, we can interpret this result according to Social Identity Theory (Tajfel, Turner 1979), even though further research is needed to prove this hypothesis: who perceives a conflict between religions could value religions in 'better and worse', inherent dignity claims dignity for all humans, if there are 'bad people' representing a religion, may they also claim inherent dignity? – in general, this predictor is not semantically uniform.

We have already seen that it was not possible to construct a reliable scale of all items because the content of the items is apparently too diverse. Given the background of public debates about Islam in Germany and elsewhere, this result could be related to anti-immigrant and anti-Islamic sentiments. It is interesting that only the differences between citizenship and religion are significant. It therefore makes sense to situate these results in a wider political and social public discourse.

The dimensions of social formation class and type of school the student attends – as representatives of the social class context – have a significant influence on respondents' attitudes towards the notion of human dignity as merit. From the lower-class perspective, there is a tendency to believe that economic and social advancement encourages acknowledgment by others – which is understood as "attributed" dignity. This predictor includes migration background, but this dimension is not significant. As far as attitudes towards the concept of inherent human dignity is concerned, no dimension of this predictor was found to be significant.

The fourth predictor is religious socialization. There is only one significant influence at all, and this concerns dignity as merit. Students whose best friends' believe in God do not support this concept of dignity. If it is true that young people are looking for friends who have a similar worldview, this shows that religious socialization can have a positive influence and this finding might be saying something about the influence of religion as a whole. However, none of the other socialization variables have any influence on a respondent's attitude towards the concept of human dignity as merit. Inherent dignity is not influenced by any of the socialization dimensions.

Finally, we measured if sex (gender) and age are important predictors for attitudes towards human dignity. The result is that neither have any influence on a respondent's attitude towards the concept of dignity as merit. Sex (gender) has a significant influence on a respondent's support of the notion of inherent dignity: girls support this understanding of dignity more than boys do.

Research Questions and Hypotheses

The first research question is: *How do young people in Germany evaluate the three different understandings of human dignity: dignity of merit, dignity of moral stature and inherent dignity?* The findings show that students evaluate the concept of inherent dignity positive, that they are less positive about the concept of dignity as moral stature and that they have a negative attitude towards the concept of dignity as merit.

With this question, we have linked two hypotheses. The first states: *Respondents support inherent dignity positively* (H 1.1). This hypothesis can be confirmed. The second hypotheses is: *Dignity of moral stature and dignity of merit are neither positively nor negatively evaluated* (H 1.2). To measure 'neither positively nor negatively', the mean scores should be found within the range of 2.75 to 3.24. This is not the case; this hypothesis cannot, therefore, be confirmed. The results show that both meanings of dignity are valued differently. One (moral stature) is valued mainly positively while the other (merit) is regarded mainly negatively. When we look at percentages and when we define the position 'I'm not sure' as 'neither positive nor negative', then 25% of respondents vote for this position with regard to dignity of merit and 31.1% with regard to dignity of moral stature. For these subgroups of 25% and 31.1% respectively, the hypothesis is valid.

The second research question is: *Are religious belief, personal qualities, social-class context, religious socialization and socio-demographic characters predictors for attitudes towards the three facets of human dignity?* We will answer this question step by step.

When we look at religious belief (belief in God; trust in religion) the first hypothesis is: *Belief has a strong positive influence on inherent dignity* (H 2.1). The result is that the dimension of trust in religion has a positive influence on a youth's attitude towards the concept of inherent dignity. This predictor is not the strongest (the strongest is empathy) predictor that explains support of inherent dignity, but the second strongest. We can partly confirm this hypothesis. The second hypothesis is: *Belief has a positive – but less strong - influence on dignity as moral stature* (H2.2). This hypothesis must be rejected because, empirically, no significant influence was found. The third hypothesis is: *Belief has a negative influence on human dignity as merit* (H 2.3). This hypothesis can be confirmed, because the dimension of belief in God has a negative influence on a respondent's attitude towards the notion of human dignity as merit.

These results show that religious belief stimulates support for the conviction that human dignity is inherent to humankind and given to everyone. In contrast, religious belief does not favour the meaning that dignity is contingent to merit. The direction of influence is in keeping with Christian theology. What is surprising about these findings is that there is no significant relationship between belief and dignity of moral stature, because moral behaviour is still a component in theological ethics. Finally, we can indicate that religious affiliation is not a significant predictor for the three understandings of human dignity.

Interpersonal awareness (empathy; sensitivity for tensions and injustice) marks the next field of predictors. The first hypothesis is: *Empathy has a positive influence on inherent dignity* (H 3.1). We can confirm this hypothesis fully. Empathy is the most important predictor and its influence on inherent dignity is strong. The second hypothesis is: *Empathy has a negative influence on dignity as merit and dignity as moral stature* (H 3.2). The first part of this hypothesis is confirmed by the empirical data. Students with a high degree of empathy reject the idea that dignity might be related to merits. The second part of the hypothesis cannot be confirmed. There is a weak influence of empathy on dignity as moral stature, but this influence is positive. Against the hypotheses we have to say that, with empathy, a positive judgment of behaviour as criterion for human dignity is connected. But as soon as other predictors are included, the explanatory power of empathy disappears.

The area of interpersonal awareness also includes sensitivity to the existence of tensions in society. As far as this dimension is concerned, we formulated the following hypothesis: *Empathy predicts inherent dignity stronger than sensitivity for tensions in society* (H 3.3). This hypothesis can fully be confirmed. Partially there are weak influences of sensitivity for tensions, but the dominating predictor is empathy. We can conclude that empathy is an important predictor for the students' ability of socio-moral reasoning.

In our theoretical reflection we stressed the importance of social class (social formation class; migration background; type of school the student attends) for attitudes towards dignity. The first hypothesis is: *The higher the social class context is, the more positive inherent dignity is valued* (H 4.1). We cannot confirm this hypothesis; a student's high-class origin does not influence his or her attitude towards the notion of inherent dignity. The complement of this hypothesis is the following: *The lower the social-class context, the more contingent concepts of dignity are valued positively* (H 4.2). This hypothesis can partly be confirmed. Both social formation class and type of school the student attends have a positive impact, but only on attitudes towards human dignity as merit. Incidentally, we can add the finding that students of a higher social formation class and students of higher secondary education reject the concept of dignity as merit.

Given that these predictors are only relevant for dignity as merit and not for inherent dignity, we can conclude that social formation class is a specific concept to that explains the differentiating principle of dignity.

With regard to religious socialization the hypotheses are: *Parental religious socialization and peers have a positive influence on the valuation of inherent dignity* (H 5.1), and *Parents have a stronger influence than peers on the valuation of inherent dignity* (H 5.2). Neither of these hypotheses can be confirmed. As far as inherent dignity is concerned, none of the predictors show a significant influence. The impact of religious socialization is very limited. Parents are not influential at all and only peers seem to be relevant for respondents' attitudes towards the notion of human dignity as merit. Students whose best friends' are believers have a negative attitude on merit as a criterion of dignity.

Finally, sex (gender) and age were taken into account. The hypotheses are: *Females support more than males the inherent concept of human dignity* (H 6.1), and *Sex has no influence on attitudes towards dignity as merit and as moral stature* (H 6.2). Both assumptions can fully be confirmed. Sex counts significantly only with regard to attitudes towards the concept of inherent dignity: girls support this concept of dignity more than boys do.

Outlook

Our research shows that students have a distinctive understanding of human dignity and that they are aware of the complexity of the concept. For the respondents, dignity is apparently not an empty phrase (as Karl Marx provocatively claimed). The majority of students favour the modern and widely shared concept of dignity as a key feature of humankind, although they show some sympathy towards the understanding that dignity does depend on moral behaviour. We may assume that people do not endorse the concept of "pure" types of dignity, that is to say, they will not support one understanding of dignity and reject other understandings. If and which mixed-types are present among people needs further exploration. We must leave this question open in this study.

More research is needed to answer the question whether different types of dignity represent different modes of the legitimization of human rights. For instance: if people make dignity dependent on behavior, will they accept the validity of human rights for murders and terrorists? May people claim the right to be equal in front of the court or to be silent during a lawsuit, when they became so seriously delinquent? Do students operate with different degrees of legitimization of rights when they count in behaviour?

Empirically, it is also an open question whether people who have an inherent understanding of dignity affirm the validity of human rights without exception. A direct connection between human dignity and human rights is made at the level of law. The normative decision is that dignity is the foundation of law and of human rights. Can this connection be found to exist empirically? In this research, this issue was not studied comprehensively.

In her historical study, Lynn Hunt points out that human rights are most accurately predicted by the ability of a person to identify with the other. Human rights flourish when people learn to think of others as their equal, as the same as them in some fundamental fashion. They learn this equality, at least partially, by experiencing identification with ordinary characters (Hunt 2008, 55–58). Hunt sees the experience of identification as connected with the ability of empathy. Our study shows that her assumption about the importance of empathy is correct. At the same time, empathy is not alone here. Our results indicate that there is an overlap of empathy and religious habit. From the viewpoint of religion this is not surprising. A remarkable source of Christian theology is the *Parable of the Good Samaritan* (Luke 10:25–37). In this parable, an expert in the law and Jesus discuss the question of how to inherit eternal life. The expert in law says (v 28): "Love the Lord your God with all your heart and with all your soul and with all your strength and with all your mind; and, Love your neighbour as yourself." But, so he concludes, who is my neighbour? Jesus tells the story about the Samaritan and the answer is clear: the neighbour is the person who had mercy on the person attacked by robbers. Speaking to the expert in the law, Jesus concludes, "go and do likewise." This parable illustrates that the ethical claim to love God and man belongs to the central convictions of Christianity. In this text, Luke focuses on the interpersonal side. He points out that faith includes concern for one's neighbour.

The relation between empathy and religious adherence is complex. The empirical finding is that empathy and religious adherence are connected. But the questions remain: how much religion is in empathy and how much empathy is in religion? What do they have in common and what distinguishes them? Further research has to clarify, empirically, how we can better understand this relationship.

What little is being studied are categories such as "social class". At this point we can finally bring in a thought of Karl Marx that not the consciousness determines the being, but the social being of man determines the consciousness. We could show that, in a few cases, there were empirical indicators that social class matters as far as the understanding of dignity is concerned. Lower-class respondents in particular experience the fact that people are not equal, that advantages are distributed differently and that dignity seems not to be granted to everyone. Will students who share these experiences accept the state's efforts to welcome asylum seekers and refugees? What is the connection between social-class background, dignity and the legitimization of certain human rights? This also marks an interesting field for further research.

The relevance of such research is obvious. The current international situation is fragile and marked by national interests, group interests, economic interests, ideologies, and many simplifications by populist movements. Countless refugees leave their country, while other countries try to close their borders. Even in European countries, individual freedoms are restricted and civil rights are under pressure. At such a time, it is easy to exploit public opinion and make human rights less important. People's opinion is easy to manipulate – it is easy to persuade people that human rights and human dignity are values, of course, but that they must be balanced with other interests. That makes rights relative to other values.

Empirical research has to provide knowledge and create insight into complex relationships. Empirical research has the power to confront prevailing ideologies with reality. In the field of human dignity and human rights, empirical research can answer the question when and under what conditions people show which degree of identification, namely with regard to immigrants, refugees, certain ethnic groups and several minorities, people who have a different life-style and a different sex-orientation, people who turned to crime – to mention a few examples only. Findings will show to which degree people think that human rights are or should be legitimized. This can stimulate the reflection that a wide-shared understanding of human rights is crucial for ourselves and our living-together in a one-world community.

References

Acock, A. C., & Bengston, V. L. (1978). On the relative influence of mothers and fathers. A covariance analysis of political and religious socialization. *Journal of Marriage and the Family, 40*, 519–530.

Baumrind, D. (1971). *Current patterns of parental authority*. Washington: American Psychological Association.

Birnbacher, D. (1995). Mehrdeutigkeiten im Begriff der Menschenwuerde. (Ambiguities in the concept of human dignity). In: Aufklärung und Kritik, Sonderheft 1 (Enlightenment and critique, Special Issue 1).

Bittlingmayer, U. H. (2006). Grundzüge einer mehrdimensionalen sozialstrukturellen Sozialisationsforschung. In Grundmann, M., Dravenau, D., Bittlingmayer, U. H., & Edelstein, W. (Eds.). *Handlungsbefähigung und Milieu. Zur Analyse milieuspezifischer Alltagspraktiken und ihrer Ungleichheitsrelevanz* (pp. 37–55). Münster: Lit.

Brummer, A., Kießig, M., & Rothgangel, M. (Eds.). (2010). *Evangelischer Erwachsenen-katechismus:* suchen - glauben – leben, *Gütersloh: Gütersloher Verlag.*

Davis, M. H. (1980). A multidimensional approach to individual differences in empathy. *Catalog of selected documents in psychology, 10*, 85.

Davis, M. H. (1983). Measuring individual differences in empathy. Evidence for a Multidimensional Approach. *Journal of Personality and Social Psychology, 44*, 113–126.

Doise, W., Spini, D., & Clémence, A. (1999). Human rights studied as social representations in a cross-national context. *European Journal of Social Psychology, 29*, 1–29.

Dravenau, D. (2006). Die Entwicklung milieuspezifischer Handlungsbefähigung. In Grundmann, M., Dravenau, D., Bittlingmayer, U. H., & Edelstein, W. (Eds.). *Handlungsbefähigung und Milieu. Zur Analyse milieuspezifischer Alltagspraktiken und ihrer Ungleichheitsrelevanz* (pp. 191–235). Münster: Lit.

Grimm, D. (2013). Dignity in a legal context: Dignity as an absolute right. In McCrudden C. (Ed.). *Understanding human dignity* (Vol. *381–391*). Oxford.

Grundmann, M. (2006). Milieuspezifische Handlungsbefähigung sozialisationstheoretisch beleuchtet. In M. Grundmann, D. Dravenau, U. H. Bittlingmayer, & W. Edelstein (Eds.). *Handlungsbefähigung und Milieu. Zur Analyse milieuspezifischer Alltagspraktiken und ihrer Ungleichheitsrelevanz* (pp. 57–73). Münster: Lit.

Grundmann, M., & Bittlingmayer, U. H. (2006). Bildungsmilieuspezifische Erfahrungsinhalte. Zur Bestimmung der isländischen Sozialisationsmatrix. In M. Grundmann, D. Dravenau, U. H. Bittlingmayer, & W. Edelstein (Eds.). *Handlungsbefähigung und Milieu. Zur Analyse milieus-pezifischer Alltagspraktiken und ihrer Ungleichheitsrelevanz* (pp. 155–189). Münster: Lit.

Hoffman, M. L. (1990a). Empathy and justice motivation. *Motivation and emotion, 14*, 151–172.

Hoffman, M. L. (1990b). The contribution of empathy to justice and moral judgment. In N. Eisenberg & J. Strayer (Eds.). *Empathy and its development* (pp. 47–80). Cambridge: Cambridge University Press.

Huber, W. (1992). Menschenrechte/Menschenwürde. In: *TRE* (Vol. 22, pp. 577–602). Berlin: de Gruyter.

Hunt, L. (2008). *Inventing human rights*. New York: W.W. Norton.

Joas, H. (2011). Die *Sakralität der Person. Eine neue Genealogie der Menschenrechte*, Frankfurt: Suhrkamp. Engl. Translation: The sacredness of the person. An new genealogy of human rights, Washington 2013.

Keller, M., & Malti, T. (2008). Sozialisation sozio-moralischer Kompetenzen. In K. Hurrelmann, M. Grundmann, & S. Walper (Eds.). *Handbuch Sozialisationsforschung* (7th ed., pp. 410–423). Weinheim: Beltz.

Keller, M., Malti, T., & Dravenau, D. (2007). Bindung, Sozialisation und die Entwicklung sozio-moralischen Denkens von der Kindheit bis zum Jugendalter. Befunde einer Längsschnittuntersuchung. In C. Hopf & G. Nunner-Winkler (Eds.). *Frühe Bindungen und moralische Entwicklung. Aktuelle Befunde zu psychischen und sozialen Bedingungen moralischer Eigenständigkeit* (pp. 125–150). Weinheim: Juventa-Verl..

Kelley, J., & De Graaf, N. D. (1997). National context, parental socialization and religious belief. Results from 15 nations. *American Sociological Review, 62*, 639–659.

Klein, S. (1999). Religiöse Tradierungsprozesse in Familien und Religiosität von Männern und Frauen. *Religionspädagogische Beiträge, 43*, 25–40.

Kohlberg, L., Levine, C., & Hewer, A. (1983). *Moral stages. A current formulation and a response to critics*. Basel: Karger.

Kramer, R.-T. (2011). *Abschied von Bourdieu? Perspektiven ungleichheitsbezogener Bildungsforschung*. Wiesbaden: VS (Studien zur Schul- und Bildungsforschung, 39).

Krappmann, L. (2001). Die Sozialwelt der Kinder und ihre Moralentwicklung. In W. Edelstein, F. Oser, & P. Schuster (Eds.). *Moralische Erziehung in der Schule. Entwicklungspsychologie und pädagogische Praxis* (pp. 155–174). Weinheim: Beltz.

Kress, H. (1999). *Menschenwürde im modernen Pluralismus*. Hannover: Lutherisches Verlagshaus.

Kriele, M. (1986). *Befreiung und politische Aufklärung. Plädoyer für die Würde des Menschen*. Herder: Freiburg.

Liebold, H. (2005). In der Hinsicht lassen wir uns eigentlich ziemlich in Ruhe. Religiöse Erziehung in christlich-konfessionslosen Familien. Ein Beitrag aus Ostdeutschland. *Wege zum Menschen, 57*, 239–252.

Lohmann, G. (2014). Nicht affektive Ergriffenheit, sondern öffentlicher Diskurs. Sakralisierte Person oder säkulare Menschenwürde als Basis der Menschenrechte. In H.-J. Große Kracht (Ed.). *Der moderne Glaube an die Menschenwürde* (pp. 13–27). Bielefeld: Transcript-Verlag.

Martin, T. F., White, J. M., & Perlman, D. (2003). Religious socialization. A test of the channeling hypothesis of parental influence on adolescent faith maturity. *Journal of Adolescent Research, 18*, 169–187.

McCrudden, C. (Ed.). (2013). *Understanding human dignity*. Oxford: Oxford University Press.

McFarland, S., & Mathews, M. (2005). Who cares about human rights. *Political Psychology, 26*, 365–385.

Montada, L., Schmitt, M., & Dalbert, C. (1986). Thinking about justice and dealing with one's own privileges. A study of existential guilt. In H. W. Bierhoff, R. L. Cohen, & J. Greenberg (Eds.). *Justice in social relations* (pp. 125–143). New York: Plenum.

Myers, S. M. (1996). An interactive model of religiosity inheritance. The importance of family context. *American Sociological Review, 61*, 858–866.

Nordenfelt, L. (2004). The varieties of dignity. *Health Care Analysis, 12*, 69–81.

Reiter, J. (2004). Menschenwürde als Maßstab. *Aus Politik und Zeitgeschichte*. (online 28.5.2004).

Rosen, M. (2012). *Dignity – Its history and meaning*. Cambridge: Harvard University Press.

Schaber, P. (2012). *Menschenwürde (human dignity)*. Stuttgart: Reclam.

Sherkat, D. (2007). Religious socialization. Sources of influence and influences of agency. In M. Dillon (Ed.), *Handbook of the sociology of religion* (pp. 151–163). Cambridge: Cambridge University Press.

Tausch, R., & Tausch, A. (1973). *Erziehungspsychologie. Psychologische Prozesse in Erziehung und Unterricht*. Göttingen: Hogrefe.

Vester, M., von Oertzen, P., Geiling, H., Hermann, T., & Müller, D. (2001). *Soziale Milieus im gesellschaftlichen Strukturwandel*. Frankfurt/Main: Suhrkamp.
Wagner, H. (1992). *Die Würde des Menschen*. Würzburg: Wesen und Normfunktion.
Wetz, F. J. (2011). *Texte zur Menschenwürde* (Texts on human dignity). Stuttgart: Reclam.
Ziebertz, H.-G., & Benzing,, T. (2012). *Menschenrechte – trotz oder wegen Religion?* Münster: LIT Verlag.
Ziebertz, H.-G., & Riegel, U. (2008). *Letzte Sicherheiten*. Freiburg: Eine empirische Untersuchung zu Weltbildern Jugendlicher. Freiburg: Herder.

Chapter 3
Understanding Human Dignity. Theoretical Groundings and Empirical Findings Among the Youth in Belarus

Olga Breskaya and Susanne Döhnert

Abstract Together with a comparative analysis of secular and theological approaches to human dignity, this article will present evidence from empirical research on attitudes to human dignity. The first findings from the international research project 'Religion and Human Rights', about the attitudes of young Belarusians (N = 458) to human dignity and their predictors, will be presented – together with attempts to discover if and how the cultural, social, and religious identity of respondents affects their distinct attitudes towards human dignity. The goal of this paper is to apply the multi-dimensional scale of human dignity suggested by Lennart Nordenfelt, and to explore the differences in attitude of Belarusian youth towards the dignity of merit, the dignity of moral stature, and inherent dignity.

In this paper, we will present an analysis of the overlapping meanings of Nordenfelt's multi-dimensional scale of human dignity, and of various approaches to the understanding of human dignity articulated in the official documents of the Russian Orthodox Church. The differences and similarities revealed in both approaches will be used for a further exploration of empirical results: to ascertain whether the position of Belarusian youth is in consensus with the convictions of the Russian Orthodox Church on human dignity.

This research is explorative in nature; it questions the relationships between religiosity, the personal characteristics of respondents and the socialising process in the family, and attitudes towards the three kinds of human dignity: dignity of merit, dignity of moral stature, and inherent dignity. We assume that empathy and authoritarianism are personal characteristics that predict the choice of attitude towards human dignity.

O. Breskaya (✉)
University of Padua, Padua, Italy
e-mail: olga.breskaya@phd.unipd.it

S. Döhnert
University of Würzburg, Würzburg, Germany
e-mail: susanne.doehnert@uni-wuerzburg.de

H.-G. Ziebertz, C. Sterkens (eds.), *Religion and Civil Human Rights in Empirical Perspective*, Religion and Human Rights 2, DOI 10.1007/978-3-319-59285-5_3

The survey outcomes show that the religiosity of young people in Belarus negatively influences the human dignity of moral stature; students with a greater predisposition to authoritarianism support the dignity of merit more strongly than those with a lesser predisposition to authoritarianism; and the empathy of young Belarusians (as a personal characteristic) and the religiosity of their fathers have the strongest influence on attitudes towards inherent dignity. We also want to establish whether the empirical outcomes support our assumption concerning the predictors of choice of attitude towards moral dignity, for the adherents of the Russian Orthodox Church (ROC).

This paper begins with a theoretical introduction, to justify the importance of the current debates on human dignity in the ROC and to introduce the scholarly discourses about the ROC's vision. In the first two sections we will compare recent official church documents on human dignity with Nordenfelt's multi-dimensional scale of human dignity, constructed through research into the philosophy of healthcare ethics. The conceptual model and research design section will follow a description of the arguments explaining the particularism of the ROC approach to human dignity presented in the relevant literature. Finally, we will submit our empirical findings, showing the relationship between religiosity, the socialising process in the family, the position of respondents concerning the function of religion in modern society, personal characteristics such as authoritarianism and empathy, and attitudes to multiculturalism. The appendixes on the operationalisation of research concepts and the bibliography are presented at the end of the chapter.

Theoretical Introduction

During the last decade, discussion of the concept of human dignity has involved diverse actors, and has both integrated and confronted a variety of approaches in countries where the ROC is a major or significant religious denomination. The discourse – formed from key ROC discussions, and from documents in 2006 to 2008 relating to issues of human dignity – contrasted with the secular vision of human dignity. It was also both challenging to and beneficial for the various interpretations of this multivocal concept. The ROC's particular vision of human dignity and human rights is explained either by the difference between the specific political context of the ROC and its authoritarian and antidemocratic character (Stoeckl 2014), or by the differences in the Christian anthropology of Eastern Orthodoxy (Kyrlezhev 2007). Whether external or internal reasons define the distinct approach to human dignity of the ROC, it is obvious that the very tensions around the concept require from theology and social theory a dialogue for its revision, and a new transdisciplinary perspective.

The empirical data will reveal the perceptions young Belarusians have of the concept of human dignity, in relation to the individual dispositions of the respondents, their family-socialising impact, and the values of the prevailing political culture. We are interested in discovering how attitudes to human dignity are formed, and what particular role the family and social institutions play in this process.

Individuals' disposition towards human dignity will be examined, with multidimensional psychometric scales measuring personality traits and personal characteristics. The data on individual religiosity (Huber 2003; Huber and Huber 2012) and disposition towards empathy (Davis 1983) will be observed as predictors of human dignity at the personal level.[1] The influence of a family-socialising process on the attitudes to human dignity of young Belarusians will be observed, together with the characteristics of the parents' education and religiosity, which we assume are also predictors of human dignity. The position of Belarusian youth in terms of authoritarianism (Manganelli Rattazzi et al. 2007; Altemeyer 1996), openness to multiculturalism, and the public role of religion will be analysed as the wider socio-cultural and political context that influences the understanding of the phenomenon of human dignity.

Two Theoretical Models of Human Dignity

The idea for this article stems from the desire to include two approaches to human dignity in the discussion. The first was developed by philosopher of medicine and healthcare ethics Lennart Nordenfelt, who integrated diverse historical visions on human dignity in the European intellectual tradition and created a multidimensional scale of four kinds of human dignity. Nordenfelt's scale appeared as a result of theoretical and empirical research on the integration of older people in Europe in the field of health care. His research, comprising both biological and holistic approaches to health, suggests the self-assessment of human dignity (self-reflective approach) together with its external assessments (dignity in the public dimension). Nordenfelt interprets human dignity as a concept closely connected to the category of quality of life; and both are viewed in their relationship to the values of health, autonomy and integrity (Nordenfelt 2009, 3).

The second approach is seen in the teachings of the ROC on the issues of human dignity, as stated in recent official ROC documents.[2] In ROC teaching, human

[1] Our hypothesis for the predictors of attitudes towards human dignity for the Belarusian sample will also rely on the results of empirical research on human dignity conducted in Germany and presented in this volume by Hans-Georg Ziebertz, Susanne Döhnert, and Alexander Unser. Using these results, personal dispositions such as empathy and openness to other religious traditions will be analysed as predictors for attitudes towards human dignity.

[2] The official position of the ROC on human rights concepts was developed in the official documents 'Bases of the Social Concept of the Russian Orthodox Church' (2000) and 'Russian Orthodox Church Basic Teaching on Human Dignity, Freedom, and Rights' (hereafter referred to as 'ROC Basic Teaching') (2008), adopted by the Bishop Councils. These official documents

dignity is viewed as a multifaceted concept encompassing both congenital and acquired dignity: "*In Orthodoxy the dignity and ultimate worth of every human person are derived from the image of God, while dignified life is related to the notion of God's likeness achieved through God's grace by efforts to overcome sin and to seek moral purity and virtue.*" (Russian Orthodox Church Basic Teaching on Human Dignity, Freedom, and Rights, art. I.2).

When we compare these two models and approaches we are interested in finding out, first of all, how the philosophical model can be translated into the theological one, and vice versa; and secondly, how our conceptual model for the empirical research of human dignity relates to the categories explaining human dignity in both approaches. This last task is essential for understanding to what extent the attitudes of Belarusian youth towards different kinds of human dignity are in line with the ROC's teachings on human dignity.

Human Dignity in ROC Teachings and in the Philosophy of Healthcare Ethics

Jürgen Habermas (Habermas 2006) and John Rawls (Rawls 1997) introduced the idea of the necessity of religious arguments translating into a secular political language as an important condition for a liberal democratic process. If we accept the statement that the "processes of clarifying arguments and giving reasons for positions must be central" (Calhoun 2005, 67) for the equal presence of religious and secular arguments in public, then we need to observe how the mutual understanding mechanism works with particular 'mutual accommodation' cases. For example, Kristina Stoeckl reflects that during her recent research on the ROC and human rights, she "realised that even when a conservative religious tradition like Russian Orthodoxy engages in the work of 'translation', what it renders understandable to a secular audience is far from reconcilable with liberal democracy" (Stoeckl 2014, VIII). By that statement, the outcomes of mutual interpretative and translation work are controversial. However, the anticipation of the continuation of this work is obvious. Kristina Stoeckl expects a new translation in the human rights debate, and she is asking the church to be part of it: "It is there – in theology – where the future trajectory of the encounter of Orthodoxy and modernity is being mapped out" (Stoeckl 2014, 131).

If we consider the initial conditions for both models of human dignity (in ROC Basic Teaching and Nordenfelt's multi-dimensional model), we will have a better understanding of both systems of reasoning. The official document of the ROC starts from the problem of the inconsistency of religious and secular reasoning about human rights in general. This is articulated in the introductory part of ROC Basic Teaching:

> In the world today, there is a widespread conviction that the human rights institution in itself can promote the development of human personality and social organisation in the best

---

reflect human rights issues, stressing the theological and legal grounds of their origin and addressing these issues simultaneously with their application.

possible way. At the same time, human rights protection is often the plea used to realise ideas that, in essence, radically disagree with Christian teaching. Christians have found themselves in a situation where public and social structures can force and often have already forced them to think and act contrary to God's commandments, thus obstructing their way towards the most important goal in human life, which is deliverance from sin and finding salvation.

It is obvious that the ROC model appeared as a response to the secular conception of human rights and human dignity. It is claimed in the introduction that 'Basic Teaching' starts from the interpretation of the category of human dignity, because "The human rights theory is based on human dignity as its fundamental notion. This is the reason why the need arises to set forth the Church's view of human dignity" (art. I. 1.). Before the category of human dignity was introduced by the ROC document in 2008, this concept was not in the active vocabulary of the ROC's social teaching.

Nordenfelt's model grew from the observation of real-life stories and situations of disease and death; it was developed according to the idea of dignified health care in particular moments of human life. This model appears in the sphere of practical application of the human dignity concept towards humans in need. The idea of 'dignity' developed through the necessity of providing 'weakening human beings' with the level of autonomy they had previously, in better health conditions. That is the goal of dignified health care – to support humans in the reintegration of body, soul, and mind, in new life circumstances.

For both models, the predetermined ideas relate to the sphere of care containing the conditions of human spiritual and biological being; the first in accordance with the vision of Christian theology, the second with the healthcare system in Europe. Both models recognise the dichotomies of congenital and acquired dignity, and maintain attributed dignity (recognised by others) and intrinsic human dignity (revealed in the process of self-reflection). Both approaches emphasise that even though human beings achieve or lose one kind of dignity, they can understand and face it in close relation to God (in a Christian theology) or to a community (in Nordenfelt's approach).

In his description of the dignity of merit, Nordenfelt declares: "The individual in many cases creates or achieves a state of affairs that constitutes the ground for a state of dignity. But dignity is not identical with its ground… Instead of saying that dignity is attributed to the individual, we now move to the idea of saying that the dignity scale has been attributed to human beings or to a particular community" (Nordenfelt 2009, 44). He compares it to this statement in ROC Basic Teaching (art. I.2): "Therefore, the human being as bearing the image of God should not exult in this lofty dignity, for it is not his own achievement but a gift of God". We observe that both models espouse a similar idea. Human dignity is assigned from the outside to humans (as a gift of God), or from the community that supports the particular human dignity model or scale. Also, if the human being should lose his or her dignity, there is a force protecting and calling for the return of this quality.

The similarities between the types of dignity in ROC Basic Teaching and Nordenfelt's models give us the opportunity to identify the overlapping interpretations of human dignity, and to clarify the difference between them. We will use the formulations of human dignity types suggested by Nordenfelt in the left column of Table 3.1 below, and compare the quotations from both texts. The empirical research will be based on the operationalisation scheme of the multi-dimensional human dignity scale suggested by Nordenfelt.

Table 3.1 Conceptualisation of human dignity by Nordenfelt and Russian Orthodox church basic teachings on human dignity, freedom, and rights

	Lennart Nordenfelt	Russian Orthodox church basic teaching on human dignity, freedom, and rights
Dignity of merit	"The dignity of merit depends on social rank and formal positions in life. There are many species of this kind of dignity and it is very unevenly distributed among human beings. The dignity of merit exists in degrees and it can come and go." (Nordenfelt 2004, 80)	Art. IV. 8 "A society has as its important responsibility to take care of those who are unable to secure their material needs. Access to education and vital medical care should not depend on the social or economic status of a person."
Dignity of moral stature	"The dignity of moral stature is the result of the moral deeds of the subject; likewise it can be reduced or lost through his or her immoral deeds. This kind of dignity is tied to the idea of a dignified character and of dignity as a virtue. The dignity of moral stature is a dignity of degree and it is also unevenly distributed among humans." (Nordenfelt 2004, 80)	Art. I.2. "therefore, in the eastern Christian tradition, the notion of 'dignity' has, first of all, a moral meaning, while the ideas of what is dignified and what is not are bound up with the moral or amoral actions of a person and with the inner state of his soul. Considering the state of human nature darkened by sin, it is important that things dignified and undignified should be clearly distinguished in the life of a person."
Inherent dignity	"The *Menschenwürde* pertains to all human beings to the same extent and cannot be lost as long as the persons exist." (Nordenfelt 2004, 80)	Art. I.1 "the incarnation of god the word showed that human nature did not lose its dignity even after the fall, for the image of god in it remained indelible, which means that an opportunity remained for restoring human life in the fullness of its original perfection."
Dignity of identity	"The dignity of identity is tied to the integrity of the subject's body and mind, and in many instances, although not always, is also dependent on the subject's self-image. This dignity can come and go as a result of the deeds of fellow human beings and also as a result of changes in the subject's body and mind." (Nordenfelt 2004, 80)	Art. II. 1. "the image of god can be either darkened or illumined depending on the self-determination of a free individual while the natural dignity becomes either more apparent in his life or obliterated by sin. The result is directly dependent on the self-determination of an individual."

All four kinds of human dignity can be found in both models; thus, the models can be viewed as more or less overlapping. However, while the dignity of merit is an autonomous parameter in Nordenfelt's conceptualisation, the Basic Teaching emphasises the necessity of equal possibilities for gaining access to social goods, regardless of the dignity of merit. The particular vision of the ROC is focused on the kind of dignity Nordenfelt calls the 'dignity of moral stature'. The moral dimension of human dignity is repeatedly emphasised in the text of the Church document: "[T]he patristic and ascetic thought and the whole liturgical tradition of the Church refer more to human indignity caused by sin than to human dignity". This is due to the need for "restoring human life in the fullness of its original perfection". According to the Basic Teaching, immoral behaviour results in a loss of dignity; however, the possibility of its recovery remains.

The idea of the necessity for the restoration of human life in a theological perspective is very close to Nordenfelt's idea of human dignity, reintegration and the necessity of recovering of human autonomy. For the purpose of healthcare ethics, Nordenfelt's model is aimed at matching inherent dignity with the dignity of identity. With the 'dignity of identity' category, Nordenfelt introduces an explicit idea that human dignity is an indivisible phenomenon, but is constructed of personal and social elements and requires internal individual retention and external encouragement.

This conversation between the philosophy of health care and theology demonstrates that human dignity is not an abstract concept, but the central category when it comes to the reintegration of various aspects of human life in challenging situations. Human dignity turns out to be an extremely practical phenomenon when human life is threatened by health changes. Dignified care could be taught in practice, and inherent human dignity is the only dignity that remains in the eyes of those who care for the terminally ill.

The Importance of Religious Arguments for Human Dignity and the Functions of Religion

Reflecting Louis Henkin's arguments explaining the difference between secular and religious approaches to human rights (Henkin 1998), we could say that the approach of the Russian Orthodox Church and Nordenfelt's model have similarities in their designation of kinds of human dignity; however, there is a difference regarding the centrality of human dignity.

The dignity of moral stature could be viewed as central in the Basic Teaching, as it is emphasised in the text; while in Nordenfelt's scheme, inherent dignity (*Menschenwürde*) and dignity of identity are central to his classification. Derived from the idea of dignified care for suffering humans, and the necessity of giving normative guidelines for fallen humans, both models introduce intrinsic and attributed kinds of dignity. Attributed dignity is more dependent on the divine or public image of the individual. Nordenfelt is talking about the public image of humans when he evaluates the dignity of merit, and also the dignity of moral status.

However, even inherent dignity is a phenomenon that has originated and is accepted in particular legal and political systems. Nordenfelt confirms that even in wealthy Western countries, inherent dignity requires a special understanding and further implementation regarding particular cases of disease treatment in healthcare systems. It is precisely this practical, active bond between the public and internal dimensions of human dignity that is at the centre of current discussions concerning Nordenfelt and ROC Basic Teaching.

According to the statements above, we can develop the following assumptions for our empirical analysis: different interpretative schemes of human dignity are relevant if they are rooted in particular practices of human dignity treatment, or their absence or the expectations for such treatment. And vice versa, if the ROC Basic Teaching on human dignity has resonance in civil society and religious arguments are taken seriously by the religious adherents of the ROC, we can determine the consensus; i.e. which Christians strongly support the human dignity approach articulated by the respective churches (i.e. the dignity of moral status). However, this correlation can only be explored if the influential public role of religion and religious arguments is clearly seen by the Belarusians, especially by those who declare their religious affiliation with the ROC.

Religiosity, Authoritarianism, and Human Dignity

In 2008, the Basic Teaching document underlined that cultural and religious contexts that are responsible for the development of human rights and concepts of human dignity do matter, and they should be taken into account when adopting these concepts: "*Actions aimed at respect for human rights and improvement of social and economic relations and institutions will not be truly successful if the religious and cultural traditions of countries and nations are ignored*" (art. III.4). While Nordenfelt's model is focused on the implementation of human dignity concepts (especially inherent dignity), mostly without any specific cultural or religious context, the ROC approach emphasises the particularities of cultural and religious environments for the interpretation of human rights and human dignity. Trying to find these specifics of the societal conditions that are underlined in the ROC documents, we are faced with recent reviews that cover the explanations of such particularities in Christian anthropology and regional political culture.

Alexander Kyrlezhev, the scientific consultant to the Synodic Theological Commission of the Russian Orthodox Church, says that "this conflict of interpretations revealing a conflict of worldviews and anthropologies is a serious challenge to both sides to have no simple solution" (Kyrlezhev 2007, 46). Kyrlezhev adopted the arguments from Christian anthropology, and explained that it is not possible just to borrow concepts of human rights and human dignity from a secular perspective without considering the differences in anthropology, models of social relations-building, creativity modes, and other concepts. The type of social relations construction (Kyrlezhev 2007) – grounded in the directionality of community building (from the bottom or from above) – is viewed as a particular constraint on the successful implementation of a secular human rights conception: "This health of society, however, is supposed to be built 'from below' on the volitions of individuals who have a fundamental distance between them. For religious awareness, quite the contrary; a community is built 'from above'. The essential difference is that, while human equality is recognised in both cases, a community is understood differently. In one case, it is a free association formed by a contract or 'constitution', while in the other case, it is a given co-belonging to a single common space of life and calling. It applies to the created natural world, a religious (church) community and, ideally, to the 'polis' community, that is the Earthly City" (Kyrlezhev 2007, 43).

The other specific feature is rooted in the context of the wider political culture (Stoeckl 2014), and can be observed at the societal level. Kristina Stoeckl emphasises that "the one thing that makes the Russian Orthodox Church's present process of clarification [towards human rights and human dignity – authors] very different ... is that the Church is engaging in this process in the context of political authoritarianism and democratic regress [...]" (Stoeckl 2014, VIII).

Whether the symmetry of hierarchal community relationship-building and authoritarianism as a political culture is simply a coincidence, or whether it is due to the consonance of processes at different levels of social, political and religious life, must still be clarified. We will try to observe the presence or absence of a significant relationship between authoritarianism and the human dignity scale between the adherents of the ROC and other religious or non-religious respondents.

From the 1970s, the relationship between particular religiosity types and authoritarianism came into the focus of empirical studies. Even the empirical data analysis based on Altemeyer's right-wing authoritarianism scale (Altemeyer and Hunsberger 1992; Altemeyer 1998) proves a definite dependency between the items of the scale (authoritarian submission, aggressiveness, and conventionalism) and religious orientation. Teymoori, Heydari and Nasiri emphasise that the direct link between religiosity types and authoritarianism – which has been re-examined repeatedly over the last 40 years – is not so obvious: "It is not the religiosity itself but the dogmatism in any ideology, whether the ideology is religious or not, that may relate to authoritarianism. It may be better to look at authoritarianism as a personality type or an attitudinal trait that is not necessarily associated with religiosity, and at fundamentalist and dogmatic forms of religion, or any other ideology, as revealing signs of authoritarianism" (Teymoori et al. 2014, 103).

These considerations (built on empirical evidence) reformulate the initial question: whether the difference in religious anthropology and cultural and religious tradition is in conflict with the human rights paradigm, or whether there are ideological differences where religious tradition and ideology collide. To understand the cultural and religious context for the attitudes of young people in Belarus towards their choice of a particular kind of human dignity, it should be explored whether religiosity and authoritarianism as a psychological predisposition of respondents, and their family-socialisation processes, have any significant influence regarding the human dignity scale.

Design of the Study

Research Question(s)

Considering the exploratory character of our research on the position of young people on the three variants of human dignity, and our inquiry about the particularities of socio-cultural conditions which could predetermine the attitude towards human dignity of young adherents of the ROC, the research questions are articulated accordingly:

1. What is the position of young people in Belarus regarding the human dignity of merit, the human dignity of moral stature, and inherent human dignity?
2. Can the role of religion in society, personal characteristics (empathy, right-wing authoritarianism, and attitudes towards multiculturalism), religion (religious belonging and religiosity) family-socialising process (religiosity and education of the parents), and socio-demographic characteristics (sex and age) predict the attitudes of young people towards the three variants of human dignity?
3. Is the position of young people who confirm their belonging to the ROC, and Christian belief in accordance with the vision of the ROC, emphasising the dignity of moral stature?

To answer these research questions we will use frequency analyses, factor analyses, and hierarchical regression models.

Procedure and Sample

This paper is based on the analysis of data collected by the international empirical research project 'Religion and Human Rights', coordinated by Professor Hans-Georg Ziebertz (University of Würzburg). The objective of the project is to explore how values, worldviews, religious beliefs and family context affect the understanding of human rights among young people in Europe and around the globe. Currently more than 25 countries are involved in the 'Religion and Human Rights' project.

However, the research on human dignity is a section within the wider survey instrument; the first findings from the Belarusian sample are presented in terms of the notion of human dignity, due to the centrality of its meaning for the conception of human rights. The questionnaire was translated from English into Russian by one of the authors of this paper. For the Belarusian respondents, the online survey was created by the project-coordinating team at the University of Würzburg. Participation in the online survey was secured by password access. The passwords were distributed among Belarusian youth between 17 and 19 years of age, mostly students in their first and second years of university undergraduate programmes.

The online survey started in 2015, and is still in progress. Due to enormous support from European university humanities students who responded and spread the passwords around different Belarusian universities, the sample has been growing in size and geography. Up to now, around 2000 passwords have been used, and 458 respondents have completed the online survey. Students from Minsk, Vitebsk, Brest, Hrodna, Gomel, Baranovichi and Mogilev have taken part in the survey. The operating sample of 458 respondents includes 55.7% Christians (Russian Orthodox Church), 25.5% non-religious students, and 18.8% who belong to another denomination (i.e. Roman Catholics, Muslims or Hindus). In terms of sex, 64.4% of the students are female and 35.6% are male.

Operationalisation and Method

The aim of the empirical part of this research paper is to explain the attitudes of young Belarusians towards the different dimensions of human dignity. The conceptualisation of human dignity is based on Nordenfelt's approach, with three dimensions of human dignity[3]: dignity of merit, dignity of moral stature, and inherent dignity (Fig. 3.2, in the appendix). We assume that the attitudes towards these three dimensions of dignity are predicted by personal and wider social factors. As personal and social factors of influence, we take into account the concepts of 'religion and society', 'personal characteristics', 'religion', 'family socialisation', and 'socio-demographic characteristics'.

The category 'religion and society' represents the students' opinion regarding the function that religion should have in society. The measuring instrument consists of 10 items that represent different functions that religion could fulfil in society, i.e. functions of religion as a public institution, influencing societal and cultural spheres, as well as being an institution for personal spiritual growth (Fig. 3.4, in the appendix). With a factor analysis of the 10 items included in the concept 'religion and society', a scale can illustrate the position of Belarusian youth regarding the role religious institutions should play in Belarusian society, and explain whether the salient public role of religion creates the conditions for the younger generation to be in consensus with the vision of the ROC on human dignity.

'Personal characteristics' consists of three scales: right-wing authoritarianism, empathy, and multiculturalism (Fig. 3.5 in the appendix).

The 'family socialisation' concept combines two variables: parents' belief, and educational background (Fig. 3.6 in the appendix).

The concept 'religion' consists of two variables: the religious belonging of the students, and their religiosity (Fig. 3.3 in the appendix).

As socio-demographic characteristics, we take into account sex and age.

[3] For the objective of our empirical research: while we explore the attitudes of young people to human dignity, the dignity of identity will be excluded from the scale. All three other varieties of dignity will be used in our empirical research, as a multi-dimensional scale of human dignity: dignity of merit, dignity of moral stature, and inherited dignity.

Conceptual Model

In the conceptual model (Fig. 3.1 below), human dignity will be viewed as a dependent variable predetermined by the personal and socio-demographic characteristics of the respondents.

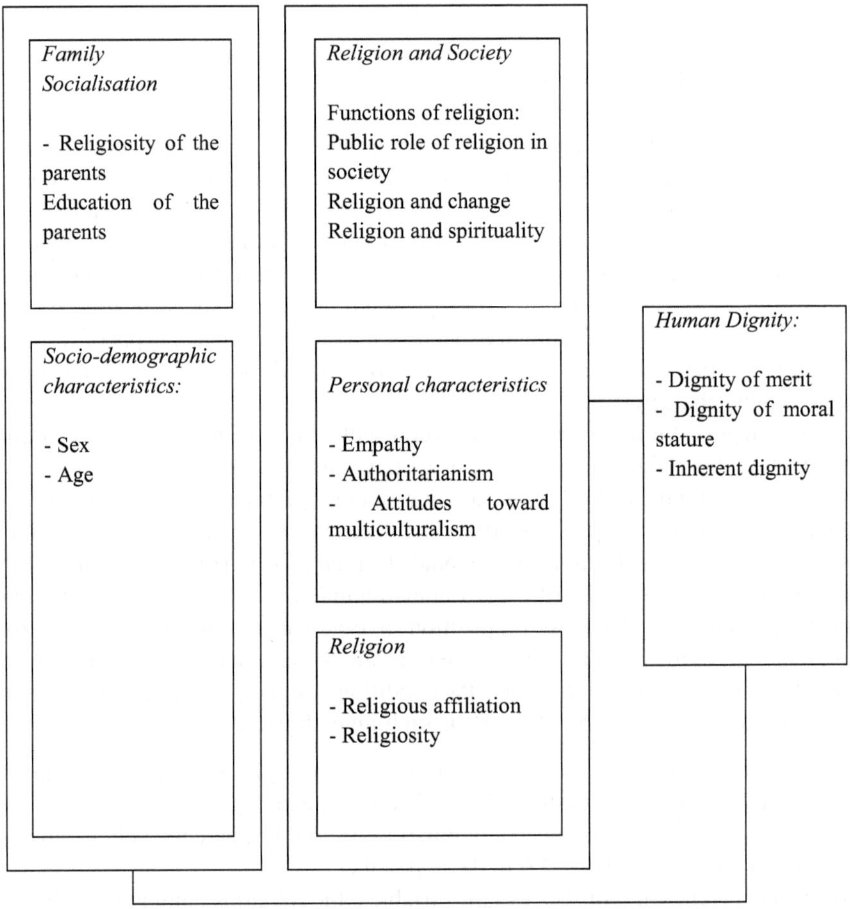

Fig. 3.1 Conceptual model

Hypotheses

The hypotheses for the Belarusian sample are based on the theoretical considerations stated above, and the empirical findings presented by Hans-Georg Ziebertz, Susanne Döhnert, and Alexander Unser in the chapter 'Predictors of attitudes towards human dignity: an empirical analysis among youth in Germany' (also published in this volume). The results of their analysis show that empathy has a negative influence on the dignity of merit and the dignity of moral stature, and a positive influence on inherent dignity. The belief of the students (their religiosity) also has a negative influence on the first two variants of dignity, and a positive one on the third variant. We will use these findings for our hypothesis about the Belarusian youth sample, together with the theoretical provisions of ROC Basic Teaching and the experts' conclusions described above.

We assume that the students' opinion of the role of religion in society, their personal characteristics, their religious belonging and religiosity, their family socialisation and their socio-demographic characteristics will predict their attitudes towards the three dimensions of human dignity – dignity of merit, dignity of moral stature, and inherent dignity. The following hypotheses will be verified in the process of the data analysis based on our theoretical considerations:

H1: Religious belonging to the ROC has a stronger positive influence on the dignity of moral stature than on inherent dignity, compared with other religiously/non-religiously affiliated respondents.

H2: The more students agree with the public role of religion in society, the stronger their support for the dignity of moral stature.

H3: Authoritarian attitudes have a positive influence on the human dignities of merit and moral stature, and a negative influence on inherent dignity.

Based on the finding from the German sample presented in this volume by Ziebertz, Döhnert & Unser, we will verify the following hypotheses:

H4: The religiosity of the students has a negative influence on the human dignity of merit and the human dignity of moral stature, and a positive influence on inherent dignity.

H5: The more the students emphasise the spiritual functions of religion in society, the stronger their support for inherent dignity.

H6: Empathy has a negative influence on the human dignity of merit and the human dignity of moral stature, and a positive influence on inherent dignity.

H7: The higher the education level of the parents of the students, the more the students reject the dignity of merit and the dignity of moral stature, and the more they support inherent dignity.

H8: The more religious the parents of the students are, the more the students disagree with the dignity of merit and the dignity of moral stature, and the more they agree with inherent dignity.

Empirical Findings

In this chapter we first present the descriptive statistics of the respondents' positions on the three dimensions of human dignity. Second, we will report on the results of the factor analyses for the concept 'religion and society'. Third, the Cronbach's alphas of the different scales will be reported; and fourth, the means and standard deviations of the scales and items. The results of the three regression models for dignity of merit, dignity of moral stature, and inherent dignity will then be introduced in the sections that follow. After that the research questions about the final comparative analysis of the regression models will be addressed, and the empirical findings will be revealed accordingly.

Descriptive Analyses

The Uncertainty in Attitudes Towards the Concept of Human Dignity Among Young People in Belarus

The empirical data demonstrate that in general, support of the three different concepts of human dignity (dignity of merit, dignity of moral stature, and inherent dignity) is quite low among Belarusian youth. For the measurement of the dignity concept a scale from 1 to 5 was suggested, where 1 = 'I totally disagree', 2 = 'I disagree', 3 = 'I am not sure', 4 = 'I agree', 5 = 'I agree fully' (Fig. 3.2 in the appendix).

The first research question – 'What is the position of young people in Belarus regarding the human dignity of merit, the human dignity of moral stature, and inherent human dignity?' – can be answered as follows: the greatest support (Table 3.2) is given to the concept of inherent dignity (mean = 3.10), the second-strongest agreement is given to the dignity of moral stature (mean = 3.07), and the dignity of merit is not supported by the students (mean = 2.55). Nearly half of the students disagree or totally disagree with dignity of merit (48.1%), about one-third are not sure (31.2%), and only one-fifth (20.7%) agree or strongly agree with this variant of dignity. In contrast, on average students agree slightly with the concept of dignity of moral stature: only one-quarter (26.2%) totally disagree or disagree with this variant of dignity; 38.4% are not sure, and 35.4% agree or totally agree.

Table 3.2 Human dignity (frequencies (%), means and standard deviation)

Items	I totally disagree	I disagree	I am not sure	I agree	I fully agree	M	SD
The value of a person depends on the appreciation given to him or her by others	21.2	26.9	31.2	17.2	3.5	2.55	1.11
The honour to be given to a person depends on his or her moral behaviour	7.6	18.6	38.4	29.5	5.9	3.07	1.01
Each human being should be recognized just because he is a human being irrespective of credit or moral behavior	10.5	18.6	32.8	26.6	11.6	3.10	1.15

In addition, it is noticeable that the concept of moral dignity causes the most uncertainty among the others, as about 40% are not sure about their position regarding this concept of dignity. The other two concepts of dignity only cause uncertainty among 30% the students in regard to their position on the items. On average, students support the concept of inherent dignity slightly more strongly than the concept of dignity of moral stature. About one-third totally disagree or disagree with the concept of inherent dignity (29.1%), about one-third are not sure (32.8%), and more than 35% agree or totally agree with it.

The Function of Religion in Society

For the independent concept 'religion and society', a principal component factor analysis with varimax rotation was computed to identify the different empirical dimensions of this survey instrument. Finally, the decision for a three-factor solution was made, since this variant represents the best balance between theoretical assumptions and empirical findings. Bartlett's test of sphericity is also significant for this solution. For the further analysis, two items must be excluded, as their factor loading is too low for one of the three identified factors. These two items are: 'Religions should take joint responsibility with the state for our national culture', and 'Religions should take public responsibility for societal development'. The full list of items is presented in the appendix (Fig. 3.4). The final factor solution is presented in Table 3.3.

The dimensions represented by the three factors can be described as follows: the first dimension can be summarised by the term 'public role of religion in society'. This dimension refers to the societal and cultural role that religion should occupy

Table 3.3 Principal component factor analysis with varimax rotation for 'religion and society'

Item	Factor I	Factor II	Factor III	h^2
Religions should try to influence public opinion on social problems.	.840			.738
Religions should publicly stand up for the underclass.	.663			.592
Religions should take responsibility for their members' spiritual growth.			.790	.687
Religions should go along with changing ideas in society.		.881		.799
Religions should use their authority to intervene in societal affairs.	.813			.671
Religions should create places for deep spiritual experiences.			.800	.684
Religions should consolidate the nation against alien influences and the deprivation of its originality.	.615			.520
Religions should always keep up with current social trends.		.900		.819
Explained variance: 68.865 — KMO = .745				

and take responsibility for. The second dimension can be described as 'religion and change', and states that religion should adapt to societal changes and be open to new developments in society. The third dimension represents the perception that the assignment of religion is to care about its members and their spiritual needs. This dimension also represents the idea that religion should not be involved in societal and secular affairs, but focus on special religious spheres. This function is summarised under the term 'religion and spirituality'.

Religiosity, Function of Religion and Personal Characteristics Scales

Table 3.4 shows the reliability of 'religion and society' (Fig. 3.4 in the appendix), religiosity, and the personal characteristics scales (Fig. 3.5 in the appendix), which will be used in a further regression analysis for the human dignity concept. As the criterion for acceptable reliability, Cronbach's alpha should have a minimum value of .60; this value is slightly undershot in three scales: 'religion and spirituality' (Cornbach's alpha = .57), 'right-wing authoritarianism' and 'multiculturalism' (Cronbach's alpha = .58). Because the values are only slightly below the reported value, the decision was made to accept these scales. The scales 'public role of religion in society' (alpha = .77), 'religion and change' (alpha = .77), 'religiosity' (alpha = .71), and 'empathy' (alpha = .68) fulfil the criterion.

Table 3.4 The reliability of the scales

Items	Cronbach's Alpha
(Religion and society: Function of religion)	
Public role of religion in society	.77
Religion and change	.77
Religion and spirituality	.57
(Religiosity)	.71
(Right-wing authoritarianism)	.58
(Empathy)	.68
(Multiculturalism)	.58

Table 3.5 shows the results of means and standard deviations for the scales and Likert-scale items. For the concept 'function of religion', the factor analysis identifies three dimensions. The first dimension, 'Public role of religion in society', is not supported by the students; the mean has a value of 2.65, which is less than three, the middle category of the scale. The perception that religion should take responsibility and be engaged in societal and cultural issues is not shared by the students. The second dimension, 'religion and change', is slightly supported by the students (mean = 3.15). They support the idea that religions should be open to societal changes and new developments. The highest agreement is with the dimension 'religion and spirituality', with a mean of 3.41. The students support the idea that reli-

Table 3.5 Scales and items (Means and standard deviation)

	Mean	Standard deviation
(Religion and society: Function of religion)		
Public role of religion in society	2.65	.80
Religion and change	3.15	.98
Religion and spirituality	3.41	.86
Religiosity	3.17	1.06
Right-wing authoritarianism	2.45	.75
Empathy	3.44	.81
Multiculturalism	3.46	.68
Religiosity of the mother	3.81	.87
Religiosity of the father	3.43	1.12

gion should care mainly about the spiritual and religious issues of its members, and should not be interwoven with societal and cultural issues.

The religiosity of the Belarusian youth is quite low as well, with a mean of 3.17, as the middle category here is three. However, an explanation could be that this is the value for the whole sample, which also includes non-religious students. In the regression models, this effect will be controlled, since religious belonging is also included in the analysis.

The descriptive statistics of the three scales of 'personal characteristics' is as follows: the perception for 'authoritarianism' is negative (mean = 2.45); the students have a non-authoritarian orientation. The situation is different for empathy and multiculturalism – the students have a positive perception for these concepts. Empathy is slightly less pronounced than openness for multiculturalism (empathy: mean = 3.44; openness to multiculturalism: mean = 3.46).

For the religiosity of the parents, we have the finding that the religiosity of the mothers is slightly stronger than that of the fathers (religiosity mothers: mean = 3.81; religiosity of the fathers: mean = 3.43).

Regression Analyses Regarding the Influence of the Independent Variables on the three Dimensions of Human Dignity

The Human Dignity of Merit and Its Personal and Socio-cultural Predictors Among Belarusian Youth

In the first regression model, we examine whether and to what degree the following five different concepts are the predictors for human dignity of merit: 'religion and society' (the youth's attitudes toward the role of religion in society); 'personal characteristics' (right-wing authoritarianism, empathy, and multiculturalism); 'religion' (religious belonging and religiosity); 'family socialisation' (religiosity and education of the parents); and 'socio-demographic characteristics' (sex and age). Dignity of merit is understood as a differentiating concept of dignity, where the value of a person depends on the appreciation given to him or her by others.

The five independent concepts are included successively in the hierarchical regression model, to investigate how much variance each independent concept can explain. Table 3.6 demonstrates that all five models are significant, but not all concepts contribute to the explained variance. The concepts of 'religion and society', 'personal characteristics' and 'religion' explain the variance to a certain degree, whereas socialisation and socio-demographic characteristics reduce the explained variance.

The first concept, 'religion and society', explains 2.8% of the variance; the second concept, 'personal characteristics', explains 1.6%; and the third concept, 'religion', explains 2%. 'Family socialisation' and socio-demographic characteristics do not contribute to the explained variance. So 'religion and society' can explain most of the variance. The second-strongest concept to explain the variance of the dignity of merit is 'religion', followed by 'personal characteristics'. In all, 5.7% of the variance of inherent dignity can be explained by the five different independent concepts.

The concept 'religion and society' consists of three scales: 'public role of religion in society', 'religion and change' and 'religion and spirituality'. 'Public role of religion in society' has a significant positive influence and 'religion and spirituality' a significant negative influence on the dignity of merit ('public role of religion in society': beta = .157; 'religion and spirituality': beta = −.126). The more the students perceive the influence of religion in society, the more they agree with the dignity of merit; and the more they support the spiritual responsibility of religion for its members, the less they support this variant of dignity.

The personal characteristic concept consists of the scales 'authoritarianism', 'empathy' and 'openness to multiculturalism'. Authoritarianism is the only significant item, and has a positive influence on the dignity of merit. Students with a higher predisposition towards authoritarianism support the dignity of merit more strongly than those with a lower predisposition to authoritarianism (beta = .144).

The concept 'religion' includes religious belonging and the religious belief of the students. Orthodox students agree significantly more strongly with the dignity of merit than non-religious students (beta = −.151). In addition, the religious belief of the students has a significant influence on the students' attitudes to this variant of dignity: the more religious they are, the more they deny the dignity of merit (beta = −.221).

The concept 'family socialisation' focuses on the religiosity and education of the parents. These indicators have no significant influence on the dignity of merit.

The variables 'sex' and 'age' – included in the regression model to control their influence – have no significant influence on this variant of dignity.

Table 3.6 Regression model for human dignity of merit

	Model 1	Model 2	Model 3	Model 4	Model 5
Religion and society (function of religion)					
Public role of religion in society	.141*	.110	.154*	.164*	.157*
Religion and change	.113*	.119*	.076	.068	.067
Religion and spirituality	−.174**	−.153*	−.128*	−.134*	−.126*
Personal characteristics					
Authoritarianism		.138*	.137*	.144**	.144**
Empathy		−.079	−.079	−.082	−.072
Multiculturalism		.006	.012	.016	.012
Religion					
Religious belonging					
Believer (ref. Orthodox)			−.034	−.042	−.045
Non-religious (ref. Orthodox)			−.157*	−.150*	−.151*
Religiosity			−.214**	−.228**	−.221**
Family socialisation					
Religiosity (parents)					
Religiosity/mother				.005	.001
Religiosity/father				.018	.021
Education (parents)					
College/mother (ref. school)				−.008	−.017
University/mother (ref. school)				−.061	−.077
College/father (ref. school)				−.141	−.138
University/father (ref. school)				−.124	−.121
Socio-demographic characteristics					
Sex					.063
Age					.024
Constant	2.368	2.202	2.884	3.165	2.746
Adj. R^2	.028	.044	.064	.058	.057
F	4.425***	3.782***	3.767***	2.485***	2.294***

N = 458
*p ≤.05; **p ≤ .01; ***p ≤ .001
Reference: Religious belonging = Russian Orthodox Church; Education father: Secondary education; Sex: Male

The Predictors for Human Dignity of Moral Stature Among Belarusian Youth

With the second hierarchical regression model, we focus on the human dignity of moral stature, and the predictors for this concept. Table 3.7 shows that all five models of the hierarchical regression model are significant, but as in the first regression model, they do not all contribute to the explained variance. Again, the first three concepts ('religion and society', 'personal characteristics' and 'religion') contribute to the explained variance, whereas socialisation and the socio-demographic characteristics reduce the explained variance. The concept 'religion and society' explains 4.1% of the variance of the dignity of moral stature; the personal characteristics of the students explain only 0.5%, and 'religiosity' 2.1%. The first concept, 'religion and society', explains most of the variance – similar to the first regression model. The second important predictor is religiosity, and the third is personal characteristics. In general, the model can explain 5.8% of the variance in human dignity of moral stature.

The concept 'religion' has one significant item; the dimension 'public role of religion in society' has a positive influence on the dignity of moral stature (beta = .244). The more students agree that religion has societal responsibility, the more they support this variant of dignity.

As with 'religion', the concept 'personal characteristics' also has one significant item. 'Authoritarianism' has a significant positive influence on the dignity of moral stature (beta = .123). The higher the students' predisposition to authoritarianism, the more they agree to the variant that the dignity of a person depends on his or her moral behaviour. 'Religiosity' is the only significant item of the concept 'religion' that has a significant negative influence on the attitudes to the dignity of moral stature (beta = -.201).

The variables of the other two concepts have no significant influence on this version of human dignity. The most important predictor for the dignity of moral stature is 'public role of religion in society', followed by 'religious belief' and then by 'predisposition to authoritarianism'.

The Attitudes Towards Inherent Dignity Among Belarusian Students

In the third regression model, we focus only on the concept of dignity, which states that every person possesses dignity simply because he or she is a human being, regardless of credit or moral behaviour. For inherent dignity, all five hierarchical regression models are significant, and contribute to the explained variance – except for the concept of 'religion' (Table 3.8). In contrast to the other two regression models that examine the differentiating variants of dignity, the socialisation and socio-demographic characteristics raise the explained variance.

The concept 'religion and society' explains 0.2% of the variance in inherent dignity; 'personal characteristics' 4.5%, socialisation 3.7%, and the socio-demographic characteristics 0.6%. So, 'personal characteristics' contribute most to

Table 3.7 Regression model for human dignity of moral stature

	Model 1	Model 2	Model 3	Model 4	Model 5
Religion and society (function of religion)					
Public role of religion in society	.210***	.174**	.230***	.222***	.224***
Religion and change	–.051	–.039	–.094	–.087	–.086
Religion and spirituality	.029	.038	.072	.079	.075
Personal characteristics					
Authoritarianism		.105	.113*	.123*	.123*
Empathy		.008	.016	.012	.006
Multiculturalism		–.036	–.028	–.024	–.023
Religion					
Religious belonging					
Believer (ref. Orthodox)			–.077	–.063	–.060
Non-religious (ref. Orthodox)			–.109	–.094	–.094
Religiosity			–.209**	–.202**	–.207**
Family Socialisation					
Religiosity (parents)					
Religiosity/mother				–.025	–.022
Religiosity/father				.038	.037
Education (parents)					
College/mother (ref. school)				.077	.080
University/mother (ref. school)				–.017	–.010
College/father (ref. school)				.042	.040
University/father (ref. school)				.104	.103
Socio-demographic characteristics					
Sex					–.032
Age					.002
Constant	2.423	2.267	2.750	2.399	2.418
Adj. R^2	.041	.046	.067	.063	.058
F	6.122***	3.891***	3.882***	2.617***	2.318***

N = 458

*p ≤.05; **p ≤ .01; ***p ≤ .001

Reference: Religious belonging = Russian Orthodox church; education father: Secondary education; sex: Male

Table 3.8 Regression model for inherent dignity

	Model 1	Model 2	Model 3	Model 4	Model 5
Religion and society (function of religion)					
Public role of religion in society	−.018	−.014	−.042	−.022	−.025
Religion and change	.103	.098	.121*	.116*	.120*
Religion and spirituality	−.008	−.036	−.043	−.061	−.066
Personal characteristics					
Authoritarianism		−.090	−.101	−.107	−.104
Empathy		.166**	.158**	.165**	.147**
Multiculturalism		.098	.106*	.117*	.116*
Religion					
Religious belonging					
Believer (ref. Orthodox)			−.044	−.054	−.042
Non-religious (ref. Orthodox)			−.029	−.048	−.053
Religiosity			.060	.062	.045
Family socialisation					
Religiosity (parents)					
Religiosity/mother				.103	.116
Religiosity/father				−.186**	−.182**
Education (parents)					
College/mother (ref. school)				.195*	.191*
University/mother (ref. school)				.188*	.196*
College/father (ref. school)				−.172	−.177
University/father (ref. school)				−.214*	−.217*
Socio-demographic characteristics					
Sex					−.050
Age					.104*
Constant	2.865	1.950	1.883	2.343	.981
Adj. R^2	.002	.047	.044	.081	.087
F	1.199***	4.004***	2.865***	3.126***	3.040***

N = 458
*p ≤.05; **p ≤ .01; ***p ≤ .001
Reference: Religious belonging = Russian Orthodox Church; Education father: Secondary education; Sex: Male

the explained variance of this variant of dignity, followed by socialisation, socio-demographic characteristics, and 'religion and society'. In all, 8.7% of the variance of inherent dignity can be explained by the five different independent concepts.

The concept 'religion and society' has one significant item. The more the students agree that religion should adapt to new societal changes, the more they agree with inherent dignity (beta = .120). Empathy and openness to multiculturalism – scales of the concept 'personal characteristics' – have a significant positive influence on this variant of dignity (empathy: beta = .147; openness to multiculturalism: beta = .116). The more empathy the students have and the more they are open to multiculturalism, the more they agree with inherent dignity.

In contrast with the previous two regression models, 'family socialisation' has a significant influence on the attitudes of the students towards inherent dignity. The religiosity of the father has a significant negative influence on this concept of dignity (beta = −.182). With an increase in the religiosity of the father, the agreement of the students with inherent dignity decreases. The education of the mother is also an important predictor for attitudes to inherent dignity. Compared with students whose mothers only have school education, students whose mothers have college and university education agree more strongly with the concept of inherent dignity. The greatest agreement with inherent dignity is for students whose mothers have a university degree (mother with a college education: beta = .191; mother with a university degree: beta = .196). As well as the mothers' education, the education of the father is also an important factor in attitudes towards inherent dignity. However, the direction of the influence is opposite: students with fathers who have a university degree agree significantly less with the concept of inherent dignity (beta = −.217) than students whose fathers have only a school education.

Socio-demographic characteristics have one significant variable. As the age of the respondents (who are between 17 and 19 years old) increases, agreement with inherent dignity also increases (beta = .104).

In contrast with the other two regression models, the family-socialisation process has an influence on attitudes towards inherent dignity. The religiosity and education of the father have the strongest influence on attitudes to this version of dignity. Empathy has the second-strongest influence, and 'religion and change' is the third-strongest variable to predict the attitudes of Belarusian youth towards inherent dignity. The variable with the least influence on this concept is the age of the respondent.

The Comparative Analysis of Human Dignity Regression Models

We observe from the data that all three regression models are statistically significant, and the independent concepts that are theoretically assumed as predictors for attitudes towards human dignity can explain the variance of the different variants of dignity to a certain extent. Nevertheless, the explained variance is not very high: our model can explain 5.7% of the variance for the dignity of merit, 5.8% for the dignity of moral stature, and 8.7% for inherent dignity. Therefore, we assume that there are still other predictors for attitudes towards dignity that are not yet identified, and that further research needs to be done.

When we look at the different concepts and their variables, it is noticeable that their influence on and significance in terms of the three variants of dignity is quite different from what was theoretically assumed. The directional effect of the concepts on the two differentiating concepts of dignity – dignity of merit and dignity of moral stature – is similar for both, and we can also see the reverse directional effects of the independent concepts on inherent dignity. For the first two variants of dignity, it can be ascertained that only the concepts 'religion and society', 'personal characteristics' and 'religion' contribute to the explained variance, and thus have significant variables. The family socialisation of the students appears to have no influence on their attitudes towards these variants of dignity. In the first two regression models, the concept 'religion and society' explains most of the variance. The second important predictor for these differentiating concepts of dignity is the concept of 'religion'. 'Personal characteristics' have the lowest power to explain.

The relevance of the independent concepts for inherent dignity is quite different. For this variant of dignity, 'personal characteristics' are most important for predicting the attitudes of the students; in second place comes 'family socialisation', then socio-demographic characteristics. 'Religion and society' has no influence on this variant of dignity. Attitudes towards inherent dignity are rooted in the family-socialising process, but the family-socialisation process has no influence on dignity of merit and moral stature.

If we compare the strength of the influence of the variables of the independent concepts on the human dignity of merit, the human dignity of moral stature and inherent dignity, we come to some unexpected conclusions:

- for the concept *'Religion and society':* the item 'public role of religion in society' has a significant positive influence on the first two variants of dignity; the item 'religion and change' has a positive influence on inherent dignity and dignity of merit; and 'religion and spirituality' has a negative influence on inherent dignity;
- for the concept *'Personal characteristics'*: 'authoritarianism' has a significant positive influence on the dignity of merit and moral stature. 'Empathy' is only significant in the third regression model, and has a positive influence on inherent dignity. 'Empathy' has no significant influence on the first two variants of dignity; but the directional effect on the dignity of merit is negative, and on the dignity of moral stature, slightly positive. 'Multiculturalism' has a significant influence on inherent dignity.
- for the concept *'Religion'*: 'religious belonging' is only significant with regard to the dignity of merit. Compared to the Orthodox students, non-religious students do support this variant of dignity to a lesser degree. More than 'religious belonging', 'religiosity' is the stronger predictor of attitudes toward the various kinds of dignity. The religious belief of the students has a significant negative influence on the first two variants of dignity, but not on inherent dignity. Even so, the influence of religious belief on inherent dignity is not significant; the directional effect is positive.

- the *'family socialisation'* and socio-demographic characteristics are not significant for the first two variants of dignity, but they are for inherent dignity. The religiosity of the father has a negative influence on inherent dignity. The education of the parents also has significant influence. The more highly educated the mother, the more the students agree with this variant of dignity; whereas they agree less with inherent dignity the more highly educated the father.

Conclusions

Among the empirical findings of this research is the uncertainty of Belarusian students regarding their attitudes towards the human dignity scale. This indicates that students do not have one established concept of human dignity. The reason could be that human dignity is viewed as an abstract and multi-dimensional concept that is difficult to perceive; or perhaps the very concept is not generally used in individuals' vocabulary and public discourse. This empirical evidence refers to the necessity of development of the educational and interpretation work on human dignity issues that could clarify the nature of this concept, making it more concrete and practical in the understanding of the young generation in Belarus.

Rethinking the comparative analysis of regression models, we must admit that young Belarusians who identify themselves with the Russian Orthodox Church do not express support for the idea that human dignity is the result of the moral deeds of the subject. On the contrary, the more the respondents' belief in God or a divine power, and the more important their belief is in their daily life, the less they support the moral aspects of human dignity. At the same time, the influence of religious belief on inherent dignity is not significant; however, the directional effect is positive. Those students who recognise the salient public role of religion in society support the dignity of merit and dignity of moral stature; thus, we can say that they are in consensus with the ROC teaching on human dignity.

We could conclude that for the first hypothesis, belonging to the ROC has only a significant influence on the dignity of merit: non-religious students agree significantly less with this variant of dignity than students who belong to the ROC. More than 'religious belonging', 'religiosity' predicts negative attitudes towards dignity of merit and dignity of moral stature, but not the inherent dignity. This finding may question whether young Belarusians are actually familiar with the position of the ROC's Basic Teaching on Human Dignity; and if they are, whether they agree or disagree with this vision, since they support inherent dignity more strongly. Or perhaps they simply do not connect religiosity with moral behaviour.

At the same time, the second hypothesis is proved: 'the more students agree with the public role of religion in society, the stronger their support for the dignity of moral stature'. Our third hypothesis, that 'authoritarian attitudes have a positive influence on the dignity of moral stature and a negative influence on inherent dignity', needs to be adjusted. Authoritarianism as a personal feature has a significant influence on the dignity of merit choice, and to a lesser degree predicts the choice regarding the dignity of moral stature. The influence of authoritarianism on inherent dignity is not significant; however, the directional effect is negative.

When we verify the hypotheses – which we developed and proved with German samples – for Belarusian youth, we find the following differences in the results of the research. We assumed that the religiosity of the students has a negative influence on the dignity of merit and the human dignity of moral stature, and a positive influence on inherent dignity. There are differences and similarities in the Belarusian and German samples regarding this hypothesis. The religiosity of Belarusian and German young people has a negative influence on the dignity of merit and no influence on inherent dignity. While there is a negative influence of religiosity on the dignity of moral stature in Belarusian sample, there is no such influence in the German case.

For German youth, empathy has a negative influence on the dignity of merit and a positive influence on the dignity of moral stature and inherent dignity; but according to the Belarusian students, empathy has no influence on the dignity of merit and moral dignity, but a positive influence on inherent dignity.

Considering which cultural, societal or family-socialisation aspects influence the attitudes of students in Belarus to the three concepts of dignity mentioned, we could clearly observe that inherent human dignity can be predicted by 'personal characteristics' (empathy and openness to others) and 'family-socialising' processes. On the other hand, the dignity of merit and moral dignity could be predicted by religiosity and the 'religion and society' concepts, while 'personal characteristics' are not involved except for the authoritarianism feature.

These findings bring us back to the theoretical basis we examined earlier in this chapter: how the human dignity scale is kept, either external to human forces (as a gift from God), or by the community which supports the particular human dignity model or scale. The empirical evidence indicates that for the younger generation in Belarus, the understanding of inherent dignity is based first and foremost on individual differences in sensitivity modes oriented to others. We observed that family relations play a particular role here; however, we could not explain why parents' religiosity and education have such an effect. Additional analysis is therefore required. The first findings clearly demonstrate that the understanding of the human dignity concept is grounded in the interplay of personal, family and other socio-cultural factors, and that differences in the perception of kinds of human dignity do matter.

Appendices (Operationalisation of the Scales and Categories)

(Human dignity of merit)
The value of a person depends on the appreciation given to him or her by others.
(Human dignity of moral stature)
The honour to be given to a person depends on his or her moral behaviour.
(Inherent human dignity)
Each human being should be recognised just because he or she is a human being, irrespective of credit or moral behaviour.

Answer scheme: 1 = I totally disagree; 2 = I disagree; 3 = I am not sure; 4 = I agree; 5 = I fully agree

Fig. 3.2 Dimensions of human dignity

(Religious belonging)
Do you belong to one of the religious communities, or would you describe yourself as 'non-religious'?

Answer scheme: 16 religions/denominations, and the categories 'other religion' and 'non-religious'

(Religious belief and importance of belief)
How often do you think about religious issues?
To what extent do you believe that God or something divine exists?
What is your position on the statement: 'My religion or worldview has great influence on my daily life'?

Answer scheme: 1 = I totally disagree; 2 = I disagree; 3 = I am not sure; 4 = I agree; 5 = I fully agree

Fig. 3.3 Scales and items of the concept 'Religiosity'

Religions should try to influence public opinion on social problems.
Religions should stand up publicly for the underclass.
Religions should take responsibility for their members' spiritual growth.
Religions should take joint responsibility with the state for our national culture.
Religions should go along with changing ideas in society.
Religions should use their authority to intervene in societal affairs.
Religions should create places for deep spiritual experiences.
Religions should take public responsibility for societal development.
Religions should consolidate the nation against alien influences and the deprivation of its originality.
Religions should always keep up with current social trends.

Answer scheme: 1 = I totally disagree; 2 = I disagree; 3 = I am not sure; 4 = I agree; 5 = I fully agree

Fig. 3.4 Scales and items of the concept 'Religion and society'

(Right-wing authoritarianism)
The majority of those who criticize proper authorities in government and religion merely create useless doubts in people's minds.
What our country really needs instead of more 'civil rights' is much more law and order.
Obedience and respect for authority are the most important values children should learn.
The facts concerning crime, sexual immorality and public disorder all show we must crack down harder on deviant groups and troublemakers, if we are going to save our moral standards and preserve law and order.

Answer scheme: 1 = I totally disagree; 2 = I disagree; 3 = I am not sure; 4 = I agree; 5 = I fully agree

(Empathy)
I often have tender, concerned feelings for people less fortunate than me.
When I see someone being taken advantage of, I feel protective towards them.
Other people's misfortunes do not usually disturb me a great deal.

Answer scheme: 1 = I totally disagree; 2 = I disagree; 3 = I am not sure; 4 = I agree; 5 = I fully agree

(Multiculturalism)
The many immigrants in our country cause unrest and tension.
The variety of customs that people have in this country is enriching.
The many points of view are good for our society and make it colourful.
In our society, there is so much diversity that you don't know in which direction to go.

Answer scheme: 1 = I totally disagree; 2 = I disagree; 3 = I am not sure; 4 = I agree; 5 = I fully agree

Fig. 3.5 Scales and items of the 'Personal characteristics' concept

(Social class context)
What is the highest educational level reached by your mother?
What is the highest educational level reached by your father?

Answer scheme: 1 = secondary education; 2 = college; 3 = university

(Parents′ belief)
How would you describe your father's belief and faith in God or a higher reality?
How would you describe your mother's belief and faith in God or a higher reality?

Answer scheme: 1 = absolutely unbelieving; 2 = rather unbelieving; 3 = doubtful; 4 = believe; 5 = absolutely believe

Fig. 3.6 Scales and items of the 'Family socialisation' concept

References

Altemeyer, B. (1996). *The authoritarian specter*. Cambridge: Harvard University Press.
Altemeyer, B. (1998). The other 'authoritarian personality'. *Advances in Experimental Social Psychology, 30*, 47–92.
Altemeyer, B., & Hunsberger, B. (1992). Authoritarianism, religious fundamentalism, quest, and prejudice. *The International Journal for the Psychology of Religion, 2*, 113–133.
Calhoun, C. (2005). *Religion, secularism, and public* reason. Comments on Helge Høibraaten's lecture. The Holberg Prize Seminar 2005, Holberg Prize Laureate Professor Jürgen Habermas: 'Religion in the Public Sphere'.

Davis, M. H. (1983). Measuring individual differences in empathy: Evidence for a multidimensional approach. *Journal of Personality and Social Psychology, 44*, 113–126.
Habermas, J. (2006). Religion in the public sphere. *European Journal of Philosophy, 14*(1), 1–25.
Henkin, L. (1998). Religion, religions, and human rights. *The Journal of Religious Ethics, 26*(2), 229–239.
Huber, S. (2003). *Zentralität und Inhalt: Ein Neues Multidimensionales Messmodell Der Religiosität.* (Veröffentlichungen der Sektion Religionssoziologie der Deutschen Gesellschaft für Soziologie). Opladen.
Huber, S., & Huber, O. W. (2012). The centrality of religiosity scale (CRS). *Religion, 3*, 710–724.
Kyrlezhev, A. (2007). Relationships between human rights concept and religious values. *Occasional Papers on Religion in Eastern Europe, 27*(1), Article 4.
Manganelli Rattazzi, A. M., Bobbio, A., & Canova, L. (2007). A short version of the right-wing authoritarianism (RWA) scale. *Personality and Individual Differences, 43*(5), 1223–1234.
Nordenfelt, L. (2004). The varieties of dignity. *Health Care Analysis, 12*(2), 69–81.
Nordenfelt, L. (Ed.). (2009). *Dignity in care for older people*. Oxford: Wiley-Blackwell.
Rawls, J. (1997). The idea of public reason revised. *University of Chicago Law Review, 64*(3), 765–807.
Stoeckl, K. (2014). *The Russian Orthodox Church and human rights*. London/New York: Routledge.
Teymoori, A., Heydari, A., & Nasiri, H. (2014). Relationship between dimensions of religiosity, authoritarianism, and moral authority. *Social Compass, 61*(1), 92–107.

Documents

(2006) 'The Declaration on Human Rights and Dignity' adopted at the 10th World Russian People's Council.
(2008) 'Russian Orthodox Church Basic Teaching on Human Dignity, Freedom, and Rights' adopted by the Bishops' Council of the Russian Orthodox Church.

Chapter 4
Religion and Civil Rights in Italy: An Empirical Exploration Among Secondary School Students

Francesco Zaccaria, Francis-Vincent Anthony, and Carl Sterkens

Abstract What is the role of religion in building up a culture of civil rights in Italy? According to Marzano and Urbinati (2013), the privileged status of the Catholic Church in Italy can result in a negative role of religion towards civil rights issues; according to these sociologists, Habermas' theory of a public role of religion in a post-secularized society is not applicable in Italy, because of the virtual Catholic religious monopoly. The present study shows the historical background of this debated relation between church and civil rights in Italy. It points out the reasons why both a negative and a positive role of religion toward civil rights can be expected. It presents the results of an empirical investigation among Italian secondary school students (N = 1087), carried out in order to explore the role of religion about civil rights among this portion of public opinion, which will shape the future of this debate in Italy. The questions of this empirical research are: What understanding of civil rights is present among the sample of students? Are there significant differences in support for civil rights in student groups as defined by their religious affiliation and practice? Is there a correlation between the students' views on civil rights and their religious attitudes? Is there a correlation between the students' views on civil rights and their background characteristics? What is the predictive strength of the students' religious attitudes and background characteristics with regard to views on civil rights?

F. Zaccaria (✉)
Apulian Theological Faculty, Bari, Italy
e-mail: frazacc@yahoo.it

F.-V. Anthony
Salesian Pontifical University, Rome, Italy

C. Sterkens
Faculty of Philosophy, Theology and Religious Studies, Radboud University, Nijmegen, The Netherlands

H.-G. Ziebertz, C. Sterkens (eds.), *Religion and Civil Human Rights in Empirical Perspective*, Religion and Human Rights 2, DOI 10.1007/978-3-319-59285-5_4

Introduction

Human rights are fragile: in order to be respected and defended they not only need to be enshrined in declarations and constitutions, but also to be embedded in people's minds and fostered by each generation. In this process of public perception of human rights, religion can be a positive, negative or neutral force in shaping a culture of human rights. In Italy, where Roman Catholicism is the religious denomination of the overwhelming majority, we need to focus on Catholicism when exploring how religion can affect human rights. Human rights span a broad spectrum, but media attention in Italy tends to focus on civil rights, as in the case of public debate about the civil rights of minorities: homosexuals and religious minorities among immigrants. In this article, we will seek to explore the civil rights culture among young Italians, who will determine the destiny of civil rights, and the role of religion with reference to civil rights.

We will begin by assessing how the Catholic Church engages with civil rights issues, focusing especially on the Italian context (section "The Catholic Church and civil rights"), before then presenting the conceptual model and the research questions (section "Conceptual model and research questions"). This will be followed by a presentation of the method used (section "Research methods"), the empirical findings (section "Empirical results"); and finally a discussion on the salient findings (section "Discussion on salient findings").

The Catholic Church and Civil Rights

In order to investigate what role religion has played in developing a civil rights culture in Italy, we will give an historical overview of the interaction between the Catholic Church and civil rights, with a focus on Italy (section "Historical overview"). Secondly, we will provide a sociological assessment of the current situation (section "Sociological assessment"), and thirdly, describe the theological foundation of the church's involvement in civil rights in contemporary society (section "Theological justification").

Historical Overview

2015 marked the eighth centenary of the *Magna Carta*, which was issued on 15 June 1215 by King John of England. The charter marks a seminal moment in the human rights tradition that culminated in the UN Universal Declaration of Human Rights in 1948. Civil rights belong to the first generation of human rights, namely those rights that prevent the state from interfering with personal freedoms, such as freedom of speech, freedom of assembly, freedom of the press, freedom of religion, etc. These "modern liberties" evolved in the 17th and 18th centuries and marked the shift from absolute monarchies to democratic states, where people are no longer subjects of a sovereign monarch but equal citizens with rights (Alexy 1985, 194ff; Van der Ven et al. 2004, 98–99). In Europe, the first solemn proclamation of these rights was the French *Déclaration des droits de l'homme et du citoyen* in 1789. These civil rights were internationally affirmed in the 1948 Universal Declaration of Human Rights and codified in the International Covenant on Civil and Political Rights in 1966. They are also enshrined in the fundamental principles of the 1948 Constitution of the Italian Republic.

How did the Catholic Church respond to the affirmation and codification of civil rights and freedoms? Obviously, this question cannot be answered all that easily. Firstly because we need to clarify what is meant here by 'the Catholic Church', and secondly because the Catholic Church's teachings on human rights has evolved and shifted over the last two centuries. Those who contributed to the evolution of the concept of civil rights, since its very beginning, included Catholic thinkers, both clergy and laity. For example, some of the members of French National Assembly who voted for the French Declaration of the Rights of Man, or Italian theologians of the same period, like Spedalieri and Tamburini, who tried to reconcile the principles expressed in modern liberties and the Gospel-based principles taught by the church (Menozzi 2012, 13–43). Nevertheless, for the purpose of our study, the position of the Catholic Church refers to official documents issued by the Catholic hierarchy on human rights issues, namely by popes, ecumenical councils and Vatican congregations. Essentially these are universal doctrines that shape the moral teachings and life of the church at its grassroots.

The Catholic Church responded to the civil rights enshrined in the 1789 Declaration with concern and opposition. In 1791, Pope Pius VI (1791), in the encyclical *Quod aliquantum*, stated that equality and freedom of all men was to be rejected on rational and biblical grounds. Pius VI (1791) argued that religious freedom was a ploy to overthrow the Catholic religion. During the French Revolution, the Catholic Church was divested of existing privileges and properties, which prevented constructive dialogue between the Catholic hierarchy and advocates of modern liberties. Furthermore, the Catholic Church was concerned that the freedoms undermined the transcendental foundations of social order, which was then subject to the will and the approval of the people, as equal and free citizens. In 1814, in a letter to the Bishop of Troyes, Pius VII expressed his concerns regarding the draft constitution which guaranteed freedom for all religions in France and the freedom of the press. Gregory XVI (1832) expressed much stronger condemnation of the modern freedoms in 1832 in the encyclical letter *Mirari Vos*, which considered freedom of conscience, freedom of thought and freedom of the press as serious errors intended to destroy both religion and society. Nevertheless, even within the upper echelons of the Catholic hierarchy, different groupings tried to influence the leadership either to take a firm stand against civil rights or alternatively to encourage a more diplomatic attitude toward the new liberal states that were emerging in those years. One such state was the Kingdom of Italy, which was formed in 1861. In this case Pius IX was directly involved, as head of the Papal States and a military enemy of the new Kingdom of Italy. Unsurprisingly, the church wing of opponents of modern liberties was further strengthened by the historical and political circumstances. The day after the proclamation of the Kingdom of Italy, in a speech to the secret consistory on 18 March 1861, Pius IX declared that Catholicism was ultimately incompatible with the modern state, not only because of the attacks on church properties and privileges, but also because of the rights it proclaimed: freedom of religion, of the press, of expression and the legal equality of all citizens. When the army of the Kingdom of Italy attacked the Papal States, the conspiracy theory about how modernity and liberties undermined religion, in order to destroy it, gained momentum in the official position of the Catholic Church (Menozzi 2012, 43–55). In 1864, at a higher doctrinal level, the encyclical letter *Quanta Cura* of Pius IX (1864a) and the related Vatican document *Syllabus Errorum* (1864b) again condemned modern liberties. Catholic liberal circles, especially in France, tried to interpret these statements as merely theoretical principles that left scope for diplomatic compromise, but the conservative Roman theologians had a far greater influence on all kinds of church statements at the end of the nineteenth century (*ibid*, 68).

According to the historian Menozzi, Pope Leo XIII (1888) maintued the negative attitudes to the human rights derived from the liberal tradition. Nevertheless, in his encyclical letter *Libertas* in 1888, he stated that he was willing to consider "tolerating" certain rights and temporarily accepting them with a view to restoring the social order according to divine law. This may have been a small step forward, but it opened the way for Catholics to participate actively in the politics in the liberal states. It should be noted that when the Italian troops conquered Rome in 1870, the Papal States were lost, while as early as 1868 Pius IX had prohibited Italian Catholics from participating in the political life of the fledgling Kingdom of Italy. Leo XIII taught that natural law, established by God, was the supreme law and the foundation of all human laws, rights and duties. In this way, he effectively authorised church members to play a role in modern states and contribute to a historical understanding of natural law, a law that can be understood by human reasoning. At the same time, however, by identifying natural law with divine law, Leo XIII could argue that the church was the ultimate interpreter of natural law (Kaufmann 1973, 126–164). It should also be pointed out that the development of social doctrine following Pope Leo XIII's (1891) encyclical *Rerum Novarum* highlights the contribution of the Catholic Church in this regard (Quinn 2003; Pontifical Council for Justice and Peace 2004).

In the twentieth century, the Catholic Church's attitude to civil rights remained closely entwined with the political situation in Italy. Under the Fascist regime in 1929, a Concordat was signed between the Holy See and the Kingdom of Italy, which put an end to the "war" between the Holy See and the Italian State. Nevertheless, it widened the gap between the church's statements and the values of liberal democracies, as when the Pope failed to openly defend the Jews against the racial laws in 1938 (Perin 2013). As a matter of fact, Pius XI (1931) spoke up against the Fascist regime with the letter *Non abbiamo bisogno* in defence of the people's right not to be controlled by the state, for example, in education.

Nonetheless, this did not indicate that the church supported the liberal tradition of human rights but rather, according to Menozzi, constituted a defence of the church's right to determine the ideal social order based on natural and divine law.

Pope Pius XII did not commend the 1948 Universal Declaration of Human Rights in any way. He was disappointed by the fact that the Declaration lacked any reference to God, an omission repeated by Catholic MPs, who failed to include any mention of God in the Italian Constitution promulgated the same year. These decisions opposed the traditional Catholic understanding that all human rights and duties should be founded on the divine law as expressed in nature. As the Italian Jesuit Messineo pointed out at the time, the Universal Declaration was therefore doomed to be frail and ineffective in defending human rights against the attacks of both liberal and totalitarian regimes (Menozzi 2012, 168). In this period, other Catholic thinkers and leaders supported the 1948 Declaration, which they deemed to be compatible with Catholic doctrine, but they were unable to influence the official position adopted by the Catholic hierarchy. In a speech to Italian lawyers in 1953, Pius XII reaffirmed that all positive rights and laws did not depend ultimately on the will of nation states but on nature and as such the Creator God (*ibid*, 188).

The Catholic hierarchy's attitude to human rights shifted with the encyclical *Pacem in Terris* of John XXIII in 1963. John XXIII listed the institution of the United Nations as one of the "signs of the times", or one of the most relevant events in that period, and stressed that the 1948 Universal Declaration was a fundamental step toward a just social order and an important tool for preserving human dignity in contemporary society. The document contained references to the traditional doctrine of human rights being founded in nature and ultimately in God, but also a certain ambivalence about specific rights (Bloch 2008). Nevertheless, it constituted a real change: for the first time the rights listed in the Universal Declaration and those officially presented by the Catholic Church pointed in the same direction, namely, to enforcing and defending the dignity of the human person. Furthermore, the use of the expression "signs of the times" gave the UN's advocacy of human rights a theological relevance. "Signs of the times" referred to relevant events in contemporary society with negative or positive features that needed to be interpreted by the church. Taking its inspiration from the Gospel, the church is to be critical of negative social developments and support positive forces and changes. This expressed the church's renewed commitment to the Gospel. It indicated a major positive shift in the church's position on the 1948 Universal Declaration: human rights are no longer seen as a temporary compromise with contemporary society, perhaps to defend the rights of the church; but are promoted for the common good and human dignity, in response to God's commission to the church.

The Second Vatican Council (1965a, b) pastoral constitution *Gaudium et Spes*, promulgated in 1965 by Paul VI, reaffirms a positive assessment of human rights, again motivated "by virtue of the Gospel", but within certain limits. Human rights are not be be defined by the autonomous will of the people, but must be grounded in human dignity, which can never be preserved if separated from divine law (*GS* 41). Another Council document indicating a new attitude to human rights was the 1965 declaration *Dignitatis Humanae*, which recognised religious freedom, or the right of individuals and communities to be free from coercion in religious matters and the inviolability of human conscience (*DH* 1). Although the declaration is not clear on certain matters, if we compare the document with the definition of the freedom of conscience in *Mirari Vos* – "absurd and erroneous proposition" – we cannot deny that there had been a radical paradigm shift in the Catholic Church on the subject of religious freedom. In the 1960s, the Catholic Church seems to have completed the shift from being a traditional ally of authoritarian regimes to a critical voice on the world stage in the face of power structures from both the extreme right and extreme left (Langan 1986).

After the Second Vatican Council, an increasing focus on natural law as the foundation of the human rights discourse appears, together with a recurring link between human dignity and the transcendental basis of this dignity (John Paul II 1979, 1995). John Paul II in *Evangelium Vitae* in 1995 points out that the democratic systems can produce just laws only when they do not oppose natural law (*EV* 70). A similar argument can be found in Benedict XVI's (2008) speech to the UN General Assembly in 2008, in which he stated that natural law was the only safe and lasting foundation for human rights. Following this line of reasoning, in 2009 the International Theological Commission issued a document maintaining that to acknowledge human rights "means to acknowledge the objective order of human relations based on the natural law" (International Theological Commission 2009, 92).

Some observers consider that the emphasis on the link between human rights and natural law shows the church to be out of touch with contemporary philosophical discourse and with mainstream human rights culture (Van der Ven et al. 2004, 243–254; Menozzi 2012, 265–266), while others hold that traditional theory, if suitably updated, can still promote universal respect for human rights (Cahill et al. 2010).

The focus on natural law may fade away in Catholic teaching under Pope Francis (2014). One indication of a possible new direction can be found in his speech on 25 November 2014 to the Council of Europe, where he did not mention natural law at all. Although Francis criticises an individualistic understanding of human rights and argues that they should be rooted in the "truth" of human beings, he does not claim that this universal truth stems from nature, but rather he relates truth to concepts such as conscience and freedom. Furthermore, Pope Francis is a firm supporter of collective rights, such as the rights of immigrants and environmental rights, which could indicate a new shift in Catholic teaching on human rights.

Sociological Assessment

What role does the Catholic Church today play in public discussions of civil rights? More specifically, what is its role in Italy, where the church's relationship with the civil rights culture has been marred for so long by divergences and differences?

In order to answer these questions, it is useful to refer to the debate surrounding the role of religion in the public sphere today. According to Habermas (2009, 27), secularisation theorists were right to suggest that religion is losing social functions.

In tandem with the differentiation of social systems, secularisation theory correctly predicted a correlation between the specialisation of social systems and the privatisation of religious practice. Nevertheless, secularisation does not mean *per se* that religion will lose relevance and influence in public political and cultural debate nor in the moral choices of believers. In other words, the secularisation equation linking modernisation and progressive decline in the public and private influence of religion might just have been wrong. Modern contemporary society can coexist with flourishing religious communities. Habermas points out that in post-secular society, democracy is safeguarded not by privatising religion entirely, but by "the public use of reason" both on the part of religious citizens and on that of nonreligious citizens (Habermas 2011, 24). Accordingly, the burden of translating religious language into a generally accessible language should fall equally on both sides, namely the secular and the religious. Both groups of citizens should actively reflect on the content of their statements and engage in a process of mutual learning. Here we should distinguish between informal communication in public and the formal deliberations of public bodies, such as Parliament, the courts and administrative bodies. Religious citizens should not be required to eliminate all religious arguments from their opinions on society when communicating informally – this would create an asymmetry in the burden for religious and secular citizens. However in formal discussions, all religious citizens should avoid using religious language and arguments. Habermas affirms that religions in a post-secular society can exercise a bottom-up influence through informal communication. Through these channels of communication, he argues, "religions can become a transformative force in the centre of a democratic civil society" (*ibid*, 25).

The question is whether the Catholic Church can take on this role in Italy. According to two Italian sociologists, Marco Marzano and Nadia Urbinati, Habermas's theory of the public role of religion in a post-secular society is not applicable in an almost single religion state like Italy. The Catholic hierarchy in Italy is said to have far too much influence on politicians and public bodies, while its influence on public opinion is weakening. This political influence is rooted in the privileged status that the Catholic Church enjoys in Italy. Italian law defines three different levels of interaction between religions and the state. On the first level, there is the Catholic Church, which enjoys a preferential legal status, due to its position as the dominant national religion and its particular significance in Italian history. This relationship is regulated by the Concordat between Italy and Holy See as amended in 1984. One example of this privileged status is that only Catholic religion can be taught in state schools by teachers employed by the state. The second level comprises those churches and religious communities who have signed an agreement (*Intesa*) with the state; currently these agreements have been established with many historical Protestant, Evangelical and Orthodox churches, with Jews, Mormons, Buddhists and Hindus. All these communities can access funds via the tax system. On the third level are religious communities that have not yet signed an agreement with the state, which are regulated by common law on associations (Ferrari 1996, 185).

According to Marzano and Urbinati, the privileged status of the Catholic Church and the effective Catholic monopoly on religion is a threat to democracy and any real separation between church and state in Italy. They refer to a "tyranny of the religious majority" at the expense of religious minorities and at risk of civil law not being independent of religious opinions. Habermas's hypothetical rational public debate, independent of religious language within public decision-making bodies could be useful in other European societies but is not applicable in Italy because of the Catholic monopoly. Even John Rawls' (1999) political liberalism, which also requires religion-free arguments at the informal level, cannot ensure that public decisions are independent of religious intervention, because there is no religious pluralism in Italy, which is taken as a given in Rawls' (1999) call for a "moral duty of civility". The two Italian sociologists argue that the only way to achieve a real separation of religion and state in Italy is to apply strict traditional liberalism as advocated by James Madison in the eighteenth century – only social and religious pluralism combined with a state that does not embrace any single secular or religious world view can ensure a true democracy. Having accepted Madison's idea that religious convictions are *per se* a source of intolerance and division because they inevitably tend to create monopolies, Urbinati states that public opinion in a society with a religious monopoly is structurally oblivious to equality and civil rights (Marzano & Urbinati 2013, 100–113).

To sum up: can the Catholic Church today in Italy be a social champion of civil rights? Sociologically, the question generates two conflicting answers. If we follow Habermas's reasoning, the answer is "yes", because religion can be a force promoting human rights through its members and their participation in public debate and their public use of reason, without giving up their religious beliefs. For Marzano and Urbinati, meanwhile, the answer is "no", because public opinion is inevitably influenced by the dominant religious tradition in a (quasi-)monopoly in such a way as to unwittingly devalue civil rights, specifically the rights of anyone who is not part of that dominant majority.

Theological Justification

We have shown how historically the Catholic Church moved from fierce opposition to the first generation of human rights – which was also associated with the Holy See losing political power to the Italian state – to greater support for the human rights culture in the 1960s. Nevertheless, Catholic Church and international declarations make a key distinction about the principles underpinning universal rights. The Catholic Church claims that rights are grounded in natural law and ultimately divine law, while international human rights declarations – such as the Universal Declaration of Human Rights – avoid the issue of whether there is a universal principle underlying human rights and focus on pragmatic agreements between different cultures, religions and world views.[1] This fundamental difference is nowadays visible not only in terms of the ultimate root of human rights – transcendent for the Catholic Church and immanent for international covenants and declarations – but also in the content. For example, there is a clear difference on so-called "new rights", such as reproductive and LGBT rights (Zaccaria 2015). We have highlighted two conflicting sociological interpretations of the Catholic Church's potential role in Italy today: a potentially transformational force in the public sphere advocating a culture of human rights or a religious monopoly that is a burden on democratic and liberal society.

If the about-face in the 1960s is taken as an irrevocable paradigm shift within the Catholic Church, a move to engage in dialogue on modernity and human rights culture, and if the Catholic Church is seen as a potentially powerful social champion of human rights based on believers applying arguments in public, it is useful to stress some elements in the Judeo-Christian tradition that could justify the church engaging in promoting a human rights culture in contemporary society.

Rather than adopting the position of those who affirm that human rights developed from the Enlightenment independently and in opposition to the Christian tradition or those who believe that all formalised modern human rights were already embedded in this tradition, it is more plausible to maintain that modern philosophy relied on a heritage of religious content and symbols that were used and translated into secular and rational discourse in order to legitimate human rights (Habermas 2009, 38). Let us look at two of these theological concepts: human beings being created in "the image of God" and the eschatological perspective of 'the *basileia* [kingdom] of God' in the life of Jesus. The first concept ties in with the principle of all humans being equal, which is at the very core of human rights; the second legitimates active engagement in order to foster equality in modern society with a view to eschatological fulfilment. Both theological concepts provide a common language for religious and secular voices and can be used in common endeavours to promote a human rights culture.

The First Testament refers to humans being created in the image of God three times (Genesis 1:26–27; 5:1–3; 9:5–6) and Psalm 8:5 also makes a clear reference to this notion. The idea of the "image of God" came into the biblical narratives from Egyptian writings. In the latter, the symbol of the image of God in relation to human beings mainly referred to the king. The king was considered the embodiment of God, not only through his priestly functions in rituals but also in his political duties of justice. As God's representative on earth, the king was expected to foster the same harmony on earth as reigns in heaven. In the biblical creation narratives, this idea is extended to all human beings: all human beings are God's representatives on earth and should uphold justice, a justice that is defined from the perspective of the poor, orphans, widows and aliens. This concern for justice with a "preferential option for the poor" is at the core of the First Testament writings, especially in the

[1] The famous debate between Habermas & Ratzinger (2006) on the pre-political foundations of the democratic constitution takes surprisingly similar opposing stances, and also includes explicit references to the different roots of human rights.

Deuteronomy tradition, and gives perhaps the best interpretation of what the "image of God" is intended to mean in this context and in the theology of the original texts (Van der Ven et al. 2004, 280–303). In this call for an emancipatory justice for all, a duty binding all human beings created in the image of God, we can find a theological legitimation for the church's concern for equality (Metz 2006). Commitment to justice from this biblical perspective means caring for those who suffer inequality: the poor, orphans and widows. The creation narratives in Genesis justify an "egalitarian universalism" within the Christian tradition (Böckenförde 2002, 212–370). Hence the metaphor of being made in the image of God and the human dignity this engenders applies here to all human beings, despite all attempts made to restrict human dignity to specific groups of people (Van der Ven et al. 2004, 299). Rediscovering the theological implications of all human beings being created in the image of God opens the door for the church to develop a public discourse based on a principle shared with a human rights culture rooted in modernity, namely, the principle of equality. In this vein, for instance, *Dialogue and Proclamation* of the Pontifical Council for Interreligious dialogue (1991, no. 28), affirms: "The whole of humankind forms one family, due to the common origin of all men and women, created by God in His own image". The idea that dignity and equality of human beings is grounded in their being created in the image of God is also present in the *Compendium of the Social Doctrine of the Church* and this idea is clearly highlighted at the beginning of the chapter on human rights (Pontifical Council for Justice and Peace 2004, no. 105–114).

The concept of the *basileia* (kingdom) of God in the Christian tradition offers an eschatological perspective on the principle of equality. This perspective means that the principle of equality has not been fully realised in the past and contains unfulfilled possibilities for today and promises for the future (Van der Ven 1998, 65–76). In Jesus' praxis, words and deeds, the *basiliea* symbol expresses God's plan and care for his people. Proclaiming the kingdom of God is a way of calling his disciples to engage and work with him to achieve that plan. As Van der Ven points out, the image is not simple, but has multiple layers of meaning. Jesus' words and deeds referring to the *basiliea* bring together two principles from the Jewish tradition that use the term: creation and salvation history. The creation tradition primarily expresses God's care for all humankind, especially those who suffer inequality, injustice, poverty and sickness. The creation symbolism in Jesus' proclamation of the *basiliea* of God means that all people, righteous and sinners alike, are called to fullness and wholeness (Schüssler Fiorenza 1983). From the salvation history tradition, Jesus emphasised that divine salvation consists of God's solidarity and mercy for all humans. According to his words and deeds, the kingdom of God is near and brings salvation for all without exception (Schillebeeckx 1979). Amid the rich, multiple meanings of the metaphors, parables and sayings of Jesus referring to the *basiliea*, one core idea emerges: God loves all humans, with a preferential love for those who experience less of the fullness of life. This is not just a statement: Jesus showed that love through his deeds and, being a paradigm of this love, he calls his disciples to follow in his footsteps and to commit themselves to making the *basiliea* a reality throughout history. From an eschatological point of view, this realisation is always temporary and is an ongoing task, working towards the future.

Both concepts – created in the image of God and Jesus' proclamation of the kingdom of God – offer a theological justification for the church engaging in discussions on human rights. When the church affirms that humans are created in the image of God, it not only expresses God's concern for justice and equality, but also reaffirms the ongoing commitment to realising the *basiliea* of God in history, with an emphasis on the marginalised, the unprotected, victims of injustice and inequality in society.

The Catholic Church has in its own theological heritage an imagery that offers inspiration and motivation for a civil rights culture. These symbols were drawn on during the process of defining and affirming human rights in the modern world. Today they can be used and reinterpreted by the church in order to establish a rational public debate in favour of civil rights, where both religious and secular voices can be heard. Nevertheless, history, especially in Italy, is laden with centuries-old antagonism between modern liberties and the church. Even now, especially in Italy, some thinkers argue that a civil rights culture is not compatible with the Catholic Church. We have sought to present the historical significance of the Second Vatican Council's shift in favour of a human rights culture and to highlight that the church can be an advocate for human rights in today's post-secular society. The church's position is inspired and determined by its own theological heritage. As we have shown in the case of the *basiliea* imagery, this heritage can function as a "qualitative more" (Van der Ven 1998, 74) which motivates and stimulates the church to social engagement and action. This offers us a theoretical framework for our empirical exploration.

Conceptual Model and Research Questions

Civil rights are recognised and protected under the Italian Constitution. The fundamental principles enshrined in the Constitution include the statement that "the Republic recognises and guarantees the inviolable rights of the person" (Article 2), and that "all citizens have equal social dignity and are equal before the law, without distinction of sex, race, language, religion, political opinion, personal and social conditions" (Article 3). Freedom of religion is included in these constitutional principles – freedom for the Catholic Church (Article 7) and for all religions, as Article 8 states that "All religious denominations are equally free before the law". Civil liberties are more specifically defined in Part I, Title I of the Constitution: personal freedom, freedom of assembly, freedom of expression, religious freedom, etc.

Nonetheless, promoting a human rights culture is an ongoing process; the task does not end with the affirmation of these rights in declarations and constitutions. The rights need to be supported and defended by public opinion, by present and future generations of citizens. Many factors can contribute to shaping people's ideas about human rights: personal background, psychological traits, political orientation, but also religious factors.

As we have seen in the previous sections, because the unique history of the Catholic Church in Italy, the role of religion in civil rights can be ambiguous. Some scholars argue that religion could be a social force contrary to certain civil rights, such as those referring to homosexuals or to religious minorities. The former could be perceived being at odds with the Catholic Church's teaching on sexuality and the latter as threatening the privileged status of the Catholic Church. Alternatively, the Catholic Church could defend civil rights within society: building on its own religious and theological heritage, it can speak out in support of the dignity and freedom of all human beings. In short, religion can take contradictory positions on civil rights and provide varying degrees of support or opposition.

For these reasons, in our research we have included civil rights in the list of dependent variables, which are ultimately enshrined in the Italian Constitution: protection against gender and sexual discrimination (Article 3), protection against inhuman treatment and the right to privacy (Articles 13–14), freedom of assembly (Article 18), freedom of religion (Articles 19–20), and freedom of speech (Article 21).

We are focussing here on the role of religion and therefore religious attitudes are considered independent variables. We can distinguish between personal and contextual religious attitudes. Personal religious attitudes may have a cognitive dimension (e.g. beliefs about God), an experiential dimension (e.g. religious experiences) and an operative dimension (e.g. religious practices). Contextual religious attitudes refer to the relation between different religions and between religion and society. Contextual attitudes can encompass ideas about how one's own religion relates to other religions, express confidence in one's own religion and the religion of others, or may describe the current public function of religion, the influence of contemporary society on religion, and the relation between religious communities and the state. Hence the list of independent variables in our research model comprises personal religious attitudes (beliefs about God, critical approach to belief, religious experiences and religious practices) and contextual religious attitudes (religious plurality, trust in religions, function of religion, religion in contemporary society, relation between religion and the state).

Background variables in our conceptual model are characteristics of the respondents which might influence their attitudes to human rights. First, we take into account personal characteristics: age and gender. The religious background of the respondents, such as belonging or not to the Catholic Church, can be linked to the degree of support for civil rights, therefore we deem religious identity (affiliation and practice) and religious socialisation (family/peer influence and interreligious contacts) to be background variables. Finally, we have considered the respondents' psychological and socio-political traits to be background variables in attitudes to social issues. These traits can predict greater or lesser support for civil rights. The list of psychological traits includes the personality tendencies in relation to authoritarianism, social dominance orientation and empathy, we have also factored in views on multiculturalism and political orientation as socio-political traits.

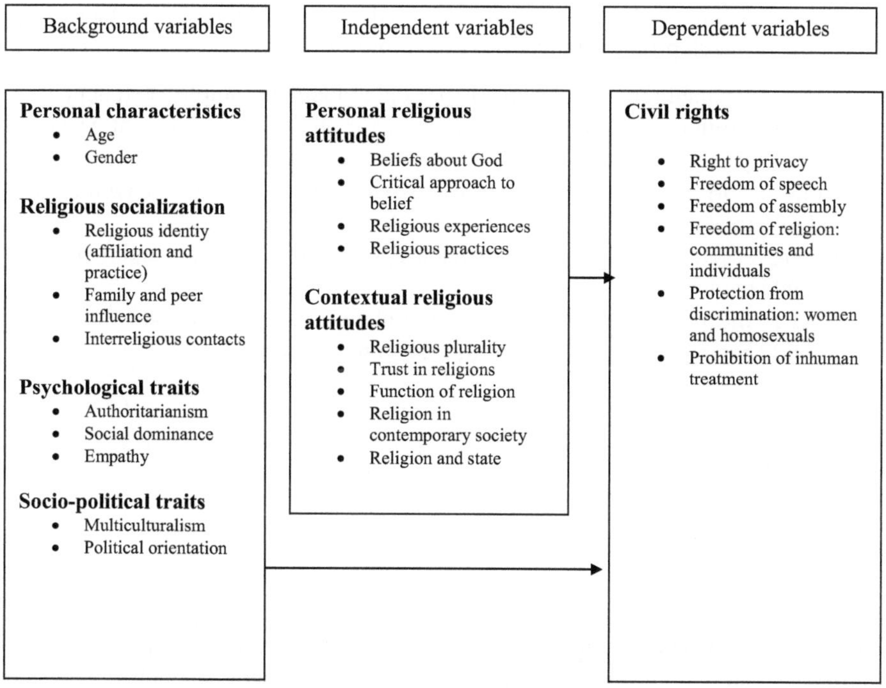

Fig. 4.1 Conceptual model

As shown in Fig. 4.1, the conceptual model underlying our exploration of the relation between religion and civil rights among Italian students comprises three groups of variables: attitudes to civil rights (dependent variables); personal and contextual religious attitudes (independent variables); and personal characteristics, religious socialisation, psychological traits and socio-political traits (background variables).

In this chapter, we seek to investigate the extent to which Italian secondary school students support or reject civil rights. We begin by exploring the relationship between civil rights attitudes and religious attitudes, both personal and contextual, and subsequently consider background characteristics – personal, religious, psychological and socio-political traits. The conceptualisation and operationalisation of these variables is part of the international research project Religion and Human Rights 2012–2019 coordinated by Hans-Georg Ziebertz from the University of Würzburg. We will therefore confine ourselves to a brief presentation of the operationalisation of the concepts from Fig. 4.1 and present the measuring instruments in the next section.

Our general aim is to understand the relationship between religion and civil rights among Italian young people. Does religion make a difference in what young people think about civil rights? We have classified religion and civil rights concepts in terms of different religious attitudes and civil rights attitudes and we can encapsulate the research problem in five *research questions*.

1. What understanding of civil rights is present among the sample of students?
2. Are there significant differences in support for civil rights in student groups as defined by their religious affiliation and practice?
3. Is there a correlation between the students' views on civil rights and their contextual religious attitudes?
4. Is there a correlation between the students' views on civil rights and their background characteristics?
5. What is the predictive strength of the students' religious attitudes and background characteristics with regard to views on civil rights?

Research Methods

Data Collection and Sample

In order to clarify the relationship between religion and civil rights among young Italians, we collected our data from students at the end of secondary education. Data were collected with the help of teachers who distributed our questionnaires in state high school classes. We found teachers willing to collaborate in three geographical Italian areas with a varied levels of urbanisation: Pordenone (a city in northern Italy with about 50,000 inhabitants), Rome (the capital in Central Italy; population approximately 2,800,000), and in Monopoli and Conversano (two cities in southern Italy with approximately 50,000 and 30,000 inhabitants respectively). A total of 1162 questionnaires were completed. As our focus was on religion, we needed religious groups within the sample of a sufficient size for the purpose of comparison. Given the monoreligious landscape in Italy, we decided to exclude from the sample all students belonging to religions other than the Catholic Church. Respondents belonging to other churches and religions made up about 5% of the sample in total. Our final sample therefore comprised 1087 students.

The sample of secondary school students comprises 54.7% women and 45.3% men. The age breakdown of students was as follows: 15 to 16 (4.6%), 17 (39.5%), 18 (41.4%), 19 (12.1%), 20 to and 21 (2.4%). In terms of geographical distribution, 372 are from northern Italy (Pordenone), 348 from central Italy (Rome) and 366 from the South of Italy (Monopoli and Conversano). The students' were classified by religious profile into four groups according to their self-professed church affiliation and practice: Catholic churchgoers (30.8%), Catholic non-churchgoers[2] (39.3%), generally religious (9.2%) and non-religious (20.7%).

[2] "Churchgoers" are defined as those who claim to go to church at least once a month; "non-churchgoers" claim to attend church a few times a year, hardly ever or never.

Measuring Instrument

The questionnaire we used in our research is a tool designed by the group of international scholars involved in the Religion and Human Rights 2012–2019 research project. The questions used to determine the respondents' backgrounds, religious attitudes and view on civil rights were selected from the broader instrument.

Background variables comprise four groups of characteristics that could play a role in shaping students' attitudes to civil rights: personal characteristics, religious socialisation, psychological traits and socio-political traits. *Personal characteristics* include age and gender. *Religious socialisation* includes the religion to which respondents say they belong and their self-professed religious practice (religious identity), the faith of their parents and best friends, their parents' expectation that they will adopt their faith (family and peer influence), and time spent with people of other religions (interreligious contacts). *Psychological traits* refer to the respondents' tendencies in terms of authoritarianism, social dominance orientation and empathy. *Socio-political traits* include support for multiculturalism and political orientation (left wing or right-wing).

Independent variables refer to the students' religious attitudes. Religious attitudes are assumed to include beliefs about religious issues and religious activities. We divided religious attitudes into two groups: personal and contextual religious attitudes. *Personal religious attitudes* comprise beliefs about God, beliefs in a personal iconic God (theism, panentheism), beliefs in a non-personal iconic God (deism, pantheism), beliefs in a aniconic God (meta-theism). Personal religious attitudes also encompass a critical approach to religious beliefs and behavioural issues, such as religious experiences (faith experiences and spirituality experiences) and religious practices (praying and attending religious services). *Contextual religious attitudes* include beliefs about religion in relation to other religions and society. For the purpose of our research, we have included beliefs about religious plurality (exclusivism and pluralism), trust in religion (trust in his/her own religion and in other religions), the function of religion (public function, cultural conformity and spiritual service), religion in contemporary society (relevance/irrelevance), and the relationship between religion and the state (separation and consultation).

Attitudes to human rights, specifically opinions about civil rights, constitute *dependent variables* in our model. Attitudes to each civil right were operationalised using two items from Table 4.1. Our respondents expressed their attitudes to the right to privacy (items 1 and 8), freedom of speech (items 2 and 14), freedom of assembly (items 6 and 9), freedom of religion: for communities (items 7 and 3) and for individuals (items 11 and 13), preventing discrimination: against women (items 15 and 10) and homosexuals (items 16 and 4), and preventing inhuman treatment (items 12 and 5).

Table 4.1 Number of respondents (N), means and standard deviations of *items on civil rights* in descending order of (average) agreement

	N	Mean	s.d.
12. Women should have the right to be protected from sexual harassment in the workplace.	1084	4.60	0.70
10. The state should protect women's right to adequate job opportunities.	1079	4.46	0.76
15. Women should have the right to be equally paid for equal work.	1085	4.38	0.86
2. People should be free to express any opinion whatsoever.	1086	4.22	0.87
5. Inhuman treatment is forbidden in any circumstances.	1085	4.18	1.13
14. People should be free to discuss all moral ideas, no matter what.	1085	4.17	0.83
4. Homosexuals should have the right to hold any public office.	1086	4.03	1.24
8. The state should not interfere in any sexual activities freely chosen by adults.	1086	3.87	1.15
16. The state should prosecute behaviour which discriminates against homosexuals.	1086	3.69	1.23
9. Radical political groups for law and order should have the right to assembly.	1080	3.54	0.86
7. The state should not interfere with missionary activities in both the majority and minority religions.	1081	3.42	0.97
6. People without criminal intent should have the right to associate, however extreme they may be.	1075	3.38	1.03
13. The state should not prevent female teachers from wearing a head scarf for religious reasons.	1082	3.25	1.33
3. The state should stay out of the public manifestations by the majority and minority religions.	1084	3.18	1.01
1. Our laws should protect people's right to live by any moral values they choose.	1082	3.11	1.09
11. Students should be offered time, space and a room in schools to do their prayers	1079	2.81	1.15

Interpretation of means: 1.00–1.79: total disagreement; 1.80–2.59: disagreement; 2.60–2.99: negative ambivalence; 3.00–3.39: positive ambivalence; 3.40–4.19: agreement; 4.20–5.00: full agreement

Statistical Methods

The data collected from the questionnaires were inserted into SPSS 20 program and analysed. Means and standard deviations were calculated for each statement on human rights (Table 4.1), in order to explore the general thrust of attitudes to civil rights among the students, with a view to answering our first question. Factor analyses (principal axis factoring) were used for the purpose of data reduction and scaling.[3] We used variance analyses (ANOVA) and Scheffé's tests to answer the second research question. These calculations indicated variations in the mean scores

[3] For the authoritarianism measurement only, principal component analysis was applied.

for different groups of students on each scale of support for the individual civil rights. The four religious groups taken into account here were Catholic churchgoers, Catholic non-churchgoers, generally religious and non-religious students. The relationships between religious attitudes and attitudes to civil rights (question 3) and background characteristics and civil rights attitudes (question 4) were investigated by calculating Pearson's r correlation coefficients.[4] Finally, the fifth question, which refers to the predictive strength of our respondents' religious attitudes and background characteristics in terms of their attitudes to civil rights, was answered by performing multiple regression analyses.

Empirical Results

Taking the five research questions in order, we will analyse the respondents' understanding of the civil rights by examining the data at item level and scale level. We will then examine the links between attitudes to civil rights, religious attitudes and background variables.

Research Question 1 What understanding of civil rights is present among the sample of students?

As the mean scores in Table 4.1 indicate, our respondents agreed or fully agreed with eleven items referring to civil rights. Three of the four items for which they expressed full support refer to women's rights. By contrast, three of the five items for which there was no clear position refer to religion.

Factor analysis (PAF, oblimin rotation) necessitated the removal of two items (1 & 3) due to low commonalities and three items (5, 7, 2) due to loading on more than one factor (at three different stages of analysis). For thematic reasons, item 14, which loaded on Factor 1 was removed. Of the remaining ten items shown in Table 4.2, our analysis highlighted four meaning factors that explain a total variance of 47%.

Three items (10, 12 and 15) that load on Factor 1 deal with the rights of women, and have therefore been named "women's rights". The reliability of this factor is high (α 0.81). Two items refering to homosexuality (4 & 16) and one item (8) linked to sexuality load on Factor 2. The reliability of this factor referred to as "gay and sexual rights" is fairly high (α 0.74).

Two items (6 & 9) representing freedom of assembly and two (11 & 13) representing freedom of religion load respectively on Factor 3 and Factor 4. The reliability of these two factors, "freedom of assembly" (α 0.46) and "freedom of religion" (α 0.42) is modest.

It is significant that two factors representing protection against discrimination (women and homosexuals) and two related to freedom of assembly and freedom of

[4] For the religious identity variable only, "eta" coefficients were calculated.

Table 4.2 Factor analysis (PAF, Oblimin rotation), communalities (h^2), percentage of explained variance, and reliability (Cronbach's alpha) of *civil rights attitudes*

	F1	F2	F3	F4	h^2
10. The state should protect women's right to adequate job opportunities.	**0.88**	−0.04	−0.02	0.00	0.72
12. Women should have the right to be protected from sexual harassment in the workplace.	**0.75**	−0.03	−0.00	0.01	0.54
15. Women should have the right to be equally paid for equal work.	**0.66**	0.13	0.03	0.02	0.57
4. Homosexuals should have the right to hold any public office.	0.01	**0.84**	−0.06	0.08	0.75
14. The state should prosecute behaviour which discriminates against homosexuals.	0.01	**0.68**	−0.05	0.11	0.51
8. The state should not interfere in any sexual activities freely chosen by adults.	0.07	**0.54**	0.12	−0.14	0.36
6. People without criminal intent should have the right to associate, however extreme they may be.	−0.09	0.00	**0.64**	0.03	0.39
9. Radical political groups for law and order should have the right to assembly.	0.09	−0.01	**0.48**	0.00	0.25
11. Students should be offered time, space and a room in schools to do their prayers.	0.01	−0.06	0.02	**0.52**	0.26
13. The state should not prevent female teachers from wearing a head scarf for religious reasons.	0.03	0.21	0.03	**0.49**	0.35
Cronbach's alpha	0.81	0.74	0.46	0.42	
Number of valid cases	1075	1084	1069	1075	

Eigenvalue = 1; Oblimin rotation with Kaiser Normalization; extraction: PAF
Explained variance = 47.0%;
F1 = Women's rights; F2 = Gay and sexual rights; F3 = Freedom of assembly; F4 = Freedom of religion
N = 1087

religion emerge as distinct factors and confirm our conceptual framework for civil rights to some extent.

Research Question 2 Are there significant differences in support for civil rights in student groups as defined by their religious affiliation and practice?

As shown in Table 4.3, there are no significant differences between groups (namely, Catholic churchgoers, Catholic non-churchgoers, generally religious, and non-religious) with reference to women's rights (strongly supported by all groups) and to freedom of assembly (supported by all groups). These rights seem to be fairly well established among the young respondents.

However, there are significant differences between the groups (F-value: 9.23; $p < .000$) in terms of *gay and sexual rights* (supported by all groups). As a general rule, religious (4.15) and non-religious students (4.06) agree more strongly with these rights than both Catholic churchgoers (3.71) and Catholic non-churchgoers

Table 4.3 Levels of agreement (mean and standard deviation) with *civil rights* for Catholic churchgoers, Catholic non-churchgoers, generally religious and non-religious students; and comparison of means between groups of respondents (Scheffé's tests)

	N	Mean	s.d.	Cath. non-churchgoers	Generally religious	Non-religious
Women's rights						
Cath. churchgoers	335	4.45	0.70			
Cath. non-churchgoers	427	4.48	0.66			
Generally religious	100	4.50	0.62			
Non-religious	225	4.52	0.64			
Gay and sexual rights						
Cath. churchgoers	335	3.71	0.92		**	**
Cath. non-churchgoers	427	3.81	1.01		*	*
Generally religious	100	4.15	0.86	*		
Non-religious	225	4.06	0.99	*		
Freedom of assembly						
Cath. churchgoers	335	3.43	0.72			
Cath. non-churchgoers	427	3.44	0.73			
Generally religious	99	3.43	0.78			
Non-religious	225	3.56	0.87			
Freedom of religion						
Cath. churchgoers	335	3.24	0.92		*	**
Cath. non-churchgoers	427	3.07	1.00			**
Generally religious	100	2.87	0.86	*		
Non-religious	224	2.73	1.02	**		

Interpretations of means: 1.00–1.79: total disagreement; 1.80–2.59: disagreement; 2.60–2.99: negative ambivalence; 3.00–3.39: positive ambivalence; 3.40–4.19: agreement; 4.20–5.00: full agreement

Inter-group differences are significant at p < 01 (**) or p < 05 level (*)

Scheffé's tests: *Gay & sexual rights* (F-value: 9.23; p < 000); *Freedom of Religion* (F-value: 13.84; p < 000)

(3.81). The fact that Catholic students (churchgoers and non-churchgoers) express less support may reflect the Catholic moral view of homosexuality as a defective tendency to be overcome.

There are also significant inter-group differences (F-value: 13.84; p < .000) on *freedom of religion*: the positive ambivalence of Catholic churchgoers (3.24) differs significantly from the negative ambivalence among non-religious students (2.73) and religious students (2.87); while the positive ambivalence of Catholic non-churchgoers (3.07) diverges only from the negative ambivalence expressed by non-religious respondents. The non-religious students seem to have some reservations about freedom of religion. This seems to reflect the growing opposition of secularism to public religious expression.

Research Question 3 Is there a correlation between the students' views on civil rights and their contextual religious attitudes?

In presenting the results of the correlation analysis we have only commented on moderate (.14 ≤ r < .30) and strong correlations (r ≥ .30).

As shown in Table 4.4, there is a moderate correlation between *women's rights* and one personal religious attitude, namely the critical approach to religious belief (r .20). This means that support for women's rights is more likely to be found among

Table 4.4 Correlations (Pearson's r) between *civil rights* and *personal and contextual religious attitudes*

	Women's rights	*Gay & sexual rights*	*Freedom of assembly*	*Freedom of religion*
Personal religious attitudes				
Beliefs about God				
Personal & pantheistic				0.26**
Deistic	0.13**			0.20**
Meta-theistic				
Relevance of God and religion				
Critical approach to relig. Belief	0.20**	0.21**		0.20**
Belief in the existence of God				0.26**
Belief in divine intervention				0.23**
Influence of religion in life	0.08**			0.23**
Religious experiences				
Faith	0.07*			0.20**
Spirituality	−0.09**			0.15**
Religious practices				
Prayer frequency				0.21**
Participation in rel. Services		−0.09**		0.23**
Contextual religious attitudes				
Religious plurality				
Exclusivism	−0.10**	−0.21**		0.12**
Pluralism		0.17**		0.17**
Trust in religion				
Trust in in-group				0.16**
Trust in out-group	0.06*	0.19**		0.31**
Function of religion				
Public function				0.19**
Cultural conformity	0.18**	0.23**	0.06*	
Spiritual service	0.21**	0.22**	0.15**	0.28**
Religion in contempor. Society				
Relevance of religion in society	0.07*			0.28**
Religion and state				
Separation	0.11**	0.13**	0.11**	−0.22**
Consultation	0.19**	0.12**	0.16**	

Correlations are significant at p < 01 level (**) or p < 05 level (*)

Interpretation of correlations: weak (r < 14); moderate (0.14 ≤ r < 30); strong (r ≥ 30)

those Italians who take a critical approach to religious belief. There are also moderate correlations with the following contextual religious attitudes: functions of religion (spiritual service: r .21; and cultural conformity: r .18) and consultation (r .19) between religion and state.

Gay and sexual rights are also more supported by those respondents with a critical approach to religious belief (r .21). There is a moderate correlation between gay and sexual rights and some functions of religion, namely cultural conformity (r .23) and spiritual service (r .22); religious pluralism (r .17); and trust in the religion of the out-group (r .19). But support for gay and sexual rights is negatively correlated with exclusivism (r – .21), which means that those who make exclusive truth claims are less likely to support these progressive civil rights concerning sexuality.

Freedom of assembly is more strongly supported by those who think that religion and state should cooperate in consultative structures (r .16) and among those who feel that religion fulfils a spiritual service function (r .15).

Freedom of religion has far stronger support from respondents who score relatively high for personal and contextual religious attitudes. Freedom of religion correlates moderately with all personal religious attitudes except meta-theism: personal-pantheistic God images (r .26); deism (r .20); belief in the existence of God (r .26); belief in divine intervention (r .23); influence of religion in daily life (r .23); a critical approach to religious belief (r .20); and faith (r .20) and spirituality (r. .15) as religious experiences. Support for freedom of religion is prevalent among students who score higher for religious activities such as attending religious services (r .23) and regular prayer (r .21). It seems logical for all personal religious attitudes to be associated with freedom of religion. Support for freedom of religion also correlates with most contextual religious attitudes. There is a strong correlation with trust in the religious out-group (r .31) and a moderate correlation with trust in the religious in-group (r .16). We also find moderate correlations with two functions of religion: spiritual service (r .28) and the public function of religion (r .19). Respondents who perceived religion as relevant to society (r .28) and were open to religious pluralism (r .17) were also more likely to support freedom of religion. By contrast, respondents who favoured a strict separation of religion and state (r – .22) expressed less support for freedom of religion.

Research Question 4 Is there a correlation between the students' views on civil rights and their background characteristics?

As shown in Table 4.5, correlation analysis reveals a range of strong, moderate and weak correlations between most civil rights and the background variables. However, freedom of assembly does not correlate significantly with any of the background variables. We have only presented the moderate ($.14 \leq r < .30$) and strong correlations ($r \geq .30$).

In the case of *women's rights*, we find relatively strong associations with all psychological traits: social dominance orientation (r – .37), empathy (r .35) and authoritarianism (r – .14). The correlation is negative for social dominance orientation and authoritarianism, meaning that women's rights enjoyed less support among respondents who scored higher on social dominance orientation and authoritarianism. For socio-political traits, we find that multiculturalism (r .34) and a left-wing political

Table 4.5 Correlations (Pearson's r) between *civil rights* and *background characteristics*

	Women's rights	*Gay & sexual rights*	*Freedom of assembly*	*Freedom of religion*
Personal characterstics				
Age		–0.08**		
Gender (male)	–0.31**	–0.31**		–0.26**
Religious socialization				
Religious identity (eta)		0.16**		0.19**
Father's belief and faith		–0.08*		0.08**
Mother's belief and faith				0.08**
Best friend's belief and faith	0.10**			0.11**
Father: important to adopt his faith		–0.14**		0.10**
Mother: import. to adopt her faith		–0.12**		0.10**
Interreligious contacts	0.07*	0.15**		0.18**
Psychological traits				
Authoritarianism	–0.14**	–0.25**		
Social dominance	–0.37**	–0.39**		–0.29**
Empathy	0.35**	0.32**		0.26**
Socio-political traits				
Multiculturalism	0.34**	0.53**		0.29**
Political orientation	–0.19**	–0.39**		–0.14**

Correlations are significant at $p < 0.01$ level (**) or $p < 0.05$ level (*)
Interpretation of correlations: weak ($r < 0.14$); moderate ($0.14 \leq r < 0.30$); strong ($r \geq 0.30$)

orientation (r – .19 for scores on a scale from left to right) correlate to greater support for women's rights. Last but not least, we found that women (gender: r – .31) were significantly more supportive of women's rights than men.

Gay and sexual rights also enjoy greater support among women than men (gender: r – .31) and have a moderate association with religious identity (eta .16). As we have indicated, there is less support for these rights among Italians who define themselves as Catholic (both churchgoers and non-churchgoers) than among generally religious or non-religious students. These progressive civil rights also reveal strong correlations with psychological traits like social dominance orientation (r – .39), empathy (r .32) and authoritarianism (r – .25). Once again these rights are negatively correlated with social dominance orientation and authoritarianism. Support for sexual rights is further related with a higher score on multiculturalism (r .53) and a left-wing political orientation (r – .39). In terms of religious socialisation aspects, we found that these emerging rights have a moderate correlation with interreligious contact (r .15) and negative correlation to the importance of adopting the father's faith (r – .14). Overall the social location of gay and sexual rights is very similar to the social location of women's rights.

Freedom of religion is also supported more by women than men (r – .26) and is linked to religious identity. So Catholics (churchgoers and non-churchgoers) express greater support for freedom of religion than generally religious or non-religious

Italians (eta .19). Higher levels of interreligious contact correlates to greater support for freedom of religion (r .18). In terms of psychological and socio-political traits, support for freedom of religion is more common among those with lower levels of social dominance (r – .29) and higher levels of multiculturalism (r .29) and empathy (r .26). People with a left-wing political orientation are also more likely to support freedom of religion (r – .14, the figure is negative because the scale runs from political left to right).

Overall, we find that support for all civil rights has a greater correlation to personal characteristics and psychological traits than religious socialisation.

Research Question 5 What is the predictive strength of the students' religious attitudes and background characteristics with regard to views on civil rights?

We used regression analyses to define the predictive strength of religious attitudes and background characteristics in terms of the individual civil rights. We only analysed variables with at least a moderate correlation with the relevant set of civil rights ($r \geq .14$).

As shown in Table 4.6, the regression analysis of *women's rights* explains about one-fourth of the variance (R^2 .27; Adj. R^2 .26). Agreement with the opinion that religions should be open to current trends in society (cultural conformity: β .11) indicates a propensity to support women's rights, as does the idea that politicians may consult religions on ethical issues (consultation: β .13). Women's rights are more likely to be supported by women than by men (gender: β – .17). Among the psychological traits, empathy (β .14) and a positive appreciation of multiculturalism (β .09) have increased the probability of support for women's rights. By contrast, social dominance orientation (β – .22) has a negative impact on support for women's rights.

Gay and sexual rights are explained for 41% of the variance (R^2 .42; Adj. R^2 .41). These rights are affected negatively by religious exclusivism (β – .10) and positively by religious pluralism (β .06). In terms of religious attitudes, conformity of religion to cultural trends (β .11) and spiritual function of religion (β .08) have a positive predictive strength for these rights. Among the personal characteristics, we find that women (gender: β – .15) support gay and sexual rights more than men, and that there is significantly less support for these rights among Catholic churchgoers compared to non-religious students (β .14), Catholic non-churchgoers (β .11) and generally religious students (β .10). Some psychological traits also affect the level of support for gay and sexual rights: social dominance orientation (β – .17) reduces agreement, while multiculturalism (β .26) and empathy (β .08) are conducive to support for these rights.

Freedom of assembly is significantly affected only by the contextual religious attitudes of spiritual service function of religion (β .12) and consultation between the state and religion (β .13). With only two predictive variables, our regression analysis for freedom of assembly is not very relevant (Adj. R^2 .04).

Freedom of religion is explained for one-fifth of the variance (R^2 .23; Adj. R^2 .20). There are no significant predictors among personal religious attitudes but some contextual religious attitudes are significant: religious pluralism (β .06), trust

Table 4.6 Regression analyses for *civil rights* with weights (β) for each variable and total explained variance (R^2 and Adjusted R^2)

	Women's rights	*Gay & sexual rights*	*Freedom of assembly*	*Freedom of religion*
Personal religious attitudes				
Personal & pantheistic beliefs				0.01
Deistic beliefs				0.00
Critical approach to relig. Belief	0.00	0.06		–0.03
Belief in the existence of God				–0.04
Belief in divine intervention				0.00
Influence of religion in life				0.09
Faith				0.00
Spirituality				0.05
Prayer frequency				0.00
Contextual religious attitudes				
Exclusivism		–0.10**		
Pluralism		0.06*		0.06*
Trust in religious ingroup				0.02
Trust in religious outgroup		0.05		0.17**
Public function				–0.02
Cultural conformity	0.11**	0.11**		
Spiritual service	0.05	0.08**	0.12**	0.09*
Relevance of religion in society				0.05
Separation (religion/state)				–0.16**
Consultation (religion/state)	0.13**		0.13**	
Personal characteristics				
Gender (male)	–0.17**	–0.15**		–0.09*
Religious socialization				
Religious identity				
Catholic churchgoers		Ref.		Ref.
Catholic non-churchgoers		0.11**		0.02
Generally religious		0.10**		–0.04
Non-religious		0.14**		0.00
Interreligious contacts		0.05		0.06*
Psychologic traits				
Authoritarianism	–0.04	0.00		
Social dominance	–0.22**	–0.17**		–0.09*
Empathy	0.14**	0.08**		0.01
Socio-political traits				
Multiculturalism	0.09*	0.26**		0.14**
Political orientation	0.02	–0.06		
R^2	0.27	0.42	0.04	0.23
Adj. R^2	0.26	0.41	0.04	0.20

Standardised regression coefficients (β) are significant at $p < 0.01$ (**) or $p < 0.05$ (*) level in religious out-groups (β .17) and spiritual service function of religion (β .09) have a positive predictive strength for freedom of religion, while a preference for a radical separation of church and state (β – .16) reduces support for freedom of religion. Once again, women appear to be stronger supporters of civil rights than men (gender: β – .09). When it comes to religious socialisation, interreligious contacts (β .06) have some predictive value. Finally, authoritarianism (β – .09) has a negative impact on support for freedom of religion, whereas multiculturalism has a positive effect (β .14).

Discussion on Salient Findings

Our empirical analysis among secondary school students has brought to light some significant findings with regard to relationship between civil rights and religion. Rather than exploring the implications of these findings in depth, in this section we will summarise and comment on the salient findings linked to our core question: public perception of civil rights in Italy and how religion affects those attitudes. We will also consider future avenues for academic investigation and church activities in support of a civil rights culture in Italy.

Firstly, four distinct sets of civil rights emerged among our sample of Italian students. In general, we observed a solid level of support for civil rights. Women's rights are strongly supported; the relatively new concept of gay and sexual civil rights is supported, as is the more traditional freedom of assembly. It is only in the case of freedom of religion that we find mixed responses within all four religious sub-groups, namely Catholic churchgoers, Catholic non-churchgoers, generally religious and non-religious students. This overall support for the civil rights culture among young Italians is encouraging. It appears that not only are fundamental liberties such as freedom of assembly (historically related to the freedom of thought, of speech, of the press, etc.) strongly rooted in the mind of younger generations, but also a firm commitment to non-discrimination, i.e. against women and homosexuals. On the other hand, variations in opinions on freedom of religion indicate that the public debate about the future of the civil rights culture in Italy should include religious issues. More research is needed in order to understand the challenges of increasing religious plurality in the Italian society and more energy might need to be devoted to developing a civil rights culture that explicitly includes the fundamental right of religious freedom in the public domain.

Secondly, we found different levels of support within the sub-groups defined by religious identity (i.e. Catholic churchgoers, Catholic non-churgoers, generally religious and non-religious students). We found no significant difference in support for women's rights and freedom of assembly among the groups. However, Catholic students, both practicing and non-practicing, are less supportive of gay and sexual rights than those who are generally religious or non-religious. This may be explained by the moral education that Catholic students receive in Catholic parishes and families, especially regarding sexual issues. Meanwhile, Catholic students expressed much clearer support for freedom of religion. This finding may be justified by the fact that those who see themselves as Catholic value their religious affiliation and are also willing to defend the right to assert their allegiance in public. This group appears to be more sensitive to the right of expressing religious beliefs and practices, also of other religious groups. These findings do not fully confirm the theory put forward by Marzano and Urbinati, who argue that the virtual Catholic monopoly in Italy hinders progress in terms of the civil rights culture and equal treatment for all. While their hypothesis appears to be true with regard to gay and sexual rights, our results indicate a different conclusion for freedom of religion. More research is needed to assess the role that Catholic identity plays in people's support for or rejection of civil rights. Our data suggest that no one broad statement can be made and that a finer distinction between different kinds of civil rights is required.

Examining the predictive value of religious variables in terms of attitudes to civil rights, we find that personal religious attitudes have no significant impact, whereas contextual religious attitudes appear to have some significant effects. An exclusivist attitude to religion reduces support for gay and sexual rights, while a pluralistic world view tends to go hand in hand with support for gay and sexual rights and freedom of religion. Trust in other religious communities has a positive impact on support for freedom of religion. The idea that religion should be open to cultural trends in society ("cultural conformity") is conducive to support for women's rights and gay and sexual rights. The view that religion should focus on providing spiritual services increases support for gay and sexual rights, freedom of assembly and freedom of religion. In terms of the relationship between church and state, a preference for a radical separation of religion and state means respondents are less likely to value freedom of religion, whereas advocating a consultative relation is associated with support for women's rights and freedom of assembly. Going back to the core question about the role of religion in fostering human rights, the question is not *whether* religion has an impact on civil rights, but *what kind* of religion has a positive impact on the civil rights culture. Our findings suggest that this would be a religion that values religious plurality positively and has a sense of trust in other religious traditions. A form of religion that favours interreligious contacts, is open to current trends in society and focuses on spiritual service is more likely to support civil rights. Finally, people who prefer a consultative relationship between religion and political institutions are more likely to agree with most of the civil rights studied. These findings represent a challenge for theological reflection, such as within ecclesiology and practical theology, which explore the identity and function of the church in relation to other religions and society at large. In our view, the church can find justification and motivation to move forward as a church *for* human rights in its own theological heritage, as demonstrated in section "Theological justification". Pastoral activities within the church are also challenged by this model of religion working for human rights. As Habermas argues, post-secular society needs a church that can exercise a positive influence "from below", through the public statements and publications of its members as part of civil society.

A fourth conclusion is that there is clear relation between identity (religious affiliation and practice) and levels of support for gay and sexual rights. Catholic churchgoers express less support for these rights than non-churchgoers, generally religious or non-religious students. Nevertheless, the average score of churchgoers on gay and sexual rights also falls within the range of support. We have measured these rights as the right of homosexuals to hold any public office and the statement that the state should prosecute behaviour which discriminates against homosexuals. While Catholic doctrine teaches that homosexuals should not be unjustly discriminated (Catechism of the Catholic Church, 2358), the church does not appear to have successfully communicated the full message to the younger generation of churchgoers. Further theological reflection is needed, for instance in moral theology, in order to better understand homosexuality and clarify Catholic teaching on "unjust discrimination" against gays. We should also not forget that the official teaching, while opposed to "unjust discrimination", also labels homosexual acts as "intrinsically disordered", "contrary to the natural law" and "not proceeding from a genuine affective and sexual complementarity" (Catechism, 2357). Confronting these issues, both in theory and in church practice, might help Catholic believers to participate in the public debate about civil rights with reasonable arguments and in a constructive way, and could overcome any ambiguity about discrimination against homosexuals.

Our last comment relates to the fact that our data show that psychological and socio-political traits of the students are strong predictors of their attitudes to civil rights. Social dominance orientation reduces support for civil rights, while empathy engenders support (for women's rights, gay and sexual rights, and freedom of religion). A positive attitude towards cultural diversity in society is also a significant predictor of support for civil rights (gay and sexual rights, freedom of religion). In terms of the role of religion in supporting a civil rights culture, we can say that these findings suggest that the church could commit to championing human rights in Italy through the numerous church-run educational institutions and programmes, which still impact a significant portion of young people in Italy. Parishes, Catholic schools and Catholic associations can contribute to a flourishing civil rights culture in Italy, not only by investing time and effort in the religious aspects of education for young people, but also by considering psychological and socio-political traits, for instance by introducing initiatives to develop empathy for others and increase acceptance of cultural differences.

Ultimately, far from having found definitive answers to questions about the role of religion in the present and future development of a civil rights culture in Italy, we have highlighted some avenues for further research in this matter. The rolc of religion cannot be dismissed within the public debate on human rights. Religious issues still have a pivotal role in this debate and religious symbols and concepts can have an impact. It is up to the church, both leaders and believers, to choose, strengthen and foster theological ideas and pastoral and educational programmes that will reinforce the positive role of religion in our human rights culture, both now and in the future.

Bibliography[5]

Alexy, R. (1985). *Theorie der Grundrechte*. Baden-Baden: Nomos.

Bloch, T. (2008). *Die Stellungnahme der römischen-katholischen Amtskirche zur Frage der Menschenrechte seit 1215*. Frankfurt a.M.: Lang.

Benedict XVI (2008). Address to the general assembly of the United Nations organization. New York, 18 April 2008.

Böckenförde E.-W. (2002/2006[2]). *Geschichte der Rechts- und Staatsphilosophie,* 2 Vols., Tübingen: Mohr Siebeck.

Cahill, L. S., Haker, H., & Metogoet, E. M. (Eds.). (2010). Human nature and natural law. *Special issue Concilium, 46*, 3.

Ferrari, S. (1996). Stato e Chiesa in Italia. In G. Robbers (Ed.), *Stato e Chiesa nell'Unione Europea* (pp. 181–203). Giuffré: Milano.

Francis. (2014). Address to the Council of Europe. Strasbourg, 25 November 2014.

Gregory XVI (1832). Mirari Vos. *Encyclical on liberalism and religious indifferentism.* Rome, 15 August 1832.

Habermas, J. (2009). La rinascita della religione: una sfida per l'autocomprensione laica della modernità? In A. Ferrara (Ed.), *Religione e politica nella società post-secolare*. Meltemi: Roma.

Habermas, J. (2011). "The political": The rational meaning of a questionable inheritance of political theology. In E. Mendieta & J. VanAntwerpen (Eds.), *The power of religion in the public sphere* (pp. 15–33). New York: Columbia University Press.

Habermas, J., & Ratzinger, J. (2006). *The dialectics of secularization: On reason and religion*. San Francisco: Ignatius Press.

International Theological Commission (2009). In search of a universal ethic: A new look at the natural law. Rome.

John XXIII (1963). Pacem in Terris. *Encyclical on establishing universal peace in truth, justice, charity and liberty.* Rome, 11 June 1963.

John Paul II (1979). Redemptor Hominis. *Encyclical on the redeemer of mankind.* Rome, 4 March 1979.

John Paul II (1995). Evangelium Vitae. *Encyclical on the value and inviolability of human life.* Rome, 25 March 1995.

Kaufmann, F. X. (1973). *Wissensoziologische Überlegungen zu Renaissance und Niedergang des katholischen Naturrechtsdenkens im 19. und 20. Jahrhundert*. In F. Böckle & E.-W. Böckenförde (Eds.), *Naturrecht in der Kritik* (pp. 126–164). Grünenwald: Mainz.

Leo XIII (1888). Libertas. *Encyclical on the nature of human liberty.* Rome, 20 June 1888.

Leo XIII (1891). Rerum Novarum. *Encyclical on capital and labor*. Rome, 15 May 1891.

Langan, J. (1986). Human rights in Roman Catholicism. In C. E. Curran & R. A. McCormick (Eds.), *Official Catholic social teaching* (pp. 110–129). New York: Paulist Press.

Marzano, M., & Urbinati, N. (2013). *Missione impossibile: la riconquista cattolica della sfera pubblica*. Bologna: Il Mulino.

Menozzi, D. (2012). *Chiesa e i diritti umani*. Bologna: Il Mulino.

Metz, J.-B. (2006). *Memoria Passionis*. Freiburg: Herder.

Perin R. (2013). *Pio XI e la mancata lettera sugli ebrei a Mussolini,* in *Rivista di Storia del Cristianesimo*, 1/2013, 181–206.

Pius VI (1791). Quod Aliquantum. *Encyclical on the subject of the civil constitution of the clergy of France*. Rome, 10 March 1791.

Pius IX (1864a). Quanta Cura. *Encyclical condemning current errors*. Rome, 8 December 1864.

[5] All (English translations of) documents of the Second Vatican Council, Apostolic Constitutions, Encyclicals, Papal public addresses and documents of Pontifical Councils and institutions have been taken from the Vatican website: www.vatican.va

Pius IX (1864b). *Syllabus Errorum* [Syllabus of errors]. Rome, 8 December 1864.
Pius XI (1931). Non Abbiamo Bisogno. *Encyclical on Catholic action in Italy.* Rome, 29 June 1931.
Pontifical Council for Inter-religious Dialogue (1991). Dialogue and proclamation. *Reflection and orientations on interreligious dialogue and the proclamation of the gospel of Jesus Christ.* Rome, 19 May 1991.
Pontifical Council for Justice and Peace (2004). Compendium of the social doctrine of the church. Rome.
Quinn, P. (2003). Christian ethics and human rights. In J. Runzo, N. M. Martin, & A. Sharma (Eds.), *Human rights and responsibilities in the world religions* (pp. 233–245). Oxford: Oneworld.
Rawls, J. (1999). *The idea of public reason revisited.* Cambridge: Harvard University Press.
Schilebeeckx E. (2014–VI/1979[1]). *Jesus: An experiment in Christology* (The collected works of Edward Schillebeeckx Vol. VI). London [etc.]: Bloomsbury.
Schüssler, F. E. (1983). *In memory of her: A feminist theological reconstruction of Christian origins.* New York: Crossroads.
Van der Ven, J. A. (1998). *Practical theology: An empirical approach.* Leuven: Peeters.
Van der Ven, J. A., Dreyer, J. S., & Pieterse, H. (2004). *Is there a god of human rights? The complex relationship between human rights and religion.* Leiden/Boston: Brill.
Vatican II (1965a). Gaudium et Spes. *Pastoral Constitution on the Church in the modern world.* Rome, 7 December 1965.
Vatican II (1965b). Dignitatis Humanae. *Declaration on the right of the person and of communities to social and civil freedom in matters religious.* Rome, 7 December 1965.
Zaccaria, F. (2015). Catholic Church, young people and human rights in Italy. In H.-G. Ziebertz & G. Crpic (Eds.), *Religion and human rights* (pp. 93–102). Zürich: Springer.

Chapter 5
The Role of Religion in Society, and Its Relation to the Attitudes Towards Human Rights in Chile

Joaquín Silva and Jorge Manzi

Abstract Among the various issues involved in the relationship between religion and human rights, there is one that seems essential to the relationship between religion and politics; and more specifically, to the understanding of the role of religion in the public sphere. In this study, we investigate Chilean youth's perception of the role of religion in the public sphere, as well as the possible relation between this perception and the practices of and attitudes shown towards human rights. We will also look at the variations this relationship might have, depending on the religious identities of the youth who participated in our survey. Incorporating exploratory research, our aim is to analyse the empirical data that we collect in order to raise questions and theoretical proposals that can be used in comparative studies, within the framework of the Research Project 'Religion and Human Rights'.

This article is structured as follows: (1) Exploration of the problem: brief theoretical discussions are presented of religion and the public sphere, and of the current Chilean context regarding this subject. (2) Presentation of the research questions and the conceptual model that will be used for data analysis. (3) Explaining the methodology used for data collection. (4) Presenting the overall empirical data. (5) Presenting the empirical data as it relates to each of the research questions. (6) Finally, offering some interpretative reflections and general conclusions based on the results.

For their contributions, we would like to thank Carla Vásquez, student at the School of Psychology of the Pontificia Universidad Catòlica; Catalina Cerda, postgraduate student at the Faculty of Theology; and Charlotte Pichuante, librarian.

J. Silva (✉) • J. Manzi
Pontificia Universidad Catolica de Chile, Santiago, Chile
e-mail: jsilvas@uc.cl; jmanzi@uc.cl

H.-G. Ziebertz, C. Sterkens (eds.), *Religion and Civil Human Rights in Empirical Perspective*, Religion and Human Rights 2, DOI 10.1007/978-3-319-59285-5_5

Exploration of the Problem

The relationship between religion and human rights is one of the main expressions of the more general question about the role of religion in the public sphere. This relationship depends partially on the comprehension that any religion has of itself, and of its role and functions in society. Some religions promote more involvement in the public sphere, making human rights issues more salient, whereas other religions distance themselves from society. At the same time, this relationship is also shaped by historical context, and by the way the public sphere is organised. Under some historical circumstances, religions have faced more pressure to get involved in society and in the protection of human rights.

Following this general view, we first present some theoretical approaches to the relationship between religion and the public sphere. We then present the historical context for this relationship in the case of Chile, where the breakdown of the democratic regime prompted religions to assume a new role in the protection of human rights.

Religion and the Public Sphere in Current Theoretical Debate

A large part of Western history is the result of a deep symbiosis between the areas of religion and politics – at some points even resulting in a merger of the two, as was the case in the relationship between the ecclesiastical and civil powers during the Roman Empire, after its conversion to Christianity (Van der Ven 2010). The situation began to change with the emergence of the modern European state, given that it assumed a certain functional differentiation of society: the emergence of the economy based on a free market, and the emergence of the democratic legitimisation of political authority (no longer based on transcendent grounds), implied a process of secularisation of politics (Habermas and Taylor 2011).

The current liberal political philosophy – whose greatest exponent has without doubt been John Rawls, in his earlier work – understands religion as a purely private matter. Each person is free to believe, celebrate and live his faith as he or she wants; but as soon as this person participates in the public sphere, he or she should leave all beliefs out of the picture, debating and arguing from what Rawls (1996) calls a "rational secularity". This is because mutual understanding between participants in the public sphere can only be achieved by avoiding religious beliefs, thereby also avoiding any hint of imposing non-political reasoning on an eminently rational discussion (Habermas 2006; Habermas and Taylor 2011).

In turn, Charles Taylor focuses on plurality, which should be maintained and encouraged in our liberal societies provided that it does not contradict the founding principles of these societies: liberty, equality and fraternity. Liberal democracies based on this triad, the author reminds us, not only protect the liberty and the individual faith of every person, but also ensure that everybody will be treated equally. Furthermore – and specifically supporting the topic at hand – to assure fraternity in a plural context in the public sphere, societies should foster valuing each worldview as different and complementary, without imposing any extraordinary requirements on religious worldviews; which would occur if they were to be asked to translate their public discourse into categories of secular rationality (Habermas and Taylor 2011).

From another perspective, Niklas Luhmann calls attention to the configuration of our modern societies, recognising that they have achieved a high level of complexity that has resulted in what is known as *functional differentiation*. The author theorises that our societies consist of diverse subsystems with their own means of communication: the economy, politics, the judicial order, ethics and religion, among others. These subsystems meet and interact incidentally, but they cannot influence each other because they are based on their own logic and make use of specific codes. Hence, Luhmann denies the claim – despite it being held by many religions themselves (e.g. Christianity) – that religion will be able to maintain a strong influence outside its own religious system, i.e. on other subsystems (Luhmann 2007, 2009).

Within the current public debate, these perspectives continue to have great influence on the understanding of our societies and the role of religion within them. This is also the case for Chile. The Chilean culture is indeed influenced by philosophical reflections originating from elsewhere, as well as by European and North American societies and politics – not least because of the globalisation of the market and the media, especially among the youth (Yaksic 2011). The debate about religion in the public sphere is not merely a theoretical issue; it lays out a framework that makes clear that the public sphere in Chile continues to be influenced and even partly determined by the ascribed role of religion. But there have been changes as well. We will elaborate on this in the next section.

Religion and the Public Sphere in Chile in Recent History

In Latin America, religion and politics were united during the conquest of the new world by the Spanish and Portuguese crowns. Throughout colonial times, political power was supported through religion, and was profoundly intertwined with Catholic evangelisation. Beginning in the nineteenth century, independent initiatives distanced themselves from the monarchical system and its transcendent foundation; but this did not involve a distancing or negation of religion itself, which has always been considered a part of Latin American national identities (Blancarte 2014; Cid 2014). The processes of independence and the emergence of new Latin American republics promoted the recognition of popular sovereignty as the base of political power, taking the first step towards distancing religion from politics. However, Catholicism continued to be the official religion of the State during the nineteenth century and part of the 20th.

In recent Chilean history, the presence of religion in the public sphere has had different expressions. In spite of the constitutional separation of Church and State in

1925, throughout much of the twentieth century Christianity has exerted major influence on politics (as well as other domains) through what may be called 'Social Catholicism'. Chilean Christianity expressed its ideal of a more equal society, with a special option for the poor, through initiatives such as 'Catholic Action'; the creation of numerous social institutions and even worker unions, based on the principles of equality and justice, and promoted by emblematic people such as Father Alberto Hurtado, Clotario Blest and Cardenal Raúl Silva (Silva 2014).

But perhaps the largest and most well-known expression of the presence of the church and the role it fulfilled in the Chilean public sphere in recent times has been its actions during the reign of the military government between 1973 and 1990. During this period, churches defended thousands of people who were detained, tortured and/or assassinated by the State and its repressive apparatus.

The Ecumenical Committee *Pro Paz* – in which the Catholic, Baptist, Methodist and Orthodox churches and the Jewish community and others participated (Yuraszeck Krebs 2013), and later the *Vicaría de la Solidaridad* (Precht 1998) – represented churches in the public debate, generating concrete opinions and actions in favour of respecting human rights.

However, since Chile's return to democracy in 1990, there has been a change in the role of Chilean churches in the public sphere. In the 1980s, the military government of Augusto Pinochet introduced a liberal regime not only in economic terms, but also in socio-political terms. This led to a strengthening of the processes of privatisation and individualism, and undermined the social dimension of coexistence in Chile, strengthening these processes to have a global reach during a time of expanding globalisation.

Complementing this socio-cultural process, many churches retreated, reducing their public roles. For many Christians, even members of the clergy, the return to democracy provided the possibility that the church could finally 'go back to its fundamentals', decreasing the energy it expended on social matters that (from this perspective) were taken on because of the situation that the country was experiencing, but which within a democratic context should be assumed by the State or civil society (Silva 2014). During the 1970s and 1980s, in the context of the dictatorship, when asked 'if your human rights were infringed, what institutions would you turn to?', the majority of Chileans would have answered 'religious institutions'; today, however, in a democratic context, only 2% state that they would turn to churches and other religious organisations (Instituto Nacional de Derechos Humanos 2013).

Of course, this does not imply that religion has disappeared entirely from the public sphere. The Catholic and Evangelical churches (mainly) have reclaimed their right to participate actively in public debates and in the legislature – especially on issues concerning the morality of life and sexuality, but also on social or economic issues, particularly in discussions about the reform of the Chilean educational system. But one could pose the following critical questions. Should churches be made aware that their opinion is increasingly perceived as just one among many others? And should churches therefore desist from any attempt to impose their worldview on society as a whole?

Youth, Religion and the Public Sphere in Chile Today

Because of these circumstances, the perception that the youth have of the relationship between religion and human rights is not at all obvious. The youth of today were born and have been raised in a democracy based on a model of neo-liberalism. Therefore, they have grown up with the privatisation and individualism of social relationships, and probably with a liberal understanding of the role of different worldviews (including religious worldviews) in the public sphere.

Furthermore, today's youth did not witness the rich historical and social collaboration of churches that characterised the decades prior to the 1990s as described above. Additionally, in the last few years the Chilean Catholic Church has been affected by a serious commitment and credibility crisis, largely due to sexual abuse scandals involving clergy members. While these scandals have been notable elsewhere as well, they have particularly affected the Chilean church. In fact, overall trust in the church is over 60% in all Latin American countries except in Uruguay and Chile – with Chile being the country with the least trust in the church, registering just 44% (Latinobarómetro 2014).

Alongside this, over the last few decades in Latin America (and specifically in Chile) there has been a process of transformation in the religious spectrum. Historical data show that for a large part of the twentieth century, from 1900 until the 1960s, at least 90% of the population of Latin America was Catholic; currently, only 69% of adults in the whole region identify themselves as Catholic. Close to 40% of the world's Catholic population lives in Latin America (425 million Catholics); however, identification with Catholicism has decreased in the whole region. Some countries continue to be predominantly Catholic (more than 70% of the population declaring themselves Catholic), such as Paraguay, Mexico and Colombia; others have a majority of Catholics, such as Chile, Costa Rica and Brazil; and some have half of their population being Catholic, such as El Salvador, Guatemala and Nicaragua. But there are others where Catholicism now represents less than half of the population, such as in Honduras and Uruguay. The latter registers the highest percentage (37%) of people who declare that they do not have any religious affiliation (Pew Research Center 2014).

In the last 10 years, religious disaffiliation among Chilean youth has almost doubled, increasing from 12% to 22%; one out of every four youth state that they do not have any religion; clearly, at least among the youth, a pattern of religious disbelief is emerging (Universidad Católica and Adimark 2014). This last fact is particularly surprising, given that Chile did not have a tradition of agnosticism until two decades ago. It should be stated that other religions, such as Islam, Hinduism and Judaism, are not (yet) significant in terms of numbers in Chile, or in the rest of Latin America.

Additionally, for some time the privatisation and de-institutionalisation of religion has been observed in the country (PNUD 2002), which is indicated by a high rate of belief (83% say that they believe in God), but dissimilar levels of religious practice: Evangelicals attend worship more regularly (41% attend once a week), while hardly 9% of those who classify themselves as Catholic do. On the other hand, the number of Catholics who never attend or almost never attend has reached 42%, as opposed to only 26% of their Evangelical counterparts (Universidad Católica and Adimark 2014).

Regarding the role of the Catholic Church in public decisions, there is a downward trend of devaluation by Chileans of what could be called the 'public role' of the church: in 2006, 47% of Chileans were in agreement that the church should be taken into consideration; in surveys from 2013, this percentage had dropped to 32% (Universidad Católica and Adimark 2014).

Finally – and in accordance with the last National Survey of Human Rights in Chile – today, in our current cultural and political context, religion and human rights appear to move along separate tracks, or at least independently: 39% of the population considers the State to be responsible for guaranteeing human rights, representing by far the most named institution among the alternatives. Barely 1% of the people considered that the church should be responsible for guaranteeing human rights (Instituto Nacional de Derechos Humanos 2013).

The data presented up to now have shown the importance of investigating the role that Chilean youth assign to religion in society today. As mentioned, it is possible to assume some privatisation of this role, given the liberal cultural context and the institutional strength of Chilean democracy. That said, it is necessary to gather more data to understand the relationship between religion and human rights in Chile. New data will not only provide the gateway to a whole range of research questions, but will also offer suggestions for concrete actions that churches can take, through education, pastoral work and participation in the public sphere, to strengthen their contributions to a culture of human rights.

Research Questions and the Model of Analysis

In light of the issues discussed above, this research seeks to clarify the value of religion among contemporary Chilean youth, and analyses the role of religion in relation to their attitudes to human rights. We will analyse each of the four main groups of religious affiliation in Chile (Catholics, Protestants,[1] generally religious and not-religious), to ascertain the differences among them.

Research Questions

The specific questions for guiding the investigation, and the configuration of the data analysis model that follows, were:

[1] The category "Protestants" includes all denominations of the Reformed Church and their posterior referrals. In terms of the questionnaire, it combines the answer categories 'Lutheran', 'Pentecostal', 'Evangelical' and 'other Christian traditions'.

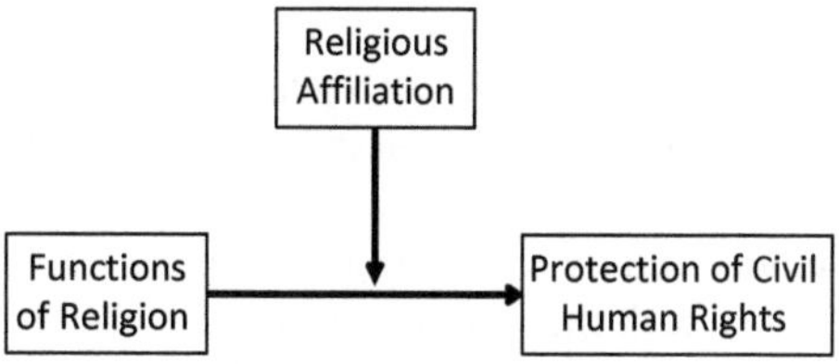

Fig. 5.1 Conceptual model

(a) *What is the perception that the youth have of the role of religion in society?*
(b) *What is the relationship between the role(s) attributed to religion and the attitudes of the youth to civil human rights?*
(c) *Are there differences in the relationship between religion and civil rights attitudes among the four main groups of religious affiliation in Chile (Catholics, Protestants, generally religious respondents and non-religious respondents)?*

Conceptual Model

Consequently, the conceptual model used (see Fig. 5.1) aims to analyse the relationship between the (attributed) roles of religion among Chilean youth and their attitudes to civil human rights. Furthermore, we will describe and comment on differences between groups based on religious affiliation.

Methodology

Procedure

Data collection was carried out between May and July 2014. The sampling took place in seven middle-sized cities in Chile, selected because they all have a population between 100 and 200 thousand: Concepción, Copiapó, Iquique, La Serena, Melipilla, Quilpué, Talcahuano, Temuco and Villa Alemana.

To increase the likelihood of reaching youth from different social contexts and from different religious affiliations, between three and five schools were selected in each city, distributed as evenly as possible according to type (municipal, charter or private school)[2] and religious denomination (Christian, Catholic, Protestant or Lay), with a total of 36 institutions.

[2] In Chile currently there is a system of mixed provision of education, with three types of education establishment in primary and secondary education: municipal schools (financed in full by the State, and managed by municipalities); private charter schools (financed by the state, but privately managed); and privately-paid schools (financed in full by the families of students). The distribution of enrolment, at the national level, is around 38% in municipal schools, 54% in charter schools, and 8% in private schools.

The questionnaires were distributed among one or two grades of high-school upperclassmen (16 to 18 years old) in each school, allowing students to participate on a voluntary basis, in their own classroom, supervised by a person trained by the research team. Beforehand, a consent form was signed by the principal of each school and by the legal guardians of the underage participants.

Overall, the sample consisted of 1307 youth. Regarding the religious conviction of the institutions at which they study, 30.2% attended a Catholic school, 23% attended a Protestant school, 5.5% attended a Christian-oriented school (without any specific denomination) and 38.1% attended a non-religiously-oriented school. At the same time, 21.1% of the participants belonged to a municipal school, 55.8% belonged to a charter school and 20% attended a private school. The average age of the participants was 16.6 years (DS = 0.83); 62.2% were in 11th grade (the penultimate year of secondary education), and the remaining 37.7% in 12th grade (final year). Distribution by gender was 49.3% females and 50.7% males.

Instruments

The survey was developed within the framework of the international 'Religion and Human Rights' research project and translated and adapted to the national context by the Chilean research team. The survey was self-reported, and the majority of the items were answered by using a five-point Likert scale, from 1 (complete disagreement) to 5 (complete agreement). Among other items, the survey incorporated various measurements of the psychological, social, moral and religious aspects of the students.

Measurements

The concepts included in the conceptual model were measured with the help of items that referred to various different scales:

Roles of Religion

The participants were asked to indicate their level of agreement with 10 items that referred to five possible roles of religion (2 items each). The items assessed the roles of the referred religions regarding: (1) 'Influence over public opinion', (2) 'Public prophetic voice', (3) 'Spiritual service', (4) 'National culture' and (5) 'Cultural conformity'.

Human Rights

The participants indicated their level of agreement with 16 items to do with civil human rights. During the analyses (explained in section "Empirical results related to factor analysis"), four additional items were added, because they were also conceptually connected with civil rights. All items were answered using a five-point Likert-type agreement scale.

Religious Affiliation

This variable was assessed by a single item in which participants reported their religious affiliation, given a list of 20 possibilities. Among these were different Catholic, Protestant and Islamic traditions and other world religions, as well as the possibility of identifying oneself as generally religious ('believing without any specific religion') or as non-religious. The following four majority groups in the sample (and in Chile) were used: Catholic (N = 497), Protestant (including diverse Christian denominations that are neither Catholic nor Anglican; N = 272), generally religious (N = 141) and non-religious (N = 269).

The items under 'Roles of Religion' and 'Human Rights' were grouped based on the results of a factor analysis. We will elaborate on this in the presentation of the empirical results (section "Empirical results related to factor analysis").

Analysis

To analyse the data, Principal Component Analysis (PCA) was used, with Varimax rotation, to generate factors based on the observed variables. Later, the reliability of each factor was calculated, using Cronbach's alpha.

In order to answer the first research question (*What is the perception that youth have of the role of religion in society?*), the procedure was carried out with all of the items under 'Roles of religion'. To tackle the second question (*What is the relationship between the role(s) attributed to religion and the attitudes of the youth towards civil human rights?*), the Principal Component Analysis was carried out with all of the items from the 'Civil Human Rights' category. Conceptual analysis of items belonging to other human rights scales led to the addition of four items – two from the political rights, and two from the socioeconomic rights – as they were conceptually and empirically related to the factors that emerged from the analysis.

To respond to the third research question (*Are there differences in the relationship between religion and civil rights attitudes among the four main groups of religious affiliation?*), Analysis of Variance (ANOVA) was conducted for each scale.

Empirical Results Related to Factor Analysis

The principal component analysis with Varimax rotation of the 10 items referring to functions of religion led to the identification of three dimensions. One was defined as the *public function* of religion. It included five items, all of which express that religion should have a public voice and influence regarding societal issues. The reliability of the scale was adequate (Cronbach's alpha $\alpha = .81$).

Two items loaded in the *conformity function* scale. These items indicate that religion should adapt to current trends in society. Finally, two other items combined in the *spiritual function*. They express the expectation that religion promotes the spiritual growth of fellowship. These scales produced satisfactory reliability estimates using Cronbach's alpha ($\alpha_{conf} = .80$; $\alpha_{spir} = .63$).

In the case of civil human rights, a similar analysis was performed on the items that addressed those rights. As previously indicated, we added four items to the analysis based on their conceptual relationship with civil rights. Four factors emerged: one addressed the *rights of women*, supporting equal rights for men and women. The scale included four items. Items addressing the *rights of homosexuals, including protection from discrimination,* loaded in a second factor. Then, four items referring to the protection of *religious rights*, including the rights of religion in education, emerged as the third factor. Finally, seven items that support freedom of expression, association and reunion combined in the fourth factor. Table 5.1 includes Cronbach's alpha estimates for the four scales. They are acceptable, although in one case (expression and association rights), reliability is just above .50.

Table 5.1 Descriptions and reliability of the civil human rights scales (number of items, mean, standard deviation and Cronbach's alpha)

Civil human rights scales	N° items	M	SD	α
Rights of women	4	4.52	.60	.78
Rights of homosexuals	3	3.82	.89	.58
Religious rights	4	3.48	.77	.67
Expression and association rights	7	3.49	.52	.52

Descriptive information about the four scales reveals that all rights are generally supported. All means are above the midpoint of the response scale (3). The rights of women receive the highest support, whereas religious and expression rights have only mild support. Variability is higher in the case of the rights of homosexuals, which indicates that the participants in the study find this issue more contentious.

Results

In considering the results of the factor analysis, the main results for each of the research questions that guided this investigation are presented.

Perception Among the Youth of the Roles of Religion in Society

Table 5.2 shows that the participants expressed higher agreement with the spiritual function (M = 3.54), followed by the social conformity function (M = 3.10), with the public function receiving the lowest support (M = 2.69, slightly below the midpoint of the response scale). The relatively high degree of variability indicates that students differ in their degree of support for each function. Moreover, the public and spiritual functions are clearly correlated (r = 0.50). This suggests that the more students support the public presence of religions, the more they also support their spiritual role. Even though these two functions are clearly different, the students do not see them as dissociated functions. In contrast, the social conformity role does not correlate with either the public or the spiritual role.

Table 5.2 Correlations and descriptive statistics of Religious functions

	Public	Conformity	Spiritual
Public		.06*	.50**
Conformity			.02
Mean	2.69	3.10	3.54
Std. deviation	.89	1.20	.98

*p < .05; **p < .01

Relationship Between the Role(s) Attributed to Religion and the Attitudes of the Youth Towards Human Rights

Table 5.3 depicts the bivariate correlations between the roles of religion and support for civil human rights. Overall, the three functions have significant correlations with most of the human rights scales. However, the correlations range from low to moderate. The rights of women and those of association and expression have low or null correlations with the functions of religions, suggesting that religion is not perceived as a relevant referent for those rights. By contrast, stronger relationships are observed for the other two dimensions of human rights, especially religious rights. The most interesting case is the support for the rights of homosexuals, which shows significant correlations with the public and conformity function of religion.

Table 5.3 Matrix of correlations of roles of religion and human rights

	Public function	Conformity function	Spiritual function
Rights of women	–.08**	.12**	.16**
Rights of homosexuals	–.20**	.27**	–.04
Religious rights	.40**	–.16**	.42**
Association and expression rights	–.02	.20**	.03

*p < .05; **p < .01

The recognition of the public function of religion is negatively associated with the support of women's and homosexual rights. In contrast, this function is positively correlated with religious rights. This pattern of correlation reveals that the participants of the study perceive that religion (mostly Catholic, in the context of this sample) does not favour civil rights for women and homosexuals. Given that the only positive correlation under the public role of religion is with religious rights, the obvious conclusion is that participants perceive the public role to be a defensive approach in society, protecting religion.

In contrast, the conformity role functions in the opposite direction: in general terms, the more people expect that religion should adapt to societal trends, the more they support all civil rights, including association and expression rights, as well as those of women and homosexuals. Moreover, this function of religion is negatively correlated with religious rights.

As expected, the spiritual function of religion is clearly and positively correlated with religious rights ($r = 0.42$). Interestingly, this function is also positively correlated with the rights of women; but this relationship is weaker ($r = 0.16$) than with religious rights. The other two correlations are not significant.

Differences in the Relationship Between the Roles of Religion and Attitudes Towards Human Rights, When Comparing the Four Main Groups of Religious Affiliation in Chile

A comparison of the four groups of religious affiliation (Catholics, Protestants, generally religious and non-religious) reveals significant differences between the groups, regarding the relationship between roles of religion and attitudes toward civil human rights. The results of the analysis are presented in three sections: first, the perception of the youth regarding the roles of religion, comparing the religious affiliation groups (c. I.); next, the differences in support for human rights when groups of religious affiliation are compared (C. II); and finally, we describe the relationship between the roles of religion and attitudes towards human rights, comparing groups of religious affiliation (c. III).

Perception of the Youth Regarding the Roles of Religion, Compared by Groups of Religious Affiliation

The first three rows of Table 5.4 show the differences in the importance attributed to each of the three functions of religion by the four groups of religious affiliation. The overall difference is significant in these three cases. Moreover, in the case of the public and spiritual function, all pairwise comparisons among the groups were significant, indicating that the four groups are statistically different. The public

Table 5.4 Scale means on functions of religion and support for civil human rights based on religious condition

	F	Protestants (n = 272)							
Public function	63.88**	2.83	a	3.05	b	2.58	c	2.13	d
Conformity function	56.07**	3.23	a	2.37	b	3.34	ac	3.54	c
Spiritual function	49.60**	3.66	a	3.94	b	3.43	c	3.01	d
Rights of women	5.23**	4.52	ab	4.41	a	4.63	b	4.57	b
Rights of homosexuals	40.49**	3.93	a	3.35	b	4.03	a	4.05	a
Religious rights	87.40**	3.58	a	3.89	b	3.44	a	2.93	c
Association and expression rights	7.61**	3.49	a	3.35	b	3.53	a	3.55	a

[a b c d]Means sharing a common subscript in each row do not differ significantly from one another (p > .5). Means having dissimilar subscripts differ significantly (p < .05). All comparisons made with Bonferroni tests

**The overall difference among the four groups is significant (p < .01)

function receives the largest support from the Protestant participants, followed by the Catholics, and then by the generally religious participants. However, no group expresses high support for this function, because even Protestants, the group with the highest average, is just above the midpoint of the response scale (M = 3.05). Clearly, this is the function less supported in our sample.

The conformity function of religion receives higher support than the public one, especially among the non-religious and generally religious groups. Moreover, those who expressed the highest support for the public function (the Protestants) now express the lowest agreement with the idea that religion should adapt to the current situation of society. This group is the only one with an average below the midpoint of the scale for this function (M = 2.37).

Finally, the spiritual function is the one receiving the highest support from all groups – except for the non-religious participants, who indicate higher support for the conformity function. As expected, religiously affiliated students (Protestants and Catholics) are the ones with the highest regard for the spiritual function.

Differences in Attitudes Towards Human Rights When Compared by Groups of Religious Affiliation

Support for civil human rights showed significant differences among groups of religious affiliation in the four scales. However, the differences were not strong, with the exception of the attitudes toward religious rights. The rights of women received the highest support from all groups. The rights of homosexuals followed, with the religious and association rights receiving less support. Groups differed in the relative support of the last two rights, in an expected way: in comparison with non-religious and generally religious participants, Catholics and Protestants favoured religious rights more than association rights.

In spite of these differences, we observed positive support for all civil human rights in all groups. In fact, the average was above the midpoint of the response scale in all cases, with the slight exception of religious rights in the case of the non-religious participants.

In general terms, Protestants were the most distinctive group. As Table 5.4 shows, this group differs from all other groups in most of the comparisons. Interestingly, they differ not only from non-religious groups, but also from Catholics in most cases, with the exception of the support for women's rights.

Table 5.4 indicates that support for the rights of women, although significantly different among groups, does not differ much overall (the distance between the highest and lowest average is less than one third of a standard deviation). The generally religious and non-religious participants show the most positive attitude toward this right, whereas Protestants had the lowest average.

In the case of the rights of homosexuals, and association rights, three of the groups had statistically equivalent averages, with Protestants being the only group with a different and lower degree of support.

Finally, religious rights were associated with stronger differences. Protestants showed the greatest support (followed by Catholics), and non-religious participants the lowest. The difference between those groups was larger than one standard deviation, indicating that this is the right with the largest range among the groups.

Relationship Between Roles of Religion and Attitudes Towards Human Rights by Groups of Religious Affiliation

In this last section, we address whether functions of religion and human rights had similar or different correlations when considering the religious affiliation of participants. Table 5.5 presents the results, showing that overall, most of the relationships are similar across groups. However, considering that the number of students differs between groups, the likelihood of obtaining a significant correlation was smaller for the groups with fewer participants (especially the generally religious group). We now present similarities and differences between the groups for each human right.

In the case of rights of women, the most consistent finding indicates that for three of the groups (with the exception of the non-religious), support for this right was positively correlated with the spiritual function of religion. This indicates that for all participants identified as having a religious orientation (including those identified as generally religious), the more they perceive that religion should have a spiritual function, the more they support the rights for equal treatment for women in society. No other function correlated with this right for these groups. However, in the case of non-religious participants, this right had significant but weak correlations with the other two functions.

The protection of homosexuals from discrimination correlated with the public and conformity functions in three of the groups (with the exception of the generally religious). In those three groups, the more students perceived that religion should have a public role, the less they supported the rights of homosexuals. The pattern of correlation was the opposite for the conformity function. This result suggests that participants clearly perceive a tension between religion and the rights of

Table 5.5 Correlations between roles of religion and civil human rights, by religious affiliation

	Catholics			Protestants			Generally religious			Non religious		
	PF	CF	SF	PF	CF	SF	PF	CF	SF	PF	CF	SF
Rights of women	−.02	.07	.22**	−.02	.02	.29**	−.01	.14	.32**	−.15*	.18**	.09
Rights of homosexuals	−.11*	.12**	.09*	−.20**	.26**	−.03	−.12	.09	.00	−.13*	.17**	.07
Religious rights	.36**	−.14**	.36**	.17**	−.03	.41**	.37**	.05	.32**	.25**	.06	.29**
Association and expression rights	.07	.12**	.09*	−.09	.25**	.04	.07	.06	.16	−.05	.10	.07

p < .05; ** p < .01

homosexuals – something that is to be expected, considering the standpoint of the Catholic Church in Chile regarding gay marriage.

Religious rights show the most consistent pattern of correlations across the four groups. In all cases, the public and spiritual function of religion was positively correlated with the protection of religious rights. In comparison with the correlations observed for other rights, these were the highest values observed.

Finally, in the case of association and expression rights, correlations were consistently low, and not significant in most cases. The only exception was the positive correlations observed for the conformity function of religion in Catholics and Protestants.

Discussion and Conclusions

In this last section, we will comment on our results in the context of the expected pattern, considering the goals and antecedents presented in the first section. We will also consider some theoretical implications of the results.

Youth Perceptions About the Functions of Religion in Society

Our analyses suggest that a combination of actively influencing society, adapting to societal changes and offering spiritual guidance reflect our participants' perceptions of the role of religion in society. Support for these functions varies; the traditional spiritual function receives the highest approval, whereas the public function receives the lowest. This suggests that young people mostly expect religion to focus on spirituality, and that religions should attempt to adapt to society rather than change it. Interestingly, even participants who identify with a specific religion do not recognise a strong role for religion in society. This finding is consistent with the idea of secularisation, but it also reveals that new generations do not seem to recognise the important role that religion once played in Chilean society, especially in fundamental issues such as the promotion of social justice and the protection of human rights.

In the introduction to this chapter we indicated that the reduction of the role of religion in society is sometimes interpreted as a manifestation of the processes of privatisation and spiritualisation of religion. However, our data show that the public and spiritual functions of religion are not dissociated. The positive correlation between these functions ($r = 0.50$) indicates that for our participants, the more that religions assume a spiritual role, the more they expect that religions should have a public and active role in society. On the other hand, the fact that the conformity function does not correlate with the other functions suggests that the demand for adaptation to societal trends is perceived to be independent of the spiritual and public roles of religion.

As a consequence, we could conclude that the results are consistent with the notion of secularisation, since our participants – even those who identify with specific religions – do not desire religion to have great influence in the public sphere. On the other hand, the individuation thesis is not clearly supported, because the important role assigned to the spiritual function of religion (which could be seen as a sign of reducing religion to the individual and private space) is not dissociated from the public function, as we confirmed in the positive correlation between these functions. Therefore, we did not find a direct tension between the public and private functions of religion. The dilemma seems to be between recognising or not recognising some role for religion in society.

Relationship Between the Role Attributed to Religion and the Attitudes of Youth Towards Human Rights

We have explained that since at least the 60s, Latin American Catholicism has been strongly associated with relevant social issues, such as the reduction of poverty and social justice. The protection of human rights became another part of the public agenda of the Catholic Church in many countries experiencing serious human rights violations. In this historical context, we wanted to test whether new generations of citizens establish a positive connection between the role of religion in society and the protection of human rights. Our results indicate that this relationship is at best moderate. With the exception of civil rights related to religious freedom, which is obviously connected to functions of religion, other civil rights are weakly related to religion, especially association and expression rights.

In fact, the public function of religion correlates positively with religious rights, while it correlates negatively with the protection of homosexuals from discrimination, and shows very low correlations with women's rights and with association and expression rights. Therefore, the public role of religion is perceived by new generations to be the defence of religion, rather than the expression of a wider concern about civil rights.

The spiritual function of religion is also linked to the protection of religious rights, but in this case is at the same time positively correlated with the protection of women ´s rights. Other civil rights are not connected to this function of religion.

Finally, the conformity role of religion is negatively correlated with religious rights and positively correlated with the other civil rights. This shows that the more young people perceive that religion should adapt to societal changes, the more they value general civil rights, and the less they value religious rights. This pattern of correlations is expressing a tension perceived by our participants between religion and society – a tension that is consistent with secularisation trends.

Differences Among Religious Groups

We also addressed potential differences among groups of different religious affiliation in the relationship between roles of religion and support for civil human rights. Overall, we observed that the general pattern of correlations discussed in the previous sections holds for most groups. In the case of the public function of religion, it consistently correlates with support for religious rights in all groups, and correlates negatively with the rights of homosexuals in three of the groups (with the exception of generally religious participants). The spiritual function shows positive correlations with religious rights in all cases, and correlates positively with women´s rights in three groups (excluding non-religious participants). Finally, the conformity function is less consistent, showing a positive correlation with homosexual rights in three groups, and positive correlations with association and expression rights in the Catholic and Protestant groups.

These results confirm that the tension between religion and the protection of civil rights is perceived by religiously affiliated youth, as well as by participants who consider themselves non-religious. In fact, correlations are slightly more consistent between Catholic and Protestant, showing that they experience a direct tension between the protection of general civil rights and the defence of religious rights: for them, association and expression rights, as well as homosexual rights, are positively correlated with the conformity function of religion, but not with the public function. This tension is not necessarily openly recognised, but is probably producing ambiguity and anxiety in religiously identified youth when having to deal with the growing demand for the general protection of civil rights in society.

In sum, this study offers three general conclusions: (1) the youth do not recognise a strong role for religion in society; (2) they do not see a clear and positive connection between religion and the protection of general civil human rights; and (3) the youth perceive that the main concern of religion in the public space is the protection of religious rights. This pattern holds (with small differences) for all relevant groups of religious affiliation in Chile. These findings indicate that new generations of Chileans have a significantly different perception to the older generations of the role of religion in society; which historically, during the second half of last century, was connected with the protection of human rights and social justice. As such, our results suggest that for most participants, religion has weakened its social role, and is focusing more on the protection of the rights in its own interest. This trend is not only troublesome for religious institutions, which are increasingly losing the trust of the citizens of Chile; it is also problematic for the political culture, since the narrowed interest that the youth see in the behaviour of religious institutions reduces their potential role in supporting public consciousness about the protection of general civil human rights – an essential condition for an effective human rights culture.

References

Blancarte, R. (2014). Dilemas del pasado y retos del presente para la laicidad en América Latina. In A. M. Stuven (Ed.), *La religión en la esfera pública chilena: ¿laicidad o secularización?* (pp. 93–127). Santiago de Chile: Universidad Diego Portales.

Cid, G. (2014). Religión, legitimidad política y esfera pública en Chile: el tránsito de la monarquía a la república (1808–1833). In A. M. Stuven (Ed.), *La religión en la esfera pública chilena: ¿laicidad o secularización?* (p. 149185). Santiago de Chile: Universidad Diego Portales.

Habermas, J. (2006). Entre naturalismo y religión (Vol. 126). Barcelona etc.: Paidós.

Habermas, J., & Taylor, C. (2011). *El poder de la religión en la esfera pública.* Madrid: Trotta.

Instituto Nacional de Derechos Humanos. (2013). Encuesta Nacional de Derechos Humanos. Retrieved from www.indh.cl/encuesta-nacional-de-derechos-humanos-2013

Latinobarómetro. (2014). *Las religiones en tiempo del Papa Francisco.*

Luhmann, N. (2007). *La religión de la sociedad.* Madrid: Trotta.

Luhmann, N. (2009). Sociología de la religión. México D.F.: Herder; UIA.

Pew Research Center. (2014). Religión en América Latina: Cambio generalizado en una región históricamente católica.

PNUD. (2002). *Desarrollo Humano en Chile. Nosotros los chilenos: un desafío cultural.* Santiago: PNUD.

Precht, C. (1998). *En la huella del buen samaritano: breve historia de la Vicaría de la Solidaridad.* Santiago, Chile: Tiberíades.

Rawls, J. (1996). *El liberalismo político.* Barcelona: Crítica.

Silva, E. (2014). Aportes del catolicismo (social) a la política: una mirada desde la recepción del Concilio Vaticano II. In A. M. Stuven (Ed.), *La religión en la esfera pública chilena: ¿laicidad o secularización?* (pp. 287–317). Santiago de Chile: Universidad Diego Portales.

Stuven, A. M. (2014). Desafíos a la confesionalidad del Estado chileno: religión y política, 1840–1883. In A. M. Stuven (Ed.), *La religión en la esfera pública chilena: ¿laicidad o secularización?* (pp. 187–213). Santiago de Chile: Universidad Diego Portales.

Universidad Católica, & Adimark. (2014). Encuesta Nacional Bicentenario. Retrieved from encuestabicentenario.uc.cl/wp-content/uploads/2014/11/Religi%C3%B3n_Encuesta-Bicentenario-20141.pdf

Van der Ven, J. A. (2010). Separation of church and state. In *Human rights or religious rules?* (pp. 304–355). Leiden: Brill.

Yaksic, M. (2011). *Política y religión: teología pública para un mundo plural.* Santiago: Pontificia Universidad Catolica de Chile.

Yuraszeck Krebs, J. F. (2013). Comité Pro Paz: la fuerza de una acción ecuménica. *Mensaje [artículo de Revista], 622*, 27–29.

Chapter 6
Social Capital and Religion in the Public Sphere: Attitudes to Visible Forms of Religion Among Norwegian High-School Students

Pål Ketil Botvar

Abstract Religion has become a contested issue in Norwegian society. Some of the ongoing debates are highly relevant to the rights and freedoms of young people, such as the debate on the use of religious symbols as part of one's attire, and the use of prayer rooms in public schools. This paper will reflect on attitudes to public forms of religion according to social capital theory. Social trust is an essential component of social capital. Trust generated in face-to-face settings develops into a more generalised social trust that has profound effects on complex modern societies. This contribution analyses the explanatory power of social-capital indicators on attitudes to religion in the public sphere. The paper will also discuss additional explanatory factors, such as gender, political views, religiosity and the education level of the parents of young people.

Introduction

Norway and the other Nordic countries have recently experienced public disputes over the use of religious symbols in the public sphere; for example, caricatures of the prophet Mohammed, the laws on blasphemy, prayer rooms in public schools, the building of mosques, and the use of religious symbols as part of the clothing of public servants. In these debates, visible religious symbols and practices in the public sphere are often discussed in relation to human-rights questions. Some argue that religion is a private matter that should be practised outside the public sphere. Others argue that people have a right to express their religious identity openly in the public sphere. What happens when religion becomes more visible in society? Will this lead to more conflict, or to increased tolerance of public forms of religion? The empirical basis for the analysis in this article is a survey conducted among high-school

P.K. Botvar (✉)
KIFO Institute for Church, Religion, and Worldview Research, Oslo, Norway
e-mail: botvar@kifo.no

H.-G. Ziebertz, C. Sterkens (eds.), *Religion and Civil Human Rights in Empirical Perspective*, Religion and Human Rights 2, DOI 10.1007/978-3-319-59285-5_6

students in the Oslo area. The survey is part of an international research project on youth, religion and human rights.[1]

The Research Problem

In 2012, the Norwegian Parliament voted to amend the constitution, in a move that formally abandoned the state church system. This formal change in relations between the state and the national Lutheran church will be implemented in new Acts in the years to come. This means that the Church of Norway will lose some of its former privilege, but at the same time enjoy greater freedom from the state. The main argument for weakening the ties between the state and the national church is the pluralisation of society, and the need for the state to treat all religious groups in society in the same way, without discrimination. When Parliament debated the amendment there was not much opposition, either from political parties or from the church itself. The most voluble opposition came from the agrarian party ('Senterpartiet'), which looks to the state church system as a guarantor that the church will remain liberal, and open to all citizens.

The shifting relationship between church and state requires new policies in the field of religion. As a step towards a new policy, a governmental committee presented a report in 2013 on the practical consequences of the principle of religious freedom (NOU 2013). According to the report, if society is to respect the principle of religious freedom it must be open and generous when it comes to religious symbols and expression in the public sphere. If important societal interests are threatened, the state has legitimate cause to intervene in religious practice.

However, the questions discussed in this article relate to ordinary religious expression and practice. If ordinary religious practice is stopped by the authorities or banned by law, the principle of religious freedom is undermined. If the government places restrictions on ordinary religious activities, in many cases this will also undermine the principle of freedom of expression. For example, if the use of head scarves is prohibited in certain public arenas, this is not only problematic in terms of the principle of freedom of religion, but also infringes on the idea of freedom of expression.

The governmental committee suggests that future policies in the field of religion should be based on human rights, and that religion should be regarded as a legitimate and natural part of society. The main principles laid down in the report are: (a) freedom of religion is a principle protecting all citizens against discrimination on the basis of belief; (b) the religious practice of certain citizens should not infringe the rights and freedoms of others; and (c) the state should not discriminate against any individual because of his or her beliefs.

The committee, consisting of politicians and religious leaders, was also concerned with the religious rights of schoolchildren and students. One of the conclu-

[1] The project is led by Professor Hans-Georg Ziebertz at the University of Würzburg, and details may be found at: www.rhr.theologie.uni-wuerzburg.de

sions in the report was that pupils should be allowed to gather to pray during school hours, and be allowed to wear religious symbols as part of their attire (NOU 2013, 181). It is still an open question if the recommendations in the report will be implemented by the government.

The recommendations from the governmental committee target the state to a large extent. If its vision of a society that is open and generous to religious expression and symbols is to become reality, not only the state but also civil society and the general population must be supportive of the ideas in the report. This is the rationale for this study – a study of which factors support and which factors undermine support for religious symbols and practices in the public sphere.

Theory and Previous Research

The theoretical framework for the empirical analysis is the theory of social capital, as developed by American political scientist Robert D. Putnam (Putnam 1993, 2000, Putnam and Campbell 2010). He is one of the theorists behind the so-called 'social capital perspective'. According to Putnam, social capital comprises features of social relations that enable individuals to cooperate and attain collective goals. In his research, Putnam distinguishes typologically between three elements of social capital: trust, norms of reciprocity, and networks of (civic) engagement, with trust playing a crucial role for the other two. Social capital improves the efficiency of society by facilitating coordinated actions. Putnam (2000, 22–23) further distinguishes between 'bonding' and 'bridging' social capital. Bonding social capital facilitates complementarity and solidarity within a group, while bridging social capital helps to connect groups together that initially are different. Contact between people with different ideological views and social backgrounds helps to prevent prejudice. According to Putnam, face-to-face interaction with others is the basis of social capital. Trust in social institutions is of importance, but more important is the generalised trust we have in our fellow citizens. A high level of social trust is seen as one of the hallmarks of the Nordic countries (Wollebæk 2013).

Putnam sees religion as one of the social capital resources (Putnam 2000, 65–80). His studies of the US suggest that religious organisations play an important role in stocking the country's social capital arsenal (Putnam 2000: 66). In an empirical analysis I will look at how religiosity and social capital are related to tolerance for religion in the public sphere. With the social capital perspective as a starting point, I assume that people who are active in networks and organisations are more likely than others to accept practices that differ from their own. Such groups may be non-governmental organisations or informal networks.

The US is highly diverse when it comes to religion. Even taking this into account, the country has high tolerance for religious symbols and expressions. In *American Grace* (2010), Putnam and Campbell find that religiously active Americans are more trusting and more involved in non-religious voluntary organisations than non-religious people. The explanation is that religiously based networks have a stronger moral component than other networks and organisations. But the US differs from Norway in many respects, not least when it comes to religion. It would therefore be interesting to see if the relationship between religion and social capital is different in Norway to its manifestation in the US.

Dag Wollebæk (2013) is a researcher who used data from Europe to examine the assumption that religious groups develop more social capital than other social groups. His analysis shows that religiosity is negatively related to measures of bridging social capital. Wollebæk questions whether Putnam's findings are transferable to a European context. An analysis based on Norwegian data confirms that a religion-based network mobilises people to engage in other volunteer networks. In his studies, however, Wollebæk finds a negative correlation between the variable 'importance of God' and generalised social trust (Wollebæk 2013, 128).

Previous studies have demonstrated that the Oslo area is more secular than other parts of Norway (Botvar et al. 2010). At the same time, Oslo has the largest proportion of immigrants from more religious countries than the Nordic ones. With the help of data from the survey of students, we will take a closer look at how both religiosity and social capital correlate to attitude to religious expression in the public sphere.

Research Questions

In this study we are interested in how students in a multicultural context in a metropolis consider visible religious symbols and other expressions in the public sphere. To what extent do social trust, participation in networks and contact with people outside your own in-group explain attitudes to religion in the public sphere? Putnam considers religious organisations to be one of the driving forces behind a country's stock of social capital. In this article we will look at social capital as an explanatory factor for attitudes to religion in the public sphere. In the empirical analysis we will also try to ascertain which other factors – both social and demographic – promote religious tolerance and which do not. The following questions will be analysed and answered:

- What attitudes do young people in the Oslo area have to religious symbols and religious expression in the public sphere?
- How do these attitudes vary according to social characteristics, such as gender, political preferences, religiosity, and parents' level of education?
- What is the effect of indicators of social capital on tolerance for public forms of religion?
- Does contact with peers with different beliefs encourage religious tolerance in young people?

Initially we assume that young people in an urban and multicultural setting are more tolerant of practical manifestations of religion than others would be. Previous research has shown that attitudes to public religion vary according to sociological variables. The 2008 Norwegian ISSP survey on religion tells us that women are more tolerant than men, young people more than the elderly, the highly educated more than the less educated; and that those living in the Oslo area are more tolerant than people in other parts of the country (Botvar 2010). We would expect to find some of the same patterns in the current data on young people in the Oslo area.

Conceptual Model

The conceptual model shown in Fig. 6.1 displays three groups of variables: (a) the dependent variables – here, the students' attitudes towards religion in the public sphere, i.e. acceptance of individual religiosity in the public sphere, acceptance of collective religiosity in the public sphere, and support for education in religion; (b) the independent variables – here, three forms of religiosity (belief in God, frequency of prayer, and collective religious activity), and three elements in social capital (institutional trust, generalised social trust, and contact across faith traditions); and lastly (c) the control variables – here, some of the population characteristics of the students, i.e. gender, place of residence, mother's birthplace, political preferences, and parents' education. The conceptual model also displays the relationships between these groups, symbolised by the arrows indicating the impact of one group on another – in this study, the impact of the social capital and religious variables on attitudes towards public forms of religion, while controlling for the impact of the population characteristics on attitudes to the public expression of religion.

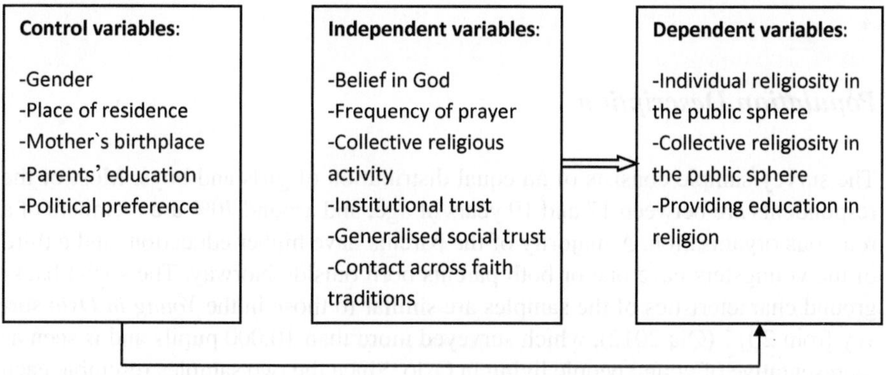

Fig. 6.1 Conceptual model: impact of social capital variables and religion on attitudes to public forms of religion, controlling for gender, place of residence, parents' education and political preferences

Method

Data Collection

The empirical basis of this study is a survey among students in the 16-to-19 age group, from 20 upper secondary schools in the Oslo area. The Norwegian questionnaire is a translation of the original English-language questionnaire, with only a few additional questions.[2] All in all, the questionnaire has 160 items. In this study, 25 of these questions or variables are used. Correlations, factor analyses and regressions are statistical techniques used in the empirical analysis.

We decided to focus on students who have been taught the subject of religion and ethics at high school. The rationale is that these students are better prepared than others to answer questions on the role of religion in the community. According to the curriculum, this particular subject contributes to the students` knowledge of and respect for various religious and ethical views. The subject is also meant to give the students room to reflect on their own identity and standpoints (Utdanningsdirektoratet 2006).

The editor of the *Norwegian Journal for Teachers in Religion* provided a list of religious education teachers in the Oslo area. A mail request was sent to about 30 teachers, 20 of whom expressed their willingness to participate in the study. The teachers distributed our questionnaires to the pupils in the classroom. After having used a school lesson to fill in the questionnaire, each pupil put his or her questionnaire in a sealed envelope and returned it to the teacher. Almost all the pupils present participated – which means about 90% of the class, as around 10% were absent at any given time. The overall response rate is therefore high, but difficult to calculate exactly.

Population Description

The survey sample consists of an equal distribution of girls and boys. Most of the respondents are between 17 and 19 years of age, and around 70% are members of a religious organisation. A majority of the parents have higher education, and a third of the youngsters have one or both parents born outside Norway. The social background characteristics of the samples are similar to those in the *Young in Oslo* survey from 2012 (Øia 2012), which surveyed more than 10,000 pupils and is seen as representative of young people living in Oslo. Since the two samples resemble each other in terms of all the background variables, we may conclude that our sample is representative of young people in upper secondary schools around Oslo.

[2] The English questionnaire was developed by a team of researchers connected with the international project and discussed by a group of about 20 researchers in a meeting in Wurzburg on 9–12 December 2012.

Measuring Instruments

Dependent Variables

This study uses six items to measure attitudes towards public forms of religion.

The first two items are intended to capture the acceptance of individual religious expressions in the public sphere.[3] The next two capture attitudes to collective religious expressions.[4] The last two items capture attitudes to society's obligation to offer education in religion. The items are formulated as statements with which respondents must agree or disagree, according to a five-point scale. The questions are organised in order to show the respondents' acceptance of the content of each item. The items are thus seen as part of the operationalisation of different forms of religion in the public sphere, called 'acceptance of individual expression', 'acceptance of collective expression' and 'supporting education in religion'.

Statements used to measure attitudes towards 'individual expression':

- Students should be offered time, space and a room in the school to conduct their prayers.
- The state should not prevent female teachers from wearing a head scarf for religious reasons.

Statements used to measure attitudes towards 'collective expression':

- The state should not interfere with missionary activities in either majority or minority religions.
- The state should not interfere with public manifestations by majority or minority religions.

Statements that measure the state's obligation to provide 'education in religion':

- The state should respect the right of religions to establish schools.
- The government should provide enough school time so that religion can be taught in schools.

Table 6.1 shows that young people tend to be divided when it comes to attitudes to religion in the public sphere. However, there is a tendency for the students to lean towards accepting religious symbols and practices in the public sphere, in the form of head scarfs among teachers, and missionary activities.

To investigate whether the six items can be used to construct indexes measuring the theoretical dimensions, we have conducted a factor analysis, and this shows that the six items constitute three separate dimensions or factors in the material (Table 6.2).

[3]The individual right to practise one's religion openly is often referred to as 'freedom to religion'.

[4]The right to form religious groups and to act collectively is often referred to as 'freedom of religion'.

Table 6.1 Descriptive statistics for attitudes towards public forms of religion (n = 988)

	Min	Max	Mean	Std. Dev.
Acceptance of prayer rooms	1	5	2.7	1.24
Acceptance of head scarves among teachers	1	5	3.2	1.35
Acceptance of religious symbols in the public sphere	1	5	2.7	1.09
Acceptance of missionary activities	1	5	3.1	1.04
Provision of religious free schools	1	5	3.2	1.13
Provision of education in religion	1	5	3.5	1.15

Table 6.2 Factor analysis (PC, varimax rotation) of the six questions relating to public religion

	Component		
	1	2	3
Acceptance of prayer rooms	.763		
Acceptance of head scarves among teachers	.873		
Acceptance of religious symbols in the public sphere		.835	
Acceptance of missionary activities		.799	
Provision of religious free schools			.718
Provision of education in religion			.838
Eigenvalue	2.55	.97	.77
Total explained variance	42%	16%	13%

A reliability test confirms that the three pairs of statements can be used to construct three indexes. The first two have Cronbach's alpha values of .66 and .59 respectively. The third has an alpha value of .51, which is a little weak as a basis for index construction. The dominant factor in the material is the dimension of 'individual expression'. The factor that measures support for 'religious education' is the weakest. There is a positive correlation between the indexes. The strongest correlation is between the index 'individual expression' and 'religious education' (Pearson r .45). The weakest is between 'collective expression' and 'religious education' (r .31).

Table 6.3 shows that young people are divided when it comes to attitudes to religion in the public sphere. The range is greatest when it comes to views on 'individual expression'. Only 'religious education' has a clear majority leaning towards the acceptance side.

Table 6.3 Descriptive statistics for the three indexes 'individual expression', 'collective expression', and 'education in religion'

	Min	Max	Mean	Std. Dev.
Individual expression	1	9	4.9	2.24
Collective expression	1	9	4.9	1.79
Education in religion	1	9	5.6	1.87

Independent Variables

In addition to a standard set of social background variables (gender, residence, political views, parents' education level), we include variables related to religion and social capital. From the social capital perspective, trust in institutions is an important issue. But more important than institutional trust is interpersonal trust in our fellow citizens. According to Putnam, social capital is produced first and foremost through contact with the people we meet in everyday situations (Putnam 1993, 171).

Being part of a social network of like-minded people can promote social capital by establishing a safe haven for the individual, and thus preparing him or her to interact with people in other groups. It is when individuals meet with people from other groups that bridging social capital may evolve (Putnam 2000, 22–23). In a societal context, the bridging form of social capital is the most important one.

In Table 6.4 we see the number of students expressing a high degree of trust in social institutions. The Norwegian economy receives the highest scores, with the healthcare system and the educational system scoring somewhat lower. This suggests that young people have a critical and reflective attitude to social institutions. The high scores for the economy, democracy and the police tell us that Norway is generally regarded as a stable and good society in which to live.

The six items in Table 6.4 are positively correlated. This means that people who have confidence in one of the institutions also tend to trust other institutions. A reliability test shows that the six items can be combined in an index measuring institutional trust (Cronbach's alpha .62).

Table 6.4 Percentage of students with a high degree of confidence in various institutions

	High degree of trust (%)
The economy	80
The democracy	79
The police	77
The healthcare system	54
The education system	49
The government	46

Degree of interpersonal trust is measured by the question 'Think of people you meet in everyday situations; in general, do you think they can be trusted or not?' As with the majority of the questions, there are five answer categories. Below we have merged the two categories for agreement and the two for disagreement. Ideally, we would have had more than one question for measuring interpersonal trust; but since this is an addition to the international dataset, we had to be selective when adding new variables (Table 6.5).

The largest group of students completely or partially agree that people they meet in everyday situations can be trusted. Only a small minority indicate that they encounter their fellow citizens with a feeling of mistrust.

Table 6.5 Degree of trust in fellow citizens

	%
High degree of confidence	41
Medium degree of confidence	33
Low degree of confidence	25
Total	99
N	988

The survey included several statements about contact with people who have other core values than theirs. Studies of immigrants show that social contact across social boundaries breaks down prejudice and creates accepting attitudes to others (Hernes & Knudsen 1990, Hagelund & Jill Loga 2009). Contact with other faith groups is measured by using three items that are combined in an index. According to the survey, young people in the Oslo area have a great deal of contact across faith traditions. In the survey we asked young people how often they had contact with other youngsters of different faith traditions to their own (Table 6.6).

Table 6.6 Percentage of young people who often or very often have contact with young people of different faiths to their own

	%
Often speak with people of another faith	65
Often meet with people of another faith during spare time	54
Often visit people of another faith	40

The three variables are all five-point scales, ranging from 'never' to 'very often'. A reliability test shows that the three variables can be combined in an index expressing degree of contact across faith traditions (Cronbach's alpha .88).

When it comes to religiosity, we focus on measures that are widely used in research on religion, such as belief in God, praying and religious-ceremony attendance. Putnam is especially concerned with participation in religious communities, because it gives people experience in dealing with others. But religions and religious organisations are different, and not all are committed to community building. In Norway, private forms of religiosity are widespread. It is true that relatively few people are engaged with religious organisations on a regular basis, and church attendance is low. However, many people believe in some sort of higher power. This kind of private religiosity may also help to promote moral behaviour. Nonetheless, according to Putnam, collective forms of religiosity are what matters most when it comes to building social capital.

In our survey we found that a majority of the students have little interest in religious questions. Oslo is a multicultural society, and also a secularised society (Table 6.7).

Of the young people in our sample, 47% stated that they do not feel that they belong to any religion or religious group. This is high when taking into account that nationally, 75% of the population belongs formally to the Norwegian Lutheran church. The corresponding figure for the municipality of Oslo is 57% (Brottveit &

Table 6.7 Percentage of upper secondary school students in the Oslo area believing or practising religion

	%
Believe in a personal god[a]	20
Pray at least once a week	13
Participate at least monthly in religious group, church etc.	11

[a]The percentage is those answering 'agree' or 'fully agree' to the statement 'I experience a personal bond between God and me'

Holberg 2014). The number specifying that they belong to other religions than the Christian religion amounts to 10%. Formal membership is not seen as important from a social capital point of view. More important is the subjective feeling of belonging to a group and participating in the collective activities of the group.

Regression Analyses

In the multivariate analysis we include a set of sociological background variables in addition to the independent variables described above. In previous studies, gender has had an impact on religion in the public sphere (Botvar 2010). Initially we assume that girls are more positive to religion in the public sphere than boys, because girls in previous studies were more interested in religion in general. Age is not a relevant factor in our analysis, since all the students are around 18 years old. Immigration background is measured by a question about the mother's birthplace. It turns out that 24% of the sample has a mother born outside of Norway. This corresponds roughly to the proportion with an immigrant background in other studies of youth in Oslo (Botvar 2014, 50).[5] The parents' level of education is included in the analysis. Parents and home are assumed to have a profound influence on the way young people reason. Education is an interesting variable when it comes to tolerating religious symbols. Previous research has shown that a high level of education goes hand in hand with tolerance (Botvar 2010). In our study, the education level of the parents is quite high – over half (53%) of the students have both a mother and a father who have undergone tertiary education.

I now present a stepwise regression analysis of attitudes to religion in the public sphere. The dependent variables are 'individual expression', 'collective expression' and 'religious education'. Regression analysis means that we isolate the effect that each of the independent variables has on the dependent variables. We want to discover how much of the variance in attitudes to religion in the public sphere is

[5]The majority of students are affiliated with schools in Oslo. A minority of the students go to schools in the neighbouring county of Akershus or in the city of Drammen, urban areas just outside of Oslo. This makes it possible to operate with the variable go to schools in Oslo/outside Oslo.

Table 6.8 Regression analysis (method: enter) with attitudes to 'individual expression' as the dependent variable. (N = 987)

	Model 1	Model 2	Model 3
Gender (Female = 0)	−.19***	−.16***	−.16***
Living in Oslo	.08***	.06*	.06
Parents' education level (1–10)	−.08*	−.06*	−.09**
Political left-right scale (1–10)	−.20***	−.20***	−.18***
Mother born outside Norway	.14***	.09**	.09**
Belief in god		.06	.05
Frequency of prayer		.15***	.15***
Collective religious activity		.04	.04
Institutional trust			.03
Generalised social trust			.09**
Contact across faith traditions			.09**
Explained variance (R^2)	13%	17%	19%

*p < .05; **p < .01; ***p < .001

explained by the independent variables, which are 'social background', 'political views', 'religiosity' and 'social capital' (Table 6.8).[6]

The final model explains 19% of the variation in attitudes to 'individual religious expression in the public sphere'. Several of the independent variables show significant effects in the regression. The social background variables are weakened when religiosity and social capital are included in the analysis. Gender, parents' education, political views and immigration have significant effect. The effect of place of residence is not significant when all the other variables are included in the analysis. Girls thus have a more accepting attitude than boys.

Parents' education level has a negative effect on acceptance of religion in the public. The effect of political views means that people who belong to the political right are more sceptical of visible religion than are people on the political left. Those with a mother born outside of Norway tend to be more positive to religion in the public sphere than others.

When it comes to religiosity, 'praying' is the only variable that has significant effect. Those who pray regularly and more often than others have a positive attitude to public forms of religion. The effect of prayer remains significant after social capital variables have been inserted into the model. Among these, 'trust in fellow citizens' and 'contact across faith' have a significant impact. 'Institutional trust' has no significant effect on this dependent variable.

In Table 6.9, the final model only explains a small proportion of the variance in attitudes (7%). Of the social background variables, only 'immigrant background' has significant effect, and when it comes to the religious variables, both 'praying' and 'attendance' have an effect. 'Belief in God' has no effect. Interestingly, the

[6] 'Political view' is self-placement on a 10-point left-to-right scale.

Table 6.9 Regression analysis (method: enter) with acceptance of 'collective expression' as the dependent variable. (N = 985)

	Model 1	Model 2	Model 3
Gender (Female = 0)	–.04	–.02	–.02
Living in Oslo	.04	.01	.01
Parents' education level (1–10)	–.02	–.01	–.03
Political left-right scale (1–10)	–.04	–.05	–.03
Mother born outside Norway	.06 *	.01	.02
Belief in god		.05	.04
Frequency of prayer		.09 *	.10 *
Collective religious activity		.13 **	.13 **
Institutional trust			–.01
Generalised social trust			.10 **
Contact across faith traditions			.05
Explained variance (R^2)	1%	6%	7%

*p < .05; **p < .01; ***p < .001

effect of religiosity ('praying' and 'attendance') remains significant after social capital variables are added to the analysis. Among these, only the variable 'social trust' has statistical effect.

The last Table 6.10 is about the degree of support for the state provision of religious education.

Table 6.10 Regression analysis (method: enter) with 'support for religious education' as the dependent variable. N = 987

	Model 1	Model 2	Model 3
Gender (Female = 0)	–.20 ***	–.16 ***	–.15 ***
Living in Oslo	.06 *	.03	.03
Parents' education level (1–10)	–.05	–.03	–.07 *
Political left-right scale (1–10)	–.08 **	–.09 **	–.08 **
Mother born outside Norway	.10 **	.04	.05
Belief in god		.12 **	.10 **
Frequency of prayer		.10 *	.11 *
Collective religious activity		.13 **	.12 **
Institutional trust			.13 ***
Generalised social trust			.06 *
Contact across faith traditions			.06 *
Explained variance (R^2)	7%	15%	18%

*p < .05; **p < .01; ***p < .001

Altogether, the set of independent variables explains 18% of the variance in attitudes. Of the background variables, 'gender', 'parents' education level' and 'political views' have significant effects. These effects resemble what we found in the analysis of 'individual expression'. Girls are more positive about 'religious education' than boys are. 'Parents' education level' has a negative effect on support for religious education. Those leaning more to the left side of the political landscape are more positive than those leaning to the right. All three religious variables have positive effects: 'belief in God', 'praying' and 'attendance' are all predictors of support for religious education. Religiosity has an effect that is independent of social capital. Moreover, the three variables related to social capital have a positive effect on attitudes to 'religious education'. In contrast to what we found in the previous analysis, 'trust in institutions' has the strongest effect. This is not surprising when the dependent variable refers to government policies in the field of education.

Discussion and Conclusion

In recent years, religion has gained a more prominent position in public life. Religious expressions and religious symbols are often a topic of public debate. While these debates have led some people to be negative to public forms of religion, others have become concerned about the human-rights aspects of visible religious symbols in the public sphere.

The abandonment of the state church model in 2012 requires new policies in the field of religion. A report from a governmental committee suggests that future policies in this field should be regarded as a legitimate and natural part of society. If this vision is to become reality, not only the state but also civil society must be supportive of it. It is especially important that the young generation of future leaders will act in accordance with the principles laid down in the report. Young people in the Oslo area have been raised in a multicultural setting, and should therefore be used to dealing with cultural diversity.

According to this study, however, young people in the Oslo area do not fully agree with the governmental report on all issues relating to public forms of religion. The data shows that young people in Oslo are quite divided when it comes to certain forms of public religion, such as visible religious symbols in the public sphere.

The empirical analysis demonstrated that social capital is a fruitful perspective when analysing attitudes to public forms of religion. As could be expected when bearing Putnam's theory in mind, what is called 'generalised social trust' is the one dimension of social capital that has a positive impact on all three dependent variables. 'Institutional trust' and 'contact across faith traditions' have an effect on some but not all of the dependent variables. The analysis suggests that 'social trust' is a significant factor when it comes to explaining attitudes to religion in the public sphere. This is an encouraging result, seen from a societal perspective.

Another interesting finding is that the religious variables tend to have an effect on the attitudes we are studying independently of the social capital variables. On one hand, this supports Putnam's claim that religion contributes to tolerance for others. On the other, our analysis does not show that the effect of religion on tolerance is through social trust, as Putnam argues. According to our analysis, both religiosity and social trust have impact on attitudes to religion in the public arena, independently of one another.

Norway is a country with a high degree of social trust. Young people in the Oslo area are also characterised a by high score on variables relating to trust. They report having a great deal of contact with people who have different beliefs from their own. This type of contact underpins an accepting attitude to public forms of religion. Even though young people in Oslo are perceived as more secular than young people elsewhere in Norway, the data suggests that there is no sharp social divide between those who believe and those who do not. On the contrary, there seems to be significant contact across all kinds of world view. Such contact does not take place randomly and without obligations, but also in the form of close relations and home visits to people of different faiths. This finding is in harmony with the vision that the governmental committee mentioned in the beginning of this article has for Norwegian society. According to their report, in order to respect the principle of religious freedom society must be open and generous when it comes to religious symbols and expression in the public sphere.

References

Botvar, P. K. (2010). 'Mellom det offentlige og det private'. (Between the public and the private). In P. K. Botvar & U. Schmidt (Eds.), *Religion i dagens Norge, Mellom sekularisering og sakralisering. (Religion in Today's Norway. Between Secularisation and Sacralisation)*. Oslo: Universitetsforlaget.

Botvar, P. K. (2014). 'Unge mennesker er skeptiske til religion i den offentlige sfære'. (young people are sceptical of religion in the public sphere). *Religion and beliefs, Tidsskrift for Religionslærerforeningen i Norge, 26*(2), 49–56.

Brottveit, Å., & Holberg, S. E. (2014). 'Survey report for the Norwegian church in 2014'. *KIFO rapport* no. 2/2014.

Botvar, P. K., Repstad, P., & Aagedal, O. (2010). 'Regionalisering av norsk religiøsitet'. (Regionalisation of Norwegian religiosity). In P. K. Botvar & U. Schmidt (Eds.), *Religion i dagens Norge. Mellom sekularisering og sakralisering. (Religion in Today's Norway. Between Secularisation and Sacralisation)*. Oslo: Universitetsforlaget.

Hagelund, M., & Loga, J. (2009). 'Voluntary, immigration, integration'. Centre for Research on the Civil Society and Voluntary Sector, 2009: 1.

Hernes, G., & Knudsen, K. (1990). 'Svart på hvitt. Norske holdninger til flyktninger, asylsøkere og innvandrere'. (Black on white. Norwegian reactions to refugees, asylum seekers and immigrants). *FAFO rapport 109*.

NOU. (2013). 1 *Det livssynsåpne samfunn.* En helhetlig tros- og livssynspolitikk. Oslo: Ministry of Culture.

Putnam, R. D. (1993). *Making democracy work: Civic traditions in modern Italy*. Princeton: Princeton University Press.

Putnam, R. D. (2000). *Bowling alone: The collapse and revival of the American community*. New York: Simon and Schuster.
Putnam, R. D., & Campbell, D. E. (2010). American grace. How Religion Divides and Unites Us. New York: Simon & Schuster.
Utdanningsdirektoratet. (2006). *Subject curriculum: Religion and ethics – Common core subject – General studies educational programme*. Utdanningsdirektoratet. (The Norwegian Directorate for Education and Training).
Wollebæk, Day. (2013). 'Religion og sosial kapital. Hva kan spørreundersøkelser fortelle oss?' (Religion and social capital: What do international surveys tell us?) *Rapport* 2013 (4). Senter for forskning på sivilsamfunn og frivillige organisasjoner.
Øia, T. (2012). 'Young people in Oslo 2012. Key measure'. *Notat 7/12*. NOVA (Norwegian Institute for Research on Adolescence, Welfare and Aging).

Chapter 7
Freedom of Religion and Freedom of Religious Clothing and Symbols in School: Exploring the Impact of Church Schools in a Religiously Diverse Society

Leslie J. Francis, Andrew Village, Ursula McKenna, and Gemma Penny

Abstract The Young People's Attitudes to Religious Diversity Project was established to compare the attitudes of students (13- to 15-years of age) educated within the state-maintained sector in church schools (Catholic, Anglican, joint Anglican and Catholic) and in schools without a religious foundation. Data provided by 2385 students recruited from England, Wales and London who self-identified as either 'no religion' or as Christian demonstrated that personal factors (especially sex), psychological factors (especially psychoticism) and religious factors (especially personal prayer) were all significantly related to attitude toward freedom of religious clothing and symbols in school. After controlling for sex and for individual differences in personality and in religiosity, students attending church schools hold neither a more positive nor a less positive attitude toward freedom of religious clothing and symbols in school (according to various religious traditions), compared with students attending schools without a religious foundation.

Introduction

The Universal Declaration of Human Rights was adopted by the General Assembly of the United Nations in December 1948. It was written in response to the atrocities of the Second World War and attempted, through its thirty Articles, to identify fundamental rights to which all human beings are entitled. In particular Article 18 deals with freedom of religion or belief, where the linkage of religion and belief may embrace non-religious worldviews.

L.J. Francis (✉) • U. McKenna • G. Penny
Warwick Religions & Education Research Unit, Centre for Education Studies, University of Warwick, Coventry CV4 7AL, UK
e-mail: leslie.francis@warwick.ac.uk

A. Village
University of York St John, York, UK

H.-G. Ziebertz, C. Sterkens (eds.), *Religion and Civil Human Rights in Empirical Perspective*, Religion and Human Rights 2, DOI 10.1007/978-3-319-59285-5_7

> Everyone has the right to freedom of thought, conscience and religion; this right includes freedom to change his religion or belief, and freedom, either alone or in community with others and in public or private, to manifest his religion or belief in teaching, practice, worship and observance.

The right to freedom of religion was also embedded within the European Convention for the Protection of Human Rights and Fundamental Freedoms (Council of Europe, 1950, Article 8), within the International Covenant on Civil and Political Rights (1966, Article 18), and within the European Union Charter of Fundamental Rights (2000, Article 10).

Van der Ven (2012), in his considered examination of 'religious liberty in political perspective', draws particular attention to the third part of Article 18 of the Universal Declaration of Human Rights that speaks of 'freedom, either alone or in community with others and in public or private, to manifest his religion or belief' as referring to the *forum externum* in which individuals are entitled to manifest their religion or belief. In this sense, religion or belief is not confined to the personal and to the interior space, but may be visible within the public arena. At the same time, van der Ven (2012) draws attention to the limitations placed on the public manifestation of religion or belief. For example, the third paragraph of Article 18 in the International Covenant on Civil and Political Rights (1965) refers to some 'limitations prescribed by law and being necessary to protect public safety, order, health, or morals or the fundamental rights and freedoms of others. One clear and visible sign of religion expressed within the public arena is seen in the form of wearing and displaying religious clothing and symbols. At the same time, there are also good reasons voiced for restricting certain religious clothing and symbols in specific contexts: labour rules may prohibit wearing veils in some professional contexts and prison rules may prohibit wearing a prayer chain.

Freedom of Religious Clothing and Symbols

The matter of wearing religious clothing and symbols in public spaces has been seen to be of sufficient significance for the Council of Europe to publish a *Manual on the wearing of religious symbols in public areas*. The aim of this manual is to clarify the concept of religious symbols and to provide guidance on the criteria used by the European Council of Human Rights in its case law (Evans 2008). In essence, the case law show that the European Court of Human Rights takes a flexible approach in which it is for individuals to determine what counts for them as religious symbols, but it does not conclude that the wearing of religious symbols may not be subject to restrictions by the states. In a ruling on 1 July 2014, in a case against France, the ECHR ruled that the French ban on veiling the face in public did not breach the European Convention on Human Rights (see http://hudoc.echr.coe.int/eng?i=001-145466#{"itemid":["001-145466"]}). In this context restrictions on the manifestation of religion or belief by students (say by displaying religious clothing or symbols) need to be objectively justified, say in the pursuit of legitimate aims of promoting public safety, personal or collective health, or civic order, or of protecting the rights of others.

According to Council of Europe (2014, p. 83) different countries within Europe have different policies on the wearing of religious dress and religious symbols. BBC News (2014) provides a detailed breakdown of the situation in various countries. A brief summary of these different European laws are now given followed by a more detailed look at the situation in France and the UK. At one end of the spectrum there are countries (for example, France, Belgium) where there are national bans in place on some religious dress and symbols in public places. A law banning the full-face veil came into effect in Belgium in 2011. At the other end of the spectrum there are countries such as The Netherlands, Turkey and Norway where there are currently no bans in force – though this may not always have been the case and may currently be subject to debate. The Netherlands did have plans to impose a ban but these collapsed when a change of government took place in 2012. In Turkey the wearing of the hijab was prohibited in 2004 in state institutions such as universities and schools (Blair and Aps 2005, p. 7). In 2013 this ban was removed – with the exception of the judiciary, military and police. Likewise, in Norway female police officers are forbidden from wearing the hijab. With the 2014 ECHR ruling supporting France's assertion that a public ban does not violate the human rights of Muslim women, Norway is also now revisiting this wider issue (see http://www.thelocal.no/20140702/norway-braced-for-burqa-ban-debate). In between these two positions there are countries where there is no national ban, but where individual regions may have their own laws which place restrictions on certain items of dress (for example, Spain, Italy, Germany). Though there is no plan for a national ban in Spain, in 2010 the city of Barcelona became the first in Spain to ban the full-face Islamic veil in public buildings. Likewise, several towns in Italy have local bans on face-covering veils and the wearing of the burka. Although during 2003 in Germany controversy arose over discrimination against a female teacher who wore the hijab, there is no national law restricting the wearing of veils. However, states can change their laws locally and at least half of Germany's 16 states have banned teachers from wearing headscarves. Where bans are in place, it tends to be the full face covering rather than the headscarf which is prohibited. Finally, there are countries where there is no national ban but where policy on wearing uniforms can come into conflict with the freedom to wear such dress and symbols (for example, UK, Denmark). In 2008, the government of Denmark announced it would bar judges from wearing headscarves and similar religious or political symbols (including the Christian crucifix, the Jewish kippah and the Sikh turban) in courtrooms. Somc have called for the ban to be extended to include school teachers and medical personnel.

Perhaps the most documented position is that of France which has long had a strict system of separation of State and Church and a rejection of any action or public expression of faith that might threaten the French ideal of equality or *Laicite*. The wearing of distinctive religious dress and symbols in public schools was banned in 2004 including the wearing of veils, headscarves and turbans. Policy guidance defined these religious symbols as those 'the wearing of which leads immediately to identification of a religious affiliation, such as the Muslim hijab, the kippah, or a cross of manifestly excessive dimensions' (Massignon 2011, p. 166). Massignon (2011, p.160) cites evidence from Chérifi (2005) that the 2004 law forbidding wearing religious symbols calmed conflicts in school caused by the expression of religious affiliation by certain pupils. Further surveys in France have shown that opinion shifted from 43% in favour of banning the hijab in school in 2003, to 76% in favour in September 2004 (Tévanian 2005, cited in Massignon 2011, p. 166). In 2010, a further act resulted in the ban on covering the face in public places whether by mask, helmet or veil and included the burka if it covered the face. France thus became the first European country to ban the full-face Islamic veil in public places.

Although there is no ban on religious dress or symbols in the UK, schools are allowed to decide their own dress codes and it is these regulations concerning school uniform which have increasingly come into conflict with the issue of religious dress and symbols. In 1990 two Muslim girls were refused entry to their classes at a Manchester school for wearing headscarves (Liederman 2000) and in 2004 a Bedfordshire schoolgirl pursued her grievance against school uniform policy, which forbade the wearing of the jilbab, to the Court of Appeal (Blair and Aps 2005, pp. 7–8). In the case of the latter, the issue went first to the High Court which found in favour of the school concluding that the girl's exclusion from school was a result of her breach of school uniform rules rather than because of her religious beliefs. The case then progressed to the Court of Appeal where judges in the case, whilst emphasising that it might be possible for the school to have a lawful policy restricting the wearing of the jilbab, found the failure of the school to consider explicitly the affected pupil's human rights in reaching a decision was a breach of those rights. As Blair and Aps (2005, p. 8) conclude, having met the needs of the majority it is not simply for the minority to obey the policy and if they do not like it to choose an alternative. The infringement needs to be acknowledged and justified.

As both Blair and Aps (2005) and more recently Berry (2013) demonstrate using legal case law from both France and the UK there is both divergence and inconsistency between the approaches taken and conclusions drawn by different human rights committees and organisations (such as the Human Rights Commission and the European Court of Human Rights) and between different sections of the legal system such as the High Court and Court of Appeal. As Berry (2013) notes, the European Court of Human Rights has been willing to accept restrictions on the right to manifest religion by wearing religious attire under article 9(2) of the European Convention on Human Rights on the grounds of the 'rights and freedoms of others', (specifically gender equality, pluralism and tolerance and State neutrality) and public order and safety. However, the wide margin of appreciation afforded to States and the failure of the Convention to probe whether restrictions on the right to manifest religion are proportionate have been subject to criticism. It is not surprising that some schools and teachers may be confused as to what approach to take in the best interests of their schools and for all their pupils.

For some 13- to 15-year-old students abstract human rights issues may seem to stand at a considerable distance from their everyday experience in general and from their classroom experience in particular. This is clearly not the case, however, for freedom of religion or belief, when religion or belief is expressed in the classroom by students who openly display their religion or belief through wearing religious clothing or religious symbols, whether the Christian cross, the Muslim headscarf, burka or Niqab, the Sikh turban, kara, or kirpan, the Jewish Star of David or the kippah/yamalke, or the Hindu bindi. Here are very visible and tangible signs and symbols of religion or beliefs.

The relevance of this issue for students was confirmed by the Council of Europe's recent document on policy and practice for teaching about religions and non-religious worldviews in intercultural education, *Signposts*, in chapter eight concerning human rights issues (Council of Europe 2014). This chapter locates religious education within the Council of Europe's wider activity related to human rights education and education for democratic citizenship. *Signposts* introduces this issue in the following way.

> One particular issue faced by some young people from religious backgrounds, and also frequently by their parents, is the wearing of religious symbols in public areas such as school. This was raised as a matter of debate within their own countries by several respondents to the questionnaire sent out to members of the Council of Europe Education Committee (Council of Europe 2014, p. 83).

The relevance of these issues for students has also been confirmed by the research project known as REDCo (Religion in Education: a Contribution to Dialogue or a factor for Conflict in Transforming Societies of European Countries) that collected the views of teenagers, between the ages of 14 and 16 years, from eight European countries on teaching and learning about religious diversity in schools. The quantitative survey (Valk et al. 2009, pp. 437–446) asked students whether they agreed or disagreed with two specific statements on the wearing of religious symbols at school: Students should be able to wear religious symbols at school… discreet ones (e.g. small crosses, etc. on necklace); Students should be able to wear religious symbols at school… more visible ones (e.g. headscarves).

The data for each country related to these two questions can be found in the relevant national chapters contained in Valk et al. (2009) though there are inconsistencies, both in how each national team reported their data and the emphasis given to these two questions, which makes direct comparison difficult. The results showed that in all countries a majority of students did not oppose the wearing of discrete religious symbols in school. The numbers agreeing were: Russia 90% (p. 329), England 85%,[1] France 78% (p. 146) and Germany over 70%. For Norway, Spain and The Netherlands no percentages are given, although, the conclusions reported by the authors, based on the data, are that a majority of students in each country favoured this position.

With regard to more visible symbols and dress there were some clear national differences, which in most cases reflect the approaches taken on this issue by the respective national governments. In Norway the numbers of students agreeing with the wearing of visible symbols was 64% (p. 287), in England 55%,[2] in Germany less

[1] Recalculated from the original data.

[2] Recalculated from the original data.

than half (p. 190), in Russia 20% (p. 329), and in France only 17% (p. 146). The Netherlands team report that a majority were in favour but to a lesser extent than the numbers agreeing to discrete symbols (p. 238) and for Spain the team report that the majority of students were against the wearing of visible symbols thus adopting a point of view in accordance with the French law of 2004 (p. 391). Thus, there are some significant differences, for example, in responses from French and Norwegian students that suggest that French students have internalised the 2004 law that only allows the wearing of discrete religious signs on school grounds in contrast to Norwegian students who are 'liberal in terms of 'visible religion' in school partly reflecting the liberal attitude prevailing in Norway in these matters' (Skeie and von der Lippe 2009, p. 291).

Church Schools

The question regarding freedom of religion and of religious clothing and symbols within schools raises an interesting political question about the position of church schools within religiously diverse societies. Church schools within England and Wales have a particularly long history, because the current system of public education had its origins in the initiative of church-related voluntary societies during the first half of the nineteenth century, including the Anglican National Society in 1811, the Free Church British and Foreign School Society in 1814 and the Catholic Poor Schools Committee in 1847. When the Government first voted a budget for building schools in 1833 money was distributed through the voluntary societies (see Cruickshank 1963; Murphy 1971; Chadwick 1997). Not until the Education Act 1870 did the Government establish a mechanism for building schools independently from the voluntary societies (Rich 1970). The continuation of church schools operating alongside schools without a religious foundation was supported by the Education Act 1902, the Education Act 1944, and the Education Reform Act 1988. Since legislation following the Education Reform Act 1988 has tended to refer to church schools by the more inclusive term 'schools with a religious character', it is this nomenclature that will be consistently employed through the rest of this paper.

During the 1980s England and Wales became increasingly self-conscious of growing cultural, ethnic and religious diversity. In particular during that decade two significant reports began to question the continuing role of church schools, suggesting that such educational provision may fail to prepare students adequately for life in face of such growing diversity. First, in their report *Race and Church Schools* from the Runnymede Trust, Dummett and McNeal (1981) argued that in areas where the black community was not Christian, church schools had the effect of preventing multiracial institutions and so were in danger of enhancing prejudice. Second, in their report *Education for All* the Government's Committee of Enquiry into the education of children from ethnic minority groups stressed misgivings about the implications and consequences of schools for established religious and ethnic groups (Swann Report 1985).

The Runnymede Trust re-voiced and sharpened its critique of the place of church schools in religiously diverse society during the late 2000s in its report *Right to Divide? Faith schools and community cohesion* (Berkeley 2008). Here was a report asking the question ‘whether a school system with faith schools could also promote equality and cohesion’ (p. 2). The project took as the starting point the guidance issued to schools as ‘their statutory duty to promote community cohesion, introduced in 2007’ (p. 3), and consulted with over a thousand people, including ‘parents, pupils, professionals, and policy makers from a range of faith backgrounds as well as those who do not subscribe to any religion’ (p. 1). The aim of the consultation was ‘to assess whether faith schools are well placed to deliver their obligations in this regard in the following areas’ (p. 4): encouraging students to share a sense of belonging; helping students develop a positive appreciation of diversity; removing barriers to inequality; and building strong partnerships between people from different backgrounds.

The six key recommendations put forward by the Runnymede Trust were, in one sense, very supportive of schools with a religious character. Such schools are supported as affirming government policies committed to increasing choice and diversity in the education sector. In another sense, however, the types of schools with a religious character being supported by the Runnymede Trust are very different from many of those currently supported within the state-maintained system in England and Wales. The first call from the Runnymede Trust is for schools with a religious character to cease to include faith criteria within their admissions policies. The argument is pitched as follows:

> Faith schools should be for the benefit of all in society rather than for just a few. If faith schools are convinced of their relevance for society, then that should apply equally for all children. With state funding comes an obligation to be relevant and open to all citizens … All parents should be given access to what faith schools claim is a distinctive ethos (Berkeley 2008, p. 4).

The recommendation is based on the following evidence:

> Our research has found that commitment to the promotion of cohesion is not universal, and for many faith schools not a priority … Too often, there remains a resistance to learning about other faiths when faith schools are seen as the spaces in which singular faith identities and traditions are transmitted (Berkeley 2008, p. 4–5).

If the Runnymede Trust is correct in its assertion that church schools are failing to equip young people for life in religiously diverse societies, we would hypothesise that students attending such schools will hold a less positive attitude toward freedom of religious clothing and symbols in schools. Before this hypothesis can be addressed with empirical data, however, consideration has to be given to the way in which the identification of school differences may be contaminated by other individual differences. In other words, consideration needs to be given to identifying appropriate control variables. Two categories of control variables may be of particular significance: personal and psychological factors, and religious factors.

Personal and Psychological Control Variables

Conceptually, attitudes toward religious diversity can be situated within the much larger domain of social attitudes. The long-established research tradition concerned with the exploration and explanation of individual differences in social attitudes has drawn attention to the significant predictive power of both personal factors and psychological factors. For example, in his review of the social scientific literature and new empirical evidence concerning factors shaping adolescent values, Francis (2001) documented the significance of two personal factors in particular (sex and age) across a range of personal and social values. Before testing for school influence, it would be prudent to control for individual differences in sex and age.

In terms of psychological factors, the Eysenckian research tradition in particular has documented the connection between social attitudes and personality. Within this framework conceptualisation has distinguished between the categories of tenderminded social attitudes (emphasising, for example, social inclusivity and acceptance) and toughminded social attitudes (including, for example, social exclusion and prejudice). In two now classic brief papers, Eysenck (1975, 1976) formulated the connection between low psychoticism scores and tenderminded social attitudes. The Eysenckian notion of psychoticism as a dimension of personality found expression in the Eysenck Personality Questionnaire (EPQ: Eysenck and Eysenck 1975) alongside the two other orthogonal dimensions styled extraversion and neuroticism. The on-going relevance of the Eysenckian dimensional model of personality for predicting individual differences in social attitudes, with special reference to prejudice, has been demonstrated by Village (2011). Before testing for school influence, it would be prudent to control for individual differences in personality.

Religious Control Variables

The two recent studies by Francis et al. (2014b) and by Village and Francis (2016) concerned with identifying the distinctiveness and effectiveness of Catholic and Anglican secondary schools, identified the way in which the influence of schools with a religious character on student values needs to be disentangled from the direct influence of the students' religiosity. This problem is one which can be addressed by including measures of individual differences in the students' religiosity as control variables within the multilevel model. While the assessment of student religiosity is itself a complex matter, four variables may be routinely introduced to capture key aspects of this multidimensional construct, namely self-assigned religious affiliation, religious attendance, personal prayer, and Bible reading. Given the possible interaction between school type and student religiosity, before testing for school influence, it would be prudent to control for individual differences in terms of these four variables (self-assigned religious affiliation, religious attendance, personal prayer, and bible reading).

Research Questions

In light of the foregoing discussion, the present analyses were established to draw on the Young People's Attitude to Religious Diversity Project to address the following three research questions. The first question employs reliability analysis to explore the internal consistency reliability of the Scale of Attitude toward Freedom of Religious Clothing and Symbols in School (SAFORCS) among a mixed group of students attending schools with a religious character and schools without a religious foundation. The second question employs correlational analysis to explore the connection between attitude toward freedom of religious clothing and symbols in schools and personal factors (age, sex), psychological factors (personality), religious factors (self-assigned religious affiliation, religious attendance, Bible reading frequency, and prayer frequency) and school factors (contrasting schools with a religious character and schools without a religious foundation). The third question employs multilevel linear analysis to explore the effects of schools with a religious character on attitude toward freedom of religious clothing and symbols in school, after taking into account individual differences in personal factors, psychological factors, and religious factors, and after taking into account that students were nested within schools and within three geographical locations.

Method

Procedure

The Young People's Attitude to Religious Diversity Project was conducted among 13- to 15-year-old students attending state-maintained schools in each of five parts of the UK: England, Northern Ireland, Scotland, Wales *and* London. In each geographical area students were recruited both from schools with a religious character (Anglican, Catholic, or joint Anglican and Catholic) and from schools without a religious character. Within the participating schools questionnaires were administered by the religious education teachers within examination-like conditions. Students were assured of anonymity and confidentiality and given the option not to participate in the project.

Sample

The present analyses were conducted on a sub-sample from the Young People's Attitude to Religious Diversity Project, drawing on information provided by 2385 students from schools in England, Wales and London who self-identified as either 'no religion' or as Christian and who gave valid replies to the items in the analysis.

Of these, 1464 (61.4%) were attending schools with a religious character and 921 (38.6%) were attending schools without a religious foundation; 658 (27.6%) were attending schools in Wales, 805 (33.8%) in London and 922 (38.7%) elsewhere in England. In terms of sex and age, 47.5% were male and 52.5% were female; 49.8% were in year nine and 50.2% were in year ten. In terms of self-assigned religious affiliation, 69.0% identified as Christian and 31.0% as 'no religion'.

Measures

Attitude toward Freedom of Religious Clothing and Symbols in School was assessed by a ten-item scale (SAFORCS) related to attitude toward allowing pupils of various religions to wear religiously-related items in school (Table 7.1). Alpha internal consistency reliability (Cronbach 1951) was .92.

Personality was assessed by the abbreviated version of the Junior Eysenck Personality Questionnaire Revised (JEPQR-A) developed by Francis (1996) who reported the following Cronbach's alpha coefficients: extraversion = .66; neuroticism = .70; psychoticism = .61; lie scale = .57.

Religious affiliation was recorded by a checklist of world faiths and Christian denominations in response to the question, 'What is your religion?' For the current

Table 7.1 Attitude toward Freedom of Religious Clothing and Symbols (AFORCS)

Cronbach's Alpha = .92	DS %	D %	NC %	A %	AS %	IRC
Christians should be allowed to wear crosses in school	4	6	20	37	33	.17
Muslims should be allowed to wear the headscarf in school	17	14	18	33	19	.76
Muslims should be allowed to wear the burka in school	23	21	28	18	9	.64
Muslims should be allowed to wear the Niqab in school	21	18	33	18	10	.68
Sikhs should be allowed to wear the turban in school	15	12	22	33	18	.81
Sikhs should be allowed to wear the Kara in school	16	12	32	27	14	.83
Sikhs should be allowed to wear the Kirpan in school	18	15	36	20	10	.70
Jews should be allowed to wear the star of David in school	11	7	23	38	21	.69
Jews should be allowed to wear the Kippah/ Yamulke in school	14	10	35	27	14	.79
Hindus should be allowed to wear the Bindi in school	14	11	28	32	16	.79

Note: *DS* disagree strongly, *D* disagree, *NC* not certain, *A* agree, *AS* agree strongly, *IRC* Item-rest of scale correlation analysis all the Christian categories were collapsed into a single group and those affiliated with other world faiths were omitted, producing a dichotomous variable: no religion = 1, and Christian = 2.

Religious attendance was assessed by the question, 'Apart from special occasions (like weddings) how often do you attend a religious worship service (e.g. in a church, mosque or synagogue). Responses were recorded on a seven-point scale: never (1), sometimes (2), at least once a year (3), at least six times a year (4), at least once a month (5), nearly every week (6), and several times a week (7).

Personal prayer was assessed by the question, 'How often do you pray in your home or by yourself?' Responses were recorded on a five-point scale: never (1), occasionally (2), and at least once a month (3), at least once a week (4), and nearly every day (5).

Bible reading was assessed by the question, 'How often do you ready holy scripture (e.g. The Bible, Qur'an, Torah)?' Responses were recorded on a five-point scale: never (1), occasionally (2), at least once a month (3), at least once a week (4), and nearly every day (5).

Sex, age and school type were recorded as dichotomous variables: male = 1 and female = 2; year nine = 1 and year ten = 2; schools with a religious character = 2 and other schools = 1.

Analysis

A multilevel linear model was employed to allow for the fact that students were nested within schools (Bryk and Raudenbush 1992; Snijders and Bosker 1999; Hox 2002; Bickel 2007). Each school was given a unique numerical code and this was employed as the subject (grouping) variable using the mixed model procedure of IBM SPSS version 20 (Norusis 2011).

Three models were fitted to the data. Model 0, the null model, had no predictor variables, and the Intraclass Correlation Coefficient (ICC) indicated what proportion of the variance in the SAFORCS scores was attributable to variations between schools. In model 1, control variables and school type were added as fixed effects. In model 2, individual-level religious variables were added to test the hypothesis that students in schools with a religious character show differences in attitude toward freedom of religious clothing and symbols in school, compared with students in schools without a religious foundation, after allowing for the fact that schools with a religious character tend to have a higher proportion of religious students than do schools without a religious foundation. The schools with a religious character included Roman Catholic schools, Anglican schools and joint Roman Catholic and Anglican Schools. Since initial separate analyses indicated similar results for these three types of schools, they were combined into a single category.

Results

Step one of the data analysis explored the scale properties of the SAFORCS in terms of the item-rest of scale correlations (see Table 7.1) and the alpha coefficient (Cronbach 1951). The alpha coefficient of .92 supports the internal consistency reliability of the instrument (DeVellis 2003).

Step two of the data analysis explored the bivariate correlations between attitude toward freedom of religious clothing and symbols in school, personal variables (sex and school year), psychological variables (extraversion, neuroticism, psychoticism, and lie scale), religious values (affiliation, attendance, prayer, and Bible reading), and school type (see Table 7.2). The key findings from the correlation matrix are that a more positive attitude toward freedom of religious clothing and symbols in school is associated with being female; with higher neuroticism scores, higher lie scale scores, lower extraversion scores, and lower psychoticism scores; with self-assigned religious afflation, and higher levels of religious attendance, Bible reading frequency and prayer frequency. It was not correlated with school type.

Step three of the data analysis employed the mixed model regression analysis to explore the combined effect on attitude toward freedom of religious clothing and symbols in school of the personal characteristics of the students (sex and age), the psychological characteristics of the students (extraversion, neuroticism, psychoticism, and lie scale scores), and of individual differences in student religiosity (self-assigned religious affiliation, religious attendance, Bible reading, and prayer frequency), while also taking into account the nesting of pupils within schools (see Table 7.3).

Model 0 indicated that around 4% of the variance in SAFORCS was attributed to differences between schools. Model 1 of the mixed model regression analysis indicated that attitude toward freedom of religious clothing and symbols was more positive among girls compared with boys, positively correlated with neuroticism scores, and negatively correlated with extraversion and psychoticism scores. School type remained uncorrelated with attitude toward freedom of religious clothing and symbols. Adding individual religious variables as predictors in model 2 significantly improve the model fit, but did not influence the effect of school type, suggesting that the individual religiosity of pupils, rather than a school's religious status *per se*, was more important in shaping attitude toward freedom of religious clothing and symbols in school.

Table 7.2 Correlation matrix of dependent and independent variables

		12	11	10	9	8	7	6	5	4	3	2
1	SAFORCS	.18***	.19***	.18***	.05*	.06**	−.24***	.10***	−.07***	−.01	.16***	−.01
2	School type	.34***	.21***	.18***	.40***	−.02	−.01	.01	.01	.03	.04*	
3	Sex	.06**	.05**	.03	.05*	.12***	−.27***	.26***	.04	−.01		
4	School year	−.02	−.04	−.03	.01	−.07***	−.03	.01	.03			
5	Extraversion	−.06**	−.06**	−.10***	−.03	−.17***	.10***	−.15***				
6	Neuroticism	−.01	.04*	.00	.00	−.04*	.01					
7	Psychoticism	−.16***	−.11***	−.13***	−.07**	−.33***						
8	Lie scale	.01	.03	.05*	.01							
9	Religious affiliation	.48***	.40***	.34***								
10	Bible reading	.62***	.67***									
11	Prayer frequency	.60***										
12	Religious attendance											

Note. * $p < .05$, ** $p < .01$; *** $p < .001$. *AFORCS* Attitude toward Freedom of Religious Clothing and Symbols. For sex, *1* male, *2* female, for year, *1* year 9, *2* year 10, for religious affiliation, *0* no religion, *1* Christian, for school type, *2* schools with a religious foundation, *1* schools without a religious foundation

Table 7.3 Mixed model regression of Attitude toward Freedom of Religious Clothing and Symbols

		Model 0	Model 1	Model 2
Intercept		27.78***	29.49***	27.46***
Sex (female)	Male		−1.76***	−1.73***
Year (year 10)	Year 9		0.37	0.27
Location (Wales)				
	England		0.93	0.69
	London		1.58	0.98
Extraversion			−0.29*	−0.24
Neuroticism			0.34**	0.33**
Psychoticism			−1.34***	−1.25***
Lie			−0.06	−0.08
Religious affiliation	Not religious			0.62
Bible reading				0.43
Prayer				0.48**
Attendance				0.22
School type	Religious		0.30	0.82
Log-2		17306.0	17142.3	17108.4
Deviance			163.7	33.9
Residual		81.5	76.3***	75.5***
Intercept		3.1	2.4**	1.6*
ICC		4%	3%	2%

Note. Grouping variable: school. Table gives unstandardized parameter estimates for fixed effects. Reference categories are in parentheses. * $p < .05$; ** $p < .01$; *** $p < .001$

Conclusion

This study began by identifying freedom of religious clothing and symbols in schools as a concrete way of accessing young people's attitude toward one of the fundamental agreed and accepted human rights, namely freedom of religion. This focus on freedom of religious clothing and symbols in schools had been suggested by the *Manual on the wearing of religious symbols in public areas* published by the Council of Europe in 2008 (Evans 2008), had been reinforced by the recent report on policy and practice for teaching about religious and non-religious worldviews in intercultural education published by the Council of Europe under the title, *Signposts* (Council of Europe 2014) and had been anticipated by the design of the quantitative strand within the European REDCo survey (Valk et al. 2009).

In order to elucidate individual differences in the attitudes of 13- to 15-year-old students in England and Wales toward freedom of religious clothing and symbols in school, the present study set out to address three specific research questions. These three research questions were tested on data provided by a sample of 2385 students, some attending schools with a religious character and others attending schools without a religious foundation. The first research question employs techniques of internal consistency reliability analysis to test the properties of the ten-item Scale of Attitude toward Freedom of Religious Clothing and Symbols in School (SAFORCS). The data demonstrated an alpha coefficient of .92, confirming that the instrument achieved a high level of internal consistency reliability among the group of students and that it is appropriate to employ this instrument to address the remaining two research questions.

A closer look at the differentiated endorsement of the ten different areas of religious clothing and symbols itemised in SAFORCS is also illuminating. These figures show that levels of support for freedom of religious clothing and symbols in school varies according to the items specified. The highest level of positive support (agreeing or agreeing strongly) is given to the Christian Cross (70%). More than half of the students support for Jews the Star of David (59%), for Muslims the Headscarf (52%), for Sikhs the Turban (51%), and almost half support for Hindus the Bindi (48%). The levels then drop in respect of the Kara for Sikhs (41%), of the Kippah/Yamalke for Jews (41%), of the Kirpan for Sikhs (30%), and of the Niqab (28%) and the Burka (27%) for Muslims.

The second research question employed correlational analysis to explore the connection between attitude toward freedom of religious clothing and symbols in school and personal factors (age, sex), psychological factors (personality), religious factors (self-assigned religious affiliation, religious attendance, Bible reading frequency, and prayer frequency), and school factors (contrasting schools with a religious character and schools without a religious foundation). The correlational data demonstrated that personal factors (especially sex), psychological factors (especially psychoticism) and religious factors (especially personal and public practices) are all associated with individual differences in attitude toward freedom of religious clothing and symbols in school. The correlational data did not, however, find any significant association between attitude toward religious clothing and symbols and type of school attended. These findings, overall, are sufficient to demonstrate that there are consistent patterns in students' attitudes toward freedom of religious clothing and symbols in school, predicted by a combination of personal, psychological and religious factors, sufficient to confirm that the individual differences are not entirely random and that any serious scientific attempt to trace connections between attitudes in this area and type of school attended properly need to control for such personal, psychological and religious factors.

Looking more closely at the significant correlations with attitude toward freedom of religious clothing and symbols in school the following points emerge. First, in terms of sex differences, females adopt a more accepting attitude than males to freedom of religion, but this simple association is also contaminated by the differences between males and females in terms of personality and religiosity. Females record higher levels of religious attendance and prayer, as consistent with the broader review of sex differences in religiosity by Francis and Penny (2013). Females also record higher levels of neuroticism and lower levels of psychoticism, as consistent with the standardisation data reported for these variables by Eysenck and Eysenck (1991).

Second, there is no significant association between attitude toward freedom of religious clothing and symbols in school and age (measured in terms of school year, distinguishing between year nine and year ten). If schools are engaged in human rights education and education for democratic citizenship during these years as suggested by the Council of Europe (2014) in *Signposts*, this finding of no effect is worth closer scrutiny.

Third, in terms of psychological factors, the major association between attitude toward freedom of religious clothing and symbols in school and personality is traced to the dimension of psychoticism. This finding is consistent with Eysenck's broader theory linking low psychoticism scores with tenderminded social attitudes and high psychoticism scores with toughminded social attitudes (see Eysenck 1975, 1976) and with Francis' conclusion that psychoticism is the major dimension of personality associated with individual differences in religious attitudes more generally (see Francis 1992).

Fourth, in terms of religious factors, among Christian and non-religiously affiliated students, frequency of religious attendance, frequency of personal prayer and frequency of Bible reading are all positively associated with greater acceptance of the rights of other religious groups to display religious clothing and symbols in school. This finding is consistent with the broader findings generated by the Young People's attitudes to Religious Diversity Project that, overall, students committed to the Christian tradition are more supportive of religious diversity than religiously non-affiliated students (see Francis et al. 2012, 2013, 2014a; Francis and Village 2014;). At the same time it is important to note that all three measures of religious practice are both intercorrelated and also correlated with self-assigned religious affiliation as Christian. This is consistent with Francis' observations that self-assigned religious affiliation is a valid (if not efficient) measure of religiosity in the absence of indices of belief and practice (see Francis 2003).

The third research question employed multilevel linear analysis to explore the effect of schools with a religious character on attitude toward freedom of religious clothing and symbols in school, after taking into account individual differences in personal factors, psychological factors, and religious factors, and after taking into account that students were nested in schools. After taking these factors into account the multilevel linear model demonstrated that none of the variance in students' attitude toward freedom of religious clothing and symbols in school can be attributed to attending schools with a religious character. Students attending Catholic, Anglican, or joint Catholic and Anglican secondary schools hold neither a more positive attitude, nor a less positive attitude toward freedom of religious clothing and symbols in school, compared with comparable students (in terms of personal, psychological, and religious factors) attending schools without a religious foundation.

This finding of no association between attitude to freedom of religious clothing and symbols in school and attending a school with a religious character challenges the theory proposed by the Runnymede Trust report, *Right to Divide?* (Berkeley 2008) that schools with a religious character prepare students less adequately than schools without a religious foundation for life in a religiously diverse society. In this sense the data did not find the hypothesised negative correlation between attending a school with a religious character and attitude toward freedom of religious clothing and symbols in school.

Taking the measure of attitude toward freedom of religious clothing and symbols in school as a key issue for human rights education, for education for democratic citizenship, *and* for religious education, as well as a key barometer for understanding students' attitudes toward living in a religiously diverse society, the first core finding of this study raises an interesting challenge both to the opponents of and to the supporters of schools with a religious character in England and Wales. If the Runnymede Trust is correct in the claim that schools with a religious character prepare students less well than schools without a religious foundation for life in religiously diverse societies, the Runnymede Trust may still need further robust data to substantiate that claim. Equally, however, if the Churches are correct in the claim that schools with a religious character give serious attention to religious education (see Church of England 2014), and if the claim is correct that religious education enhances community cohesion, the Churches may still need further robust data to substantiate those claims. At present the evidence of the current study concurs with that of the earlier study published by Francis and Village (2014), employing a different dependent variable, but drawing on the same data, namely that in England and Wales today schools with a religious character are a source neither for good nor for ill in terms of shaping student attitudes either toward freedom of religious clothing and symbols in school or toward religious diversity more generally assessed.

The present study has concentrated specifically on England and Wales because the place of schools with a religious character within the state maintained system of education has been shaped by a common history and a common legislative framework. The Young People's Attitude to Religious Diversity Project has the capacity to address similar questions on data collected in Northern Ireland and Scotland. Such analyses may well help to explore the generalisability of the findings from England and Wales.

Note

Young People's Attitudes to Religious Diversity Project (AHRC Reference: AH/G014035/1) is a large scale mixed methods research project investigating the attitudes of 13- to 16-year-old students across the United Kingdom. Students from a variety of socio-economic, cultural, ethnic and religious backgrounds from different parts of England, Wales, Northern Ireland and Scotland, with the addition of London as a special case, took part in the study. Professor Robert Jackson was principal investigator and Professor Leslie J Francis was co-investigator. Together they led a team of qualitative and quantitative researchers based in the Warwick Religions and Education Research Unit, within the Institute of Education at the University of Warwick. The project was part of the AHRC/ESRC Religion and Society Programme, and ran from 2009 to 2012.

References

BBC News. (2014, July 1). *The ban on the veil across Europe*. See http://www.bbc.co.uk/news/world-europe-13038095. Accessed 24 Nov 2014.

Berkeley, R. (2008). *Right to divide? Faith schools and community cohesion*. London: Runnymede.

Berry, S. (2013, October 10). Freedom of religion and religious symbols: Same right – Different interpretation? *Blog of the European Journal of International Law.* Available at http://www.ejiltalk.org/freedom-of-religion-and-religious-symbols-same-right-different-interpretation/

Bickel, R. (2007). *Multilevel analysis for applied research: It's just regression!* New York: Guildford Press.

Blair, A., & Aps, W. (2005). What not to wear and other stories addressing religious diversity in schools. *Education and the Law, 17*, 1–22.

Bryk, A. S., & Raudenbush, S. W. (1992). *Hierarchical linear models: Applications and data analysis methods* (Vol. 1). London: Sage.

Chadwick, P. (1997). *Shifting alliances: Church and state in English education*. London: Cassell.

Chérifi, H. (2005). *L'application de la loi du 15 mars 2004 sur le port des signes religieux ostensibles dans les établissements d'enseignement publics* [The application of the law of 15 March 2004 on the wearing of ostentatious religious symbols in state educational establishments]. ftp://trf.education.gouv.fr/pub/edutel/rapport/rapport_cherifi.pdf

Church of England. (2014). *Making a difference? A review of religious education in Church of England schools*. London: Church of England's Archbishops' Council Education Division.

Council of Europe. (2014). *Signposts: Policy and practice for teaching about religions and non-religious worldviews in intercultural education*. Strasbourg: Council of Europe Publishing.

Cronbach, L. J. (1951). Coefficient alpha and the internal structure of tests. *Pscyhometrika, 16*, 297–334.

Cruickshank, M. (1963). *Church and State in English education*. London: Macmillan.

DeVellis, R. F. (2003). *DeVellis: Theory and applications*. London: Sage.

Dummett, A., & McNeal, J. (1981). *Race and Church Schools*. London: Runnymede Trust.

Evans, M. D. (2008). *Manual on the wearing of religious symbols in public areas*. Leiden: Brill.

Eysenck, H. J. (1975). The structure of social attitudes. *British Journal of Social and Clinical Psychology, 14*, 323–331.

Eysenck, H. J. (1976). Structure of social attitudes. *Psychological Reports, 39*, 463–466.

Eysenck, H. J., & Eysenck, S. B. G. (1975). *Manual of the Eysenck personality questionnaire (adult and junior)*. London: Hodder and Stoughton.

Eysenck, H. J., & Eysenck, S. B. G. (1991). *Manual of the Eysenck personality scales*. London: Hodder and Stoughton.

Francis, L. J. (1992). Religion, neuroticism, and psychoticism. In J. F. Schumaker (Ed.), *Religion and mental health* (pp. 149–160). New York: Oxford University Press.

Francis, L. J. (1996). The development of an abbreviated form of the revised Eysenck personality questionnaire (JEPQR-A) among 13- to 15-year-olds. *Personality and Individual Differences, 21*, 835–844.

Francis, L. J. (2001). *The values debate: A voice from the pupils*. London: Woburn Press.

Francis, L. J. (2003). Religion and social capital: The flaw in the 2001 census in England and Wales. In P. Avis (Ed.), *Public faith: The state of religious belief and practice in Britain* (pp. 45–64). London: SPCK.

Francis, L. J., & Penny, G. (2013). Gender differences in religion. In V. Saroglou (Ed.), *Religion, personality and social behaviour* (pp. 191–209). New York: Psychology Press.

Francis, L. J., & Village, A. (2014). Church schools preparing adolescents for living in a religiously diverse society: An empirical enquiry in England and Wales. *Religious Education, 109*, 264–283.

Francis, L. J., Croft, J., Pyke, A., & Robbins, M. (2012). Young people's attitude to religious diversity project: Quantitative approaches from social and empirical theology. *Journal of Beliefs and Values, 33*, 279–292.

Francis, L. J., Penny, G., & Pyke, A. (2013). Young atheists' attitudes toward religious diversity: A study among 13- to 15-year-old males in the UK. *Theo-web: Zeitschrift für Religionspädagogik, 12*(1), 57–78.

Francis, L. J., ap Sion, T., & Penny, G. (2014a). Is belief in God a matter of public concern in contemporary Wales? An empirical enquiry concerning religious diversity among 13- to 15-year-old males. *Contemporary Wales, 27*, 40–57.

Francis, L. J., Lankshear, D. W., Robbins, M., Village, A., & ap Siôn, T. (2014b). Defining and measuring the contribution of Anglican secondary schools to students' religious, personal and social values. *Journal of Empirical Theology, 27*, 57–84.

Hox, J. (2002). *Multilevel analysis: Techniques and applications*. Mahwah: Lawrence Erlbaum Associates.

Liederman, L. M. (2000). Religious diversity in schools: The Muslim headscarf controversy and beyond. *Social Compass, 47*, 367–381.

Massignon, B. (2011). Laicite in practice: The representation of French teenagers. *British Journal of Religious Education, 33*, 159–172.

Murphy, J. (1971). *Church, state and schools in Britain 1800–1970*. London: Routledge and Kegan Paul.

Norusis, M. (2011). *IBM SPSS statistics 19: Statistical procedures companion*. Chicago: SPSS.

Rich, E. E. (1970). *The Education Act 1870*. London: Longmans.

Skeie, G., & von der Lippe, M. (2009). Does religion matter to young people in Norwegian schools? In P. Valk, G. Bertram-Troost, M. Friederici, & C. Beraud (Eds.), *Teenagers' perspectives on the role of religion in their lives, schools and societies: A European quantitative study* (pp. 269–301). Münster: Waxmann.

Snijders, T. A. B., & Bosker, R. J. (1999). *Multilevel analysis: An introduction to basic and advanced multilevel modelling*. London: Sage.

Swann Report. (1985). *Education for all*. London: Her Majesty's Stationery Office.

Tévanian, P. (2005). *Le voile médiatique. Un faux débat: l'affaire du foulard islamique* [The media veil. A false debate: The affair of the Muslim headscarf]. Paris: éditions Raison d'Agir.

Valk, P., Bertram-Troost, G., Friederici, M., & Beraud, C. (Eds.). (2009). *Teenagers' perspectives on the role of religion in their lives, schools and societies. A European quantitative study*. Münster: Waxmann.

van der Ven, J. A. (2012). Religious liberty in political perspective. In J. A. van der Ven & H.-G. Ziebertz (Eds.), *Tensions within and between religions and human rights* (pp. 95–145). Leiden: Brill.

Village, A. (2011). Outgroup prejudice, personality and religiosity: Disentangling a complex web of relationships among adolescents in the UK. *Psychology of Religion and Spirituality, 3*, 269–284.

Village, A., & Francis, L. J. (2016). Measuring the contribution of Roman Catholic secondary schools to students' religious, personal and social values. *Journal of Catholic Education, 19, 86–115.*

Chapter 8
Attitudes Towards Freedom of Religion Among Nigerian Students

Modestus Adimekwe and Hans-Georg Ziebertz

Abstract The question of religious freedom is as old as the human rights endeavour itself. Freedom of religion is a central theme in human rights and, in the last five decades, has come to dominate discussions in international circles. In Nigeria, human rights, especially fundamental rights, have long been adopted as legitimate moral and legal standards. The term 'fundamental rights' here refers to those basic human freedoms which are recognized worldwide as necessary for the development of the human person. Freedom of religion is one such fundamental right. However, recurring incidents of religious unrest in Nigeria have raised questions about the definition, exercise and enforcement of this right within the country. The aim of this study, therefore, is to find out what Nigerians, especially Nigerian youth, think about religious freedom, both individually and collectively as a group. Students in the last year of their secondary education constituted the research population (n = 1191). The survey was conducted in six states of the federation, plus the Federal Capital Territory, Abuja. The sample includes Christians (Catholics and Protestants) and Muslims. Initially, it was assumed – in the context of a lack of precise definition of this right in Nigeria's Constitution – that the surveyed youth had negative attitudes towards religious freedom. However, the results reveal that this is not the case; on the contrary, their attitude towards this right is definitely positive.

The purpose of this paper is to explore how young Nigerians assess the right to freedom of religion and how this view influences their attitude. The paper opens with an examination of the relevant concepts (1), followed by the research design (2). In the empirical section (3), the researchers set out to explore exactly what the youth who constituted the research population think (in the said context). We then discuss the empirical findings (4) and, finally, come to clear conclusions (5).

M. Adimekwe (✉) • H.-G. Ziebertz
Faculty of Theology, University of Würzburg, Würzburg, Germany
e-mail: madimekwe@gmail.com

H.-G. Ziebertz, C. Sterkens (eds.), *Religion and Civil Human Rights in Empirical Perspective*,
Religion and Human Rights 2, DOI 10.1007/978-3-319-59285-5_8

Introduction

The United Nations' introduction of the Universal Declaration of Human Rights (UDHR) in 1948 was met with global optimism. Coming in the wake of World War II with all its horror, the document was regarded as a rainbow after the storm. Thus it gained widespread acceptance, even though some groups had reservations about the document.

Today, human rights resemble a religion. They have become a global subject with global appeal. Based, as they are, on the transcultural, philosophical principle of the inherent dignity of the human person, human rights are now regarded as a common standard of behaviour among the international community (Dada 2012, 68).

Nigeria is the 100th member of the United Nations and it has signed the major international and regional human rights instruments.[1] Accordingly, human rights have long been adopted and command a pride of place in Nigeria's Constitution. Nevertheless, there have been varying instances of violation of basic and fundamental freedoms in Nigeria. The abduction of schoolgirls in Chibok, Borno State, by Boko Haram (a militant and violent Muslim sect) in 2014, is only the tip of the iceberg. This and other ethno-religious incidents, are the reason that the country is designated in the *2014 Annual Report of the US Commission on International Religious Freedom* as one of the countries with particular concern (CPC).[2] As in other countries, the violation of the right to freedom of religion is Nigeria's major problem. It is, in fact, the Achilles' heel in Nigeria's attempts at national cohesion and is attributed to a lack of consensus on the meaning of this right.

Religious Patrimony of Nigeria

Perhaps we should start by saying that defining the word 'religion' has not been an easy task. Over the centuries, scholars have attempted to give an umbrella definition of the term 'religion'. However, these attempts have tended to reveal more about the person supplying the definition than about the phenomenon of religion itself (Sundermeier 1999, 11). This paper does not wish to meddle in this, simply because defining what is meant by 'religion' is outside the paper's limited scope. For a working definition, 'religion' here refers to humankind's endeavours relating to the Supernatural, or a supernatural Being. Over the millennia and centuries, these endeavours have given rise to religious systems and civilizations in their bewildering variety throughout the world.

---

[1] Nigeria is signatory to, among others, the Universal Declaration of Human Rights (1948), the International Covenant on Civil and Political Rights (1966), the International Covenant on Economic, Social and Cultural Rights (1966), and the African Charter on Human and Peoples' Rights (1981).

[2] For details of this report, see www.uscirf.gov/reports-briefs/annual-report/2014-annual-report. Retrieved on 20.10.2014.

Historically, the very existence of the term 'religion' was thought to be European, and the definitions, typologies and associated terminologies were all Western. However, the discovery of new cultures during the seventeenth and eighteenth centuries broadened existing horizons and left in its wake "a dilemma concerning the relation between religions" (Beyers 2010). This caused a construction of religious categories premised on the acceptance of the evolutionistic development of religions. Consequently, the term 'traditional' was used to combine religions that share structural similarities. The indigenous religions of the African peoples thus became the African Traditional Religion (ATR) (Ekwunife 1992, 44–45; Figl 2003, 73), a term that refers to their ancient origin. It describes a religion of the diverse peoples of the geographical area which eventually became known as Nigeria. But this term belies the fact that Africa is home to a huge diversity of religious systems. As Maluleke (2001, 37) declares: "If Africa is anything, it is various and there are million ways of being an African." It is therefore difficult to talk of African religion in the singular. However, African scholars of religion maintain firmly that the multiplicity of cults have enough in common to name them in the singular (Mbiti 1989, 1). Actually, it would not be incorrect to speak of the diversity in the sense of pluriformity, though not in the sense of organized religions. Ignorance of this fact has resulted in a description of the indigenous religion of the African peoples as polytheism, heathenism, animism, totemism, etc. (Magesa 2002, 14–15).

However, the African understanding of reality holds the key to its understanding of human existence and the divine. Reality can only be comprehended from the perspective of religion (Mbiti 1989, 15). The divine is inscrutable. It cannot be exhaustively captured in the lexicon of any religious system. Every religious tradition represents "a particular excellence" (Tapasyananda 1984, 28); none has the monopoly of the whole, divine truth. The truth has its source in the supernatural Being, and not in humans. Hence, a diversity of opinions, of religious expressions are appreciated in the collective search of the knowledge of the transcendence. This understanding of pluralism is the key to the African acceptance of the equality of religions (Turaki 1999, 29).

Next is the question of individual identity. The individual is unique, but does not exist outside his or her community. As Atado (1988, 7) points out, "the individual exists within and for the community…." In other words, his or her identity is incorporated in the identity of the whole group, the community, and is meaningful only in this context. Thus, the individual person is always an inseparable part of the life and the religion of the group, "…for to do so is to be severed from his roots, his foundation, his context of security…" (Mbiti 1989, 2).

African Tradition Religion is the oldest religion in Nigeria, much older than Christianity and Islam. Both religions were officially introduced in Nigeria only in 1804 and 1841, respectively, although earlier attempts to do so are documented, (Odeme 2011, 93, 107; Onwubiko 1967, 310–312; Onwubiko 1973, 200–207). However, those two religions have taken root and spread among the citizens of Nigeria. In fact, all the states of the federation have a mixed religious population. It should be emphasised that both religions arrived as full-fledged civilizations, and both religions had confessional branches. For instance, Islam already consisted of different sects, like the older Ahmadiyya, Quadriyya, Tijanniyya and Sanusiyya, while the Christian denominations included Catholicism and the mainstream Protestant churches.

In the last four decades in Nigeria, Christianity has seen the rise of more branches in the several Pentecostal sanctuaries, as well as Islam in the upsurge of sects like the Izala movements, the Maitatsine, the Shiites and Talibans. In both religions, these new groups appear more zealous in their activities than the older, traditional divisions, and they have a greater number of followers among the youth. To put it differently: these offshoots and sects represent the fundamentalist groups (in both religions) and their activities have sometimes been "a major precipitant of religious conflicts" (Osaghae and Suberu 2005, 11).

Today, Islam and Christianity command a large number of followers among the Nigerian population. Basically, most Hausa-Fulanis in the north are Muslims, and most Igbos in the south-east are Christians. The Yorubas in the south-west are either Christians or Muslims (Lemu 2014). Believers (again, of both religions) are also found among the many minority groups. Precise and official census figures stating the religious affiliations of the Nigerian population are hard to come by, some sources though, set it down to about 50% Muslims, 40% Christians, and 10% adherents to indigenous beliefs.[3] We can therefore say that the country has an evenly split population of Muslims and Christians (Paden 2007). Although other smaller religious systems such as Judaism, Ogboni confraternity, etc. also have followers among the Nigerians, the dominant religions are Islam, Christianity and African Traditional Religion.

Religious Diversity and Freedom

Prior to European expansion into Africa, pluralism existed among the indigenous African societies, but not in the technical sense of the term. Pluralism was not the effect of the expansion of Islam and Christianity. Instead, the arrival of these religions introduced a new dimension of differentiated religious pluralism.

Of the three dominant religions, African Traditional Religion is the least active regarding politics and intolerance. Even though the masquerade activities normally associated with the indigenous beliefs have sometimes been a source of conflict in some parts of the country, African Traditional Religion is the least politically active (Etuk 2002, 35; Osaghae and Suberu 2005, 11). This lack of political activism is based on ATR's understanding of reality, which it considers to be beyond the exclusive grasp of humans. All humans should therefore widen their knowledge and understanding through social interaction. The religious heritage of Africa possesses the unique belief that all religions worldwide are concerned with providing a source for humankind's search for the knowledge of reality. Even though the advent of the two

[3] See Democracy Web (2010), http://www.democracyweb.org/about/democracyweb.php. Retrieved on 01.10.2014.

religions did not meet *prima facie* the enthusiasm of the local peoples (for instance, the coming of Christianity was perceived as disruptive to the existing Igbo world order, as Achebe (1958) explained in the introductory note of his classic, *Things fall apart*) the indigenous religion of the African peoples still maintains that a one-way reaction to "the appeal of the transcendence of the human spirit" does not exist (Turaki 1999, 29). Indigenous African religion believes that there is salvation outside the church, and it neither proclaimed an idea of holy war, or any mutual condemnation and discrimination, if anything, it thrived on the principle of 'live and let live'.

The same cannot be said of either Islam or Christianity – both Abrahamic religions – with their logic of monotheism. These religions, according to Ziebertz and Reindl (2012, 224), "offer a worldview which establishes…an overarching canopy providing interpretations of the world". Islam's and Christianity's belief in the existence of only one God implies that there is also only one correct way of relating to this deity. Thus, the truth claims and counter-claims of those two religions have been the foundation of religious differentiation and conflicts within Nigeria (Ekwunife 1992, 18; Ibrahim 1989, 65–82; Igwe 2008).

Context is essential for an exact understanding of everything, including the religious situation in Nigeria. As noted earlier, Islam and Christianity arrived at their various confessional levels and with methods of evangelism that remind one of the Scramble.[4] In Nigeria, and indeed in Sub-Sahara as a whole, Christianity was introduced after the Reformation; that means, conversion was not the major issue, but rather membership of *our denomination*. Scholars of African history aptly captured the mood of those times when they described Africa as 'a battle ground for converts'. Partly because of this, Christianity in Nigeria, if not in Africa, still bears the stigma of colonialism (Ayandele 1966, 22; Ozigboh 1993, 58).

The same is true for Islam since Muslims belong to different sects and their truth claims are the source of rivalries and ongoing conflicts (Osaghae and Suberu 2005, 11, 20). But, more importantly, Nadel (in Mbiti) referring to the impact of Islam on the Nupe tribe of northern Nigeria (as a case study) hinted that the Islamic evangelizing strategy at that time was characterized primarily by "the assimilation to upper-class culture and, only secondarily, the deliverance from unbelief." This statement is based on the assertion that the religion "came to Nupe as a religion of conquerors and the ruling class…" (Mbiti 1999, 240). Consequently, conversions were *ab initio* more social than spiritual for both religions. Therefore, the denominational and elitist evangelisms that were based on religious cosmological exclusivism, introduced rivalry and/or diametrically opposed identities, thus introducing virtual time-bombs.

After Nigeria's Independence (1960), this 'rivalry' has been dragged into all facets of national life, including the educational sector. Religious crises in Nigeria's educational institutions erupt again and again: to mention just a few, there has been religious conflict at the University of Sokoto (1986), Queen Amina College Kaduna (1987), Ahmadu Bello University Zaria (1988), and the Government Girls' College

[4] A technical term employed by Onwubiko (1973, 219) to refer to the approach used by the colonialists to annex Africa.

Jalingo (1992). In some secondary schools in Oyo State, there have been Muslim/Christian clashes over the hijab. The abduction of about 270 school girls from the Government Secondary School in Chibok, Borno State by Boko Haram as well as many other similar incidents are examples of how religion has a negative impact on Nigeria's educational system.

Initially, Nigeria's government schools were established by religious groups, mainly early Christian missionaries from Europe, as tools for conversions. But even after the government took over these schools in 1970, the Nigerian educational system has retained its religious character – Islamic in the north and Christian in the south. This is the reason why religion is believed to maintain a stifling influence on Nigeria's schools, allowing little or no veritable space for free, independent and secular scholarship (Eno-Abasi 2014; Igwe 2008).

Ethno-religious Identity and Religious Freedom

Over the years, ethnicity has been regarded as the most salient identity factor in Nigeria, and studies to ascertain the exact number of ethnic groups in the country have already been carried out. However, official figures have remained elusive (Osaghae and Suberu 2005, 9).[5] Nevertheless, the Hausa-Fulani, Yoruba and Igbo are evidently the three dominant ethnic groups and together they constitute more than half of the entire population. The assumption of ethnicity as a distinguishing feature has been supported by a number of demographic studies, for instance, the survey on "Attitudes to Democracy and Markets in Nigeria" (Lewis and Bratton 2000, 27). According to this survey, 48.2% of Nigerians prefer to identify themselves in terms of their ethnic regional groups; 28.4% opted for class identities, while 21% prefer to be classified according to their religious identity. Thus, almost two-thirds of the population regard themselves as members of a specific ethnic, regional or religious group. Ethnic clusters are indeed the most enduring behavioural units in the country, and they have been encouraged by the colonial and the post-colonial Nigerian governments (see also Nnoli 1978, 113; Okeke 2013, 65).

Identity politics (otherwise known as regionalism) date back to colonial times. This form of politics evolved from the structures that were created by colonial masters in the state formation process of their colony. The administration of the colonisers established terms such as 'Muslim-Christian', 'Northerner-Southerner', etc., and their developmental policies and projects were implemented accordingly. Together, this caused various imbalances in the system that later became a significant element in the dynamic of identity consciousness (Okpanachi 2012). However, given Nigeria's relatively long history, it is fair to point out that successive govern-

[5]According to Osaghae and Suberu (2005), the following estimations to the number of ethnic groups in Nigeria have been advanced: 248 (Coleman 1958), 62 (Murdock 1975), 161 (Gandonu 1978), 143 (Odetola 1978), and 374 (Otite 1990) and Ca. 500 (PEFS 2001). Democracy Web (2010) puts the estimate at about 250.

ments have failed to generate the necessary structures to aid the integration of the country's diverse identities. Instead, identities are politicized and often manipulated in the visionless quest for political power. Consequently, the nation has drifted towards "particularistic forms of political consciousness and identity with religion and ethnicity as its stronghold" (Ezeh and Okonkwo 2010).

In short, ethnicity has been considered to be the most potent source of identity in the country. This position has been challenged by more recent studies, for instance, the survey (2006) by the PEW Research Center on Religion and Public Life which demonstrates, *inter alia,* that Nigerians are more likely to define themselves in terms of religion than any other dimension. According to this study, 76% of Christians and 91% of Muslims consider their religious identity to be more important to them than their identity as Africans, Nigerians or members of a specific ethnic group. Thus, religion, not ethnicity, is judged to be the most potentially salient identity. Experiences confirm this claim, even though more empirical proofs are required for its actual confirmation. The same study further reveals that underneath this new wave of religiosity there is an equally deep mutual distrust. 62% of the Christians state that they do not trust people of other religions or only marginally. This position is shared by 61% of Nigeria's Muslims (Lewis 2007; Ruby and Shah 2007).

Basically, the concept of trust is defined by psychologists as a cognitive process (Colquitt et al. 2007, 909–927; Lewis and Weigert 1985, 970; McKnight and Chervany 2001, 36). Cognition involves the way in which information received is perceived, interpreted, understood, coded in the mind, stored and retrieved for future use. Perception is an integral part of the cognitive process and depends on a "complex set of variables such as psychological disposition, past experience, cultural expectations and social relationships" (Folarin 1998, 65). Usually, our perceptions, especially the ones mediated by socio-cultural factors, leave us with biases and prejudices. Differentiation, demonization and stereotyping etc. (some of the features of competitive evangelism), can influence our perception and cause distrust. Luhmann (1979, 71) points out that distrust does not reduce the complexity of the social system, whereas trust does. Christianity and Islam have undoubtedly contributed immensely to the growth of the country, but they have also favoured unhealthy competitive evangelical strategies and, in the process, promoted a culture of intolerance in Nigeria. In short, the time-bomb referred to earlier on has exploded in the form of the upsurge of Christian extremism and fundamentalist Islam.

The Nigerian Constitution and Religious Freedom

Nigeria is a pluralistic society (Odoeme 2011, 41). The Constitution of the Federal Republic of Nigeria (FRN) acknowledges that and provides, in section 10, that "the Government of the Federation or of a state shall not adopt any religion as State Religion".[6] The margin note to the same section also confirms, according to inter-

[6] See website for the text of Nigeria's Constitution: www.nigeria-law.org/ConstitutionOfTheFederalRepublicOfNigeria.htm

pretation: “Prohibition of State Religion”. This provision is further strengthened by section 38 of the Constitution, which guarantees the right of every citizen to freely choose their religion and to demonstrate his or her adherence to their religion in worship, teaching and practice. The International Covenant on Civil and Political Rights (1966) that has long been adopted by the nation restricts in article 18(3) the right to demonstrate adherence to one’s religion only when public safety, health, morals or order are in danger.

Given these constitutional provisions, it can be said that Nigeria is a secular state. However, this issue has been subject of ongoing public debate, with some claiming that the phrase “secular state” was intended even though it is not literally mentioned. Legal scholars tried to settle the matter by resorting to the legal principle of attributing the ordinary meaning to a constitutional provision where the wordings of the provision are unambiguous. Still, the fact remains that a juridical interpretation is still in want for this section, regardless of several opportunities (Adegbite 2012).

The Constitution has also made other provisions complicating the matter further: In sections 275 and 280, the creation of the Sharia Court of Appeal and the Customary Court of Appeal respectively are supported, despite its position on secularity in section 10. Consequently, there is a judicial divide in the country: common law in the south and penal code in the north. This stance of the Constitution appears not only contradictory in terms, but also strengthens existing ethnic and regional ties of the predominant religions (Adegbite 2012; Okeke 2013, 67). Thus, the main issue with religious freedom in Nigeria is the divergent understanding of the term ‘religious freedom’. Partly as a result of this state of affairs, successive Nigerian governments (constitutional and otherwise) have interfered immensely in religious matters, through programmes such as building of faith-based schools, Mosques and Cathedrals, funding of pilgrimages etc. Some of Nigeria’s leaders have even operated on the age-old principle of ‘cuius regio, euis religio’ (‘whose region, his religion’), resulting, for instance, in the enrolment of the nation as member of the Organization of Islamic conference (O.I.C.) in 1986 and the ongoing introduction of the Sharia legal code in the northern States of the federation, starting in 2000. Since then, religious freedom has been an issue of life or death.

Summary

So far, we have presented the context of religious freedom in Nigeria with reference to the dominant religions and relevant ethnic identities in the country, to clarify that the country is both culturally and religiously diverse.

A closer look at the relationship between the religions in Nigeria reveals a ‘clash of civilizations’ underneath. This problem could be traced back to the initial stages of the evangelical activities of the dominant religions. Although this took place before Nigeria’s nationhood, it has continued to define the interactions between Nigeria’s religious traditions, especially since the country has gained its independence.

The Nigerian Constitution is aware of this and regards religious freedom as a way to foster harmonious living among all of Nigeria's citizens. However, the same Constitution makes also some provisions that tend to compromise the secularity model, a model that is a necessary condition for the guarantee of the right to freedom of religion. Consequently, a precise model that clearly explains the practice of this right is still missing. This loophole has been exploited by interest groups, including Nigeria's government and politicians, for selfish reasons, given the precarious relationship between the diverse religious identities in the country.

The young people in Nigeria are aware of what is going on in their society, as far as the right to freedom of religion is concerned, and this awareness affects their attitudes towards this right. We are interested in the positions and attitudes of those young people, because they will determine Nigeria's future. Hence the question: how do young people in Nigeria view the right to freedom of religion? What are their attitudes towards the right to freedom of religion and the predictors of their attitudes towards this right?

Research Design

In their work, Botvar and Sjöborg (2012, 68) explain Dobbelaere's compartmentalization thesis[7] as the strategy that is adopted by individuals to cope with cross-pressures resulting from conflicting roles, models etc. This paper attempts to find out how adolescents in Nigeria deal with the pressures arising from the conflicting models of religion (as a source of social cohesion and, again, as a cause of conflicts in their society), as well as those arising from the discrepancy between the theory and practice of the right to freedom of religion in Nigeria – in other words, the aim of this research is to find out how respondents classify and differentiate these pressures. We also want to find out how these pressures influence the youth's attitudes towards this right. Van der Ven and Ziebertz (2012, 5) have recently indicated that the impact of religion on attitudes towards religious freedom "is limited". We want to figure out whether this also applies to the Nigerian context.

Data Collection

The data for this work was collected between March and May 2014. Six states, namely Abia, Ebonyi, Lagos, Imo, Kaduna, Sokoto, plus the Federal Capital Territory, Abuja were covered. They were chosen to get a wider picture of the views

[7] See the following works of Karel Dobbelaere: "Secularization: a multi-dimensional concept" (1981), "Secularization" (1998) and "Secularization: an analysis at three levels, gods, humans and religions" (2002). These works are quoted in Botvar and Sjöborg (2012, 80).

held by Nigeria's youth. Kaduna, Sokoto and Abuja are more or less northern states, the others belong to the southern bloc.

Senior secondary school students (SSS3) of eighteen secondary schools participated in this study. Seven of them are private, faith-based schools. At least two schools from every state mentioned above were included in the sample. The selections were based on the schools' relevance to the research project, meaning that only schools where there are interactions between the research population subgroups (namely Catholics, Muslims and Protestants) were considered.

The instrument used was the English version of the questionnaire elaborated by the International Programme on Religion and Human Rights.[8] We only had to make some marginal adjustments. Nevertheless, several students indicated that the grammar and vocabulary were difficult and that they had problems understanding some of the questions.

The questionnaire was handed over directly to the students. All in all, 1800 copies were distributed, 1682 were returned and only 1191 of these were actually usable. We have to keep in mind though that we did not use a random sample – the results should therefore not be generalized.

Conceptual Model

As stated earlier, our intention was to undertake research on how young people in Nigeria regard freedom of religion and what determines their views, i.e. the predictors. To measure attitudes to freedom of religion, the students were asked to answer questions concerning political non-interference, prayer in public schools, and the hijab. The item of political non-interference covers government's interference in religion and religious issues (one of the common features of the violation of the right to freedom of religion in Nigeria). Usually prayer is part of the beginning and the end of the daily school programme. Thus, they are familiar with the problem regarding 'prayer in public school'. The hijab is another issue; should female students be allowed to wear a hijab at school? In some states, this has even resulted in open conflicts among students of the different religious groups; therefore the students are well aware of the content of the questions regarding this topic. These three issues have been operationalized in the concepts we adopted for this study and they are used to measure attitudes towards religious freedom, our dependent variable.

To evaluate the dependencies we have generated a different set of variables, the independent variables. They will be used to explain differences in attitudes towards freedom of religion and/or the factor(s) on which they depend. The independent variables are subdivided into micro-, meso- and macro-levels.

Age, sex and religious belonging are the background variables. Since the research focussed entirely on a group of secondary school students, the age of the respondents is about the same. Societal gender roles are still an issue in Nigeria. Gender

[8] For more information, see: www.rhr.theologie.uni-wuerzburg.de

still determines a person's social status and level of involvement in society, and males have a higher status and are more involved in the public than females in Nigeria. Women are generally regarded as mothers and therefore they are chiefly restricted to the home. Because of this withdrawn role, women and girls are more often victims of human rights violation than men or boys. Since we are interested in perspectives, sex was included in the respondents' personal characteristics. As far as religious belonging is concerned, our interest was to compare Christian and Muslim attitudes. We divided Christians into Catholics and Protestants, and intended to divide the Muslims as well, therefore we offered different denominations of Islam such as Sunnite, Shiite, Alawite and others in the questionnaire. However, the respondents did not use these sub-categories, and ticked only the column for Muslim. Thus, we only have three research groups: Catholics, Muslims and Protestants.

At the micro-level, in the independent variables, we included individual belief, even though religious belonging was already part of the personal characteristics. This is not a duplication of data; we know that young people usually belong to the religion of their parents, but we also wanted to know more about the individual beliefs of the students. Therefore, we included an additional item about individual belief.

After the issue of belief we consider religious systems, institutions, etc. In the theoretical section we mentioned that religions still have an influence on public schools, thus they influence society directly at the meso-level, (that is, at institutional level) and the school system is a typical example of this. But how convincing are these religions in their institutions? Are the religions trustworthy according to the surveyed students? That is a possible predictor of attitudes towards freedom of religion.

The third issue of importance concerns the visibility of religion in society, and whether or not religion is accepted as a societal actor. We are especially interested in the perceptions of the students regarding the function of religion in society: do the respondents believe that the religions referred to contribute towards social equality, development, peace, etc. or do they think that these religions just cause tensions and injustice?

In summary, we distinguish three sets of variables in our conceptual model: dependent, independent and background variables. Freedom of religion is our dependent variable. We consider only three dimensions of freedom of religion: political non-interference, prayer in public schools and the hijab. The independent variables are sub-divided into micro-, meso- and macro-levels. The micro-level contains an item on individual belief. At thc meso-level, we have 'trust in religion'. Finally, the respondents' perception of religion and conflicts in society constitutes the macro-level. As far as socio-demographic characteristics are concerned, we consider sex, age and religious belonging. These form our background variables. The arrows in Fig. 8.1 simply indicate the direction of impact.

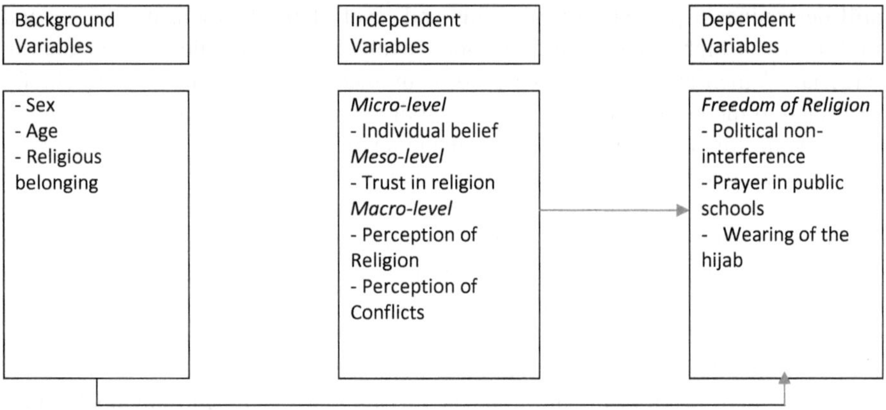

Fig. 8.1 Conceptual model

Description of Instruments

All the concepts for this paper – freedom of religion, individual belief, trust in religion, perception of religion, perception of conflicts in society and the socio-demographic characteristics of sex, age and religious belonging – are taken from the questionnaire. In this part of the paper, they will be presented as operationalized.

Freedom of Religion

We will now measure attitudes towards freedom of religion. The concept of religious freedom is an integral part of both the Islamic tradition and Christianity (see *Dignitatis Humanae* 2, in Paul VI 1965; Holy Qur'an, S. 2: 256). The term 'freedom of religion' is a broad concept that includes a number of indicators. Our operationalisation of the term does not cover all the aspects. That would exceed our study by far. For our purpose, it is enough to consider the three specific aspects mentioned before: political non-interference, prayer in public schools, and the hijab.

Political non-interference refers to "the vertical operation of civil liberties" (Van der Ven 2010, 286). Above, we claimed that Nigerian governments have been involved in religious matters by establishing faith-based schools, places of worship, and by funding pilgrimages, etc. We have also indicated that they sometimes pursue policies with religious objectives instead of maintaining a 'healthy distance' from religion, a necessary condition for the guarantee of freedom of religion (Duniya 1993, 45). Hence the relevance of this item.

The item on prayer in public schools also fits into our context, "as a specific interpretation of the freedom of religion" (Sjöborg 2012, 154). Most Nigerian schools (state- and private-owned) conduct daily 'Morning' and 'Dismissal assemblies' with prayer sessions. In some schools, the Moral Instruction lessons even turn into elaborate prayer sessions, which religious leaders are sometimes invited to conduct. However, even though the Nigerian Constitution provides for the public manifestation of belief (Section 38), it also grants the freedom from an imposition of religious practice of any form.

Lastly, the wearing of the hijab, whether by female teachers or students is a subject of unending controversies in schools, in some parts of the country. For instance, the government of Kano (a state of the federation) ordered all girls attending state schools to wear the hijab, regardless of their religion.[9] This caused a school-uniform versus religious-outfit controversy in the country. Thus, the surveyed students are familiar with the issue, even though the reference was made to female teachers in the operationalisation of this concept, and not to female students.

These three concepts are operationalized in the following statements (5-point Likert scale: 1 = I totally disagree; 2 = I disagree; 3 = I am not sure; 4 = I agree; 5 = I fully agree) and we asked the students to make it clear how they feel about the items by their answers:

- The state should not interfere with missionary activities in both the majority and minority religions.
- Students should be offered time, space and a room in schools to pray.
- The state should not prevent female teachers from wearing the hijab.

Individual Belief

Individual belief relates to individual aspects of religion and belief. Here, we want to measure the personal beliefs of our respondents. We want to know how and to what extent they value their belief. Thus we chose an item on the importance of religion: "My religion or worldview has great influence on my daily life." This item pays particular attention to "the individual person and the importance of religion for his or her life" (Ziebertz and Reindl 2013, 134). Individual belief is understood as a possible predictor of attitudes towards freedom of religion. Hence its inclusion in the regression analyses. The answering scheme is: 1 = I totally disagree; 2 = I disagree; 3 = I am not sure; 4 = I agree; 5 = I fully agree.

Trust in Religion

Regarding the concept 'trust in religion', we are interested in the institutional aspects of religion, particularly the activities of religions in society and whether people have trust in religion. We assume that trust refers to the "cognitive perceptions about the attributes…of the trustee" (McKnight and Chervany 2001, 36) i.e. of the religions in question, Islam and Christianity. We asked the students how they rate the credibility of their own religion and others they are familiar with. In order

[9] For more information, see http://www.irinnews.org/report/45857/nigeria-kano-state-directs-all-school-girls-to-wear-muslim-scarf Retrieved on 01.10.2014.

to analyse the scale properly as a possible predictor of attitudes towards freedom of religion, and with reference to its peculiar answering Scheme (1 = low – 10 = high), we will draw up the responses into four trust sub-categories. The questionnaire items concerning trust in religion are:

- If you are committed to a religion, to what degree do you generally trust your religion?
- To what degree do you generally trust other religions in your country?

Perception of Religion in Society

The perception of the function of religion in society is important for the overall evaluation of attitudes towards freedom of religion, because it reveals the function of religion and its impact on society. As we stated earlier, our respondents are young, and relatively inexperienced, their opinions and beliefs are mainly influenced by their everyday perceptions. We are using the answering scheme 1 = I totally disagree; 2 = I disagree; 3 = I am not sure; 4 = I agree; 5 = I fully agree, to measure their perceptions of the relevance of religion and how they assess actual ways religions contribute to their society. Thus, the students were asked to answer the following questions:

- Religious convictions, rituals and symbols do not fit into these modern times.
- For the morality of contemporary society, it is good that there is religion.

Perception of Conflicts in Society

Similar to the perception of religion, perception of conflicts in society is also considered as a possible predictor of attitudes in our study. This concerns the visibility of religion as a societal actor and, specifically, its contribution as a cause of tensions in society or as a source of social cohesion. Attitudes, whether they are positive or negative, towards freedom of religion do not develop in a vacuum. The students' awareness of their socio-cultural context is therefore relevant for their valuation of this right. Thus, we included six single items grouped into two sets of three items each, with the sub-titles 'perceived conflicts' and 'perceived maltreatments', respectively. They are operationalized in the form of questions (as follows) and will feature later in the correlation and regression models:

In Your View:

- to what degree are there tensions or conflicts in society between rich and poor?
- to what degree are there tensions or conflicts in society between religions?
- to what degree are there tensions or conflicts in society between races or ethnic groups?

In Your View:

- how often have you been personally treated in an unjust manner because you are rich or poor?

- how often have you been personally treated in an unjust manner because of your religion?
- how often have you been personally treated in an unjust manner because of your race or ethnic group?

The answering scheme runs as follows: 1 = never; 2 = very seldom; 3 = occasionally; 4 = often; 5 = very often.

Socio-demographic Characteristics

We included age, sex and religious belonging in the regression models as control variables. For this research, only secondary students were selected, so the age bracket ranges from 14 to 22 years, while the average is 17.36 years.

By sex we mean the different attitudes between male and female respondents. As stated above, Nigerian society has more withdrawn role patterns for girls than boys. Girls are primarily observed as future mothers, they are more reserved and tend to be more religious than boys. We therefore expect sex to be relevant to our findings. Of the 1191 students that were sampled, 656 (55.1%) are female and 535 (44.9%) are male. Sex featured in the regression models as a dummy-variable. The reference is male.

As far as religious belonging is concerned, our research focussed on Christians and Muslims. We obtained the following data on students' religious belonging from their responses. In the questionnaire the students were asked to indicate their religions, 36.6% defined themselves as Catholics, 33.8% as Muslims and 24.3% as Protestants. The rest (consisting of adherents of Judaism, other religions, religion in a general sense, non-religious and African Traditional Religion – referred to from now on as "others") came to 5.2%. Religious belonging is particularly important for our hypotheses. In the regression analyses it is included as a dummy variable, with Catholics as the reference.

Statistical Methods

Our empirical analysis consists of three stages. First, we carry out descriptive analyses involving all concepts used in the paper. These will enable us to obtain the means of and variations in attitudes towards freedom of religion, among Catholic, Muslim and Protestant students. Next, we conduct correlation analyses in order to determine the interrelationships between individual beliefs, trust in religion, the perception of religion and conflicts in society, and attitudes towards freedom of religion. Finally, the regression analyses will enable us to find out the extent of the impact of these predictor-concepts on students' attitudes towards this right, while controlling for socio-demographic characteristics.

The scale for the interpretation of the mean is: 1.00–1.79 = total disagreement; 1.80–2.59 = disagreement; 2.60–2.99 = negative ambivalence; 3.00–3.39 = positive ambivalence; 3.40–4.19 = agreement; 4.20–5.00 = full agreement.

Research Questions and Hypotheses

Questions

In the introduction, we presented our research questions in rather general terms, i.e.: how do young Nigerians view the right to freedom of religion? What are their attitudes towards the right to freedom of religion and the predictors for their attitudes towards this right? Some terms in the questions such as 'young Nigerians', 'predictors' etc. are rather unspecific and have to be defined first. The questions therefore are as follows:

1. What are the attitudes of secondary school students in Nigeria towards the three dimensions of freedom of religion, namely political non-interference in religious affairs, prayer in public schools and the hijab?
2. How far are individual belief, trust in religion, perception of religion and conflicts in society related to the different dimensions of freedom of religion?
3. Are demographic characteristics, religious belonging, individual belief, trust in religion, perception of religion and conflicts in society predictors of Nigerian students' attitudes to the three aspects of the right to freedom of religion?

Hypotheses

In relation to the questions, the following hypotheses have been formulated. With regard to Question 1, we expect that:

H 1: the students support the dimension of freedom of religion of prayer in public schools (a); do not support the dimension of political non-interference (b), and (c) are ambivalent to the dimension of the hijab.

With regard to Question 2, we expect that:

H 2.1: individual beliefs of the students show a strong positive correlation with attitudes towards freedom of religion.

H 2.2: trust in religion has a strong negative correlation with attitudes towards freedom of religion.

H 2.3: the perception of religion as good for morality correlates positively with freedom of religion.

H 2.4: the attitude towards religion as unfit for modern society shows negative correlations with freedom of religion.
H 2.5: perception of conflicts has a strong positive correlation with attitudes towards religious freedom.

With regard to Question 3, we expect that:

H 3.1: individual belief has a strong positive impact on attitudes towards freedom of religion.
H 3.2: an attitude of high trust in one's own religion with a low trust in other religions has a strong negative impact on freedom of religion (a), while a high trust in one's own religion and in other religions as well, has a strong positive influence on religious freedom (b).
H 3.3: the more religion is seen as good for morality, the more freedom of religion is supported (a), but freedom of religion will not be supported when religion is considered to be unfit for modern society.
H 3.4: perception of conflicts has a strong positive influence on freedom of religion.
H 3.5: the perception of conflicts in society between religions has a more positive influence on attitudes towards freedom of religion than the perception of conflicts between ethnic groups.
H 3.6: age has no significant impact on students' attitudes towards freedom of religion.
H 3.7: women show more support for freedom of religion than men.
H 3.8: Muslim students support freedom of religion in terms of political non-interference less than the other sub-groups.

Context

Generally, prayer is a religious practice our respondents are familiar with since it is practised in their homes. It is also part of the normal religious socialization by religious organizations. Moreover, prayer in schools, particularly during the assemblies is a 'custom' that our respondents have come to imbibe. The practice goes back to the early beginnings of schools in Nigeria and reinforces indirectly the culture of praying, which already existed in the indigenous belief system of Nigeria (Mbiti 1969, 55–56). Religious identities or differences are not important as far as prayer is concerned. Thus, there are no convincing reasons to assume that the students would abandon this practice; instead, they would rather resort to it in the case of insecurity or any form of national conflict.

The position is quite different regarding the hijab while at school. Generally speaking, religious outfits serve as a mark of identification and differentiation. However, the perception of religiosity has changed among the youths; the emphasis is no longer on the external manifestations of religion but rather on spiritual religiosity. This is partly the result of the steady transformation of Nigerian society via globalization. Secondly, the use of religious outfits or symbols in Nigerian schools has remained an open issue, one that is subject to regional bias. Still, our survey was carried out in different regions of the country, so we expect attitudes towards this dimension of religious freedom to be ambivalent.

The average person in Nigeria opposes any form of political interference in religious issues, largely because of the poor perception of national politics by the general public. However, given the insecurity caused by recurring conflicts, we expect the minority groups in particular to welcome the involvement of the government in religious affairs. Nigerian Muslims appear more politically alert than the other subgroups and are less likely to support freedom of religion in terms of political non-interference.

Empirical Findings

Our empirical findings are divided into three parts. First, we present the descriptive analyses of our concepts. Then, we correlate our variables with freedom of religion. And finally, we run the regression analyses for religious freedom. Our empirical findings will enable us to answer the research questions and to know whether or not our hypotheses are proved true or false.[10]

Descriptive Analyses for Religious Freedom

This first analysis is dedicated to freedom of religion, the most important variable in our research study. Freedom of religion is operationalized in three dimensions: political non-interference, prayer in public schools and the hijab.

Freedom of Religion

The students were provided with questions concerning these three dimensions. According to their responses, freedom of religion receives a high positive valuation overall. The dimension of prayer in public schools gets the highest agreement (mean = 4.35), followed by the hijab (mean = 3.97) and, then, political non-interference which is also positively evaluated (mean = 3.74).

[10] We would like to thank Mrs. Susanne Döhnert for her friendly support in data analysis.

Of all the students, 63.3% fully agree or agree with the dimension of political non-interference (FR 1), 22.8% are not certain about this issue, while 13.8% totally disagree or disagree.

Regarding the hijab (FR 3), 11.8% totally disagree or disagree according to the responses, 17.3% are ambivalent, while 70.8% fully agree or agree.

Prayer in public schools (FR 2) has the highest acceptance. Here, 85.8% of the respondents fully agree or agree, only 8.8% are not sure, and the rest (5.4%) either totally disagree or disagree (Table 8.1).

Table 8.1 Freedom of religion (frequencies (%), means and standard deviation)

Items	––	–	+ –	+	++	M	SD
Political non interference	4.1	9.7	22.8	34.4	28.9	*3.74*	*1.10*
Prayers in public schools	2.3	3.1	8.8	28.6	57.2	*4.35*	*.93*
Wearing the hijab	5.2	6.6	17.3	28.1	42.7	*3.97*	*1.16*

It is remarkable though that religious freedom is so positively valued by the students in the three dimensions, not only prayer in public schools, as we had anticipated. We assumed that security concerns would stampede our respondents into accepting government's interference in religious issues. In fact, despite these security concerns the students still show a strong support for religious freedom; probably because the schools have not succumbed to the influence of the religions.

Individual Belief

We used the item on the importance of religion to measure individual belief, and the answering scheme is the same as the one above (cf. Table 8.2). 81.8% of the respondents fully agree or agree that religion in fact has an influence on their lives, in other words, that their beliefs are an important issue for them. 13.8% of the respondents are not sure, and 4.4% disagree with the statement. Overall we can say, that religious belief is very highly valued by the students (mean = 4.10) as Table 8.2 shows.

We already mentioned that Nigerians, like typical Africans, "…do not know how to exist without religion…" (Mbiti 1989, 2). The finding corresponds to our expectations. We further anticipate this attitude to be a strong predictor of attitudes towards freedom of religion.

Table 8.2 Individual belief (frequencies (%), means and standard deviation)

	––	–	+ –	+	++	M	SD
Importance of religion	0.5	3.9	13.8	48.3	33.5	*4.10*	*.82*

Trust in Religion

Trust in religion was also included as a possible predictor of students' attitudes towards freedom of religion. From the two items used to measure the concept, we obtained sub-categories depicting four different trust attitudes: low trust in one's own religion and low trust in other religions (from now on referred to as low-low trust), low trust in one's own religion and high trust in other religions (from now on referred to as low-high trust), high trust in one's own religion and high trust in other religions (high-high trust) and lastly, high trust in one's own religion and low trust in other religions (high-low trust). These sub-categories allow a better evaluation, as Table 8.3 illustrates.

Table 8.3 Trust in religion (frequencies (%))

		Trust in other religions	
		Low	High
Trust in own religion	Low	5.3	1.8
	High	58.4	34.5

The table shows that more than half of the respondents (58.4%) belong to the high-low trust sub-category (i.e. high trust for one's own religion and low trust for others). Next to it is the high-high trust sub-category with 34.5%, followed by low-low trust, 5.3%, and finally, 1.8% for the low-high trust.

In the first part of this paper, we cited a recent study by the PEW Research Center (2006) on Religion and Public Life, specifically on the issue of trust. Our findings here further support the conclusions of the survey, especially, that there is widespread mutual distrust between the different religious traditions in Nigeria. We suppose that this state of affairs is caused by the biases and stereotypes resulting from the competitive evangelical strategies of the religions.

Perception of Religion in Society

Two single, parallel items were used to measure the perception of religion in society. From the submissions, 41.9% totally or simply disagree with the statement that religion does not fit into modern society, 24.6% are unsure about this and 33.5% agree. In other words, our respondents are negatively ambivalent as far as the negative statement is concerned (mean = 2.87).

On the other hand, the item 'religion is good for morality' has a high positive valuation (mean = 4.25). Of all respondents, 83.3% agree with this statement, 9.2% are uncertain of their position, and only 7.6% totally disagree or disagree. The finding confirms, in general terms, our assumption of the acceptance of religion in Nigeria as a societal actor (Table 8.4).

Table 8.4 Perception of religion (frequencies (%), means and standard deviation)

Items	−−	−	+ −	+	++	M	SD
Religion unfit for society	19.4	22.5	24.6	18.3	15.2	*2.87*	*1.33*
Religion good for morality	2.2	5.4	9.2	32.0	51.3	*4.25*	*.98*

Perception of Conflicts in Society

The perception of conflicts in society affects students' awareness of their socio-cultural context. Here, we measure how our student respondents perceive their society with regard to conflicts and what they believe to be high conflict potential, whether it is between the rich and the poor or between religions and/or between the different ethnic groups. Furthermore, we want to know whether our respondents have had any personal experience of maltreatments, and if, what they believe to be the reasons; do these derive from social status (poor or rich), from their religious belonging or from their ethnic origins. The questions were to be answered using the scale from 1 ("never") to 5 ("very often") (Table 8.5).

Table 8.5 Perception of conflicts (frequencies (%), means and standard deviation)

Items	Never	Very seldom	Occasionally	Often	Very often	M	SD
Perceived conflicts							
Between rich and poor	2.4	11.2	26.0	27.6	32.8	*3.77*	*1.09*
Between religions	0.9	4.5	15.6	28.0	50.9	*4.23*	*.94*
Between ethnic groups	3.7	13.7	26.4	28.2	28.0	*3.63*	*1.14*
Perceived maltreatments							
Because of rich/poor	25.6	29.3	27.1	12.7	5.3	*2.43*	*1.15*
Because of religion	21.3	21.5	33.2	16.0	7.9	*2.68*	*1.20*
Because of race/ethnicity	41.2	26.9	21.4	8.0	2.5	*2.04*	*1.08*

According to their responses, conflicts between religious groups are perceived as most rampant (means = 4.23), followed by conflicts between the rich and the poor (mean = 3.77), and then conflicts between ethnic groups (mean = 3.63). Of the students, 78.9% perceive conflicts between religions as being often or very often, 15.6% say occasionally, and only 5.4% think that the conflicts never happen or are very seldom. When we look at tensions between the rich and the poor, 60.4% declare that conflicts between the rich and the poor occur often or very often, 26% perceive these conflicts as being occasionally, while 13.6% state that such conflicts never happen or at most, very seldom. Of the respondents, 56.2% affirm that they observe tensions between ethnic groups often or very often, 26.4% notice such conflicts occasionally, whereas 17.4% say that they never or hardly ever happen.

On whether they have personally been maltreated for reasons of religion, 42.8% of the respondents said that they have never or very seldom been maltreated because of their religion, 33.2% affirm that they have been maltreated occasionally, and 23.9% state that this has happened often or very often (mean = 2.68). Of the students, 18% reveal that they have been maltreated because of their social status (rich or poor), 27.1% confirm the occurrence of such an abuse occasionally, while the rest (54.9%) declare it has never happened or only rarely (mean = 2.43). Finally, 68.1% of our respondents affirm that they never, or very seldom, experienced maltreatments based on their ethnic origins, 21.4% say they happen occasionally, whereas 10.5% maintain they have often or very often been maltreated because of their ethnic origins.

These responses support our claim that there is indeed rivalry between the diverse religious groups in Nigeria. The term 'ethno-religious', which is sometimes used in this connection, refers to its complex forms. Our respondents are still in school. Some of them may not have been victims of these conflicts and/or maltreatments personally, but they perceive what is going on around them. These perceptions affect their attitudes, which are important for our research.

Variance Analyses

We will now perform additional analyses (variances), in order to understand the differences in attitudes of trust concerning religious freedom.

Freedom of Religion (Political Non-interference) and Trust in Religion

Table 8.6 shows no significant differences between the four trust attitudes in the evaluation of freedom of religion, when considered from the viewpoint of political non-interference. Students who have an attitude of high trust in their own religion with low trust in other religions (that is, a high-low trust attitude) evaluate this dimension of religious freedom the highest (mean = 3.77), followed by those with a high-high trust attitude (mean = 3.74). Respondents with a low-high trust attitude

Table 8.6 Variance analyses for political non-interference (FR 1) and trust in religion

Trust in religion	N	1
low_low	63	3.51
low_high	21	3.67
high_high	411	3.74
high_low	696	3.77
Sig.		.649

Scheffé's test F-value: 1.105; sig. < .346

(that is, low trust in one's own religion and high trust in others) are next with the mean value of 3.67, while those with a low-low trust attitude evaluate this dimension the lowest (mean = 3.51).

Freedom of Religion (Prayer in Public Schools) and Trust in Religion

In Table 8.7, however, there are significant differences between the different trust attitudes in terms of prayer in public schools. Students with a low-high trust attitude and those with a low-low trust attitude differ significantly in their evaluation of this dimension of freedom of religion from those with a high-high trust attitude and others with a high-low trust attitude. In other words, there is no statistical significant difference between students with a low-high trust attitude and those with a low-low trust attitude considering prayer in public schools. Similarly, students with a high-high trust attitude do not differ in their evaluation of this item from those with a high-low trust attitude.

Table 8.7 Variance analyses for prayer in public schools (FR 2) and trust in religion

Trust in religion	N	1	2
low_high	21	3.38	
low_low	63	3.78	
high_high	411		4.32
high_low	696		4.45
Sig.		.130	.897

Scheffé's test F-value: 19.353; sig. < .000

Compared with the first dimension (FR 1), this dimension of religious freedom is very important for students with a high-low trust attitude (mean = 4.45). Again, they are followed by those with a high-high trust attitude (mean = 4.32). In the third place are those with a low-low trust attitude, with 3.78 (mean) and, at the end, are those with a low-high trust attitude (mean = 3.38). Thus, students with a low trust in their own religion (low-high, low-low) support this dimension of the right to freedom of religion less than students with a high trust in their own belief (high-high, high-low trust).

Freedom of Religion (Wearing the Hijab) and Trust in Religion

Table 8.8 presents a slightly different picture. The students with a low-low trust, a low-high trust and a high-high trust have no significant difference in attitudes to the wearing of hijabs. On a similar note, those with a low-high trust, a high-high trust and a high-low trust do not differ significantly in their evaluation of the same item. The only significant difference is between those in low-low and high-low trust categories, at both ends of the range. Students with a low-low trust attitude show the lowest support for the wearing of hijab with 3.43 (mean), followed by those with a

Table 8.8 Variance analyses for wearing the hijab (FR 3) and trust in religion

Trust in religion	N	1	2
low_low	63	3.43	
low_high	21	3.57	3.57
high_high	411	3.93	3.93
high_low	696		4.05
Sig.		.133	.162

Scheffé's test F-value: 6.811; sig. < .000

low-high trust attitude (mean = 3.57). Respondents who have a high-high trust attitude evaluate it slightly higher with the mean value of 3.93, whereas those with a high-low trust attitude show the highest support for this dimension of religious freedom (mean = 4.05).

Finally, the results show no statistically significant difference between the four trust attitudes with regard to political non-interference, whereas the opposite is the case in the other two dimensions. Political non-interference is not 'a purely religious issue'. In short, it means that politicians should not interfere in the affairs of religion. As stated earlier, most Nigerians would accept political non-interference simply because they do not trust politicians that much. This might be the reason for the homogeneous response in this case. On the other hand, prayer in schools and the hijab are strictly matters of personal beliefs and convictions and, as such, likely to differ.

In general terms, freedom of religion is supported by the four sub-categories of the 'trust' concept. Students with a high trust in their own religion show more support for freedom of religion in terms of political non-interference, prayer in public schools and the hijab, than those with a low trust in their own religion. Respondents who have an attitude of high trust in their own religion with a low trust in other religions evaluate these dimensions of religious freedom the highest. They are followed by those with a high trust in both their own and other religions. In the third place are those who have a low trust attitude in their own religion with a high trust in other religions, whereas students with a low trust in both their own religion and other religions evaluate the same items the lowest, of the four sub-categories.

Socio-demographic Characteristics

Here we include religious belonging and sex as socio-demographic characteristics; age will feature later in the regression models. For religious belonging, we have also four sub-groups: Catholics, Muslims, Protestants and others, but our focus is solely on the first three.

Freedom of Religion (Political Non-interference) and Religious Belonging

There are no statistically significant differences between Catholics, Muslims, Protestants and 'others' in their attitudes towards political non-interference in religious issues. Comparatively, the Muslims show the highest support (mean = 3.91), followed by the sub-group 'others' (mean = 3.68). Catholics are in the third place with 3.66 (mean), while Protestants evaluate this item the lowest (mean = 3.64) (Table 8.9).

Table 8.9 Variance analyses for political non-interference (FR 1) and religious belonging

Religious belonging	N	1
Protestants	289	3.64
Catholics	436	3.66
Others	63	3.68
Muslims	403	3.91
Sig.		.185

Scheffé's test F-value: 4.688; sig. < .003

It is not surprising though that there are no significant differences between the sub-groups in their attitudes towards non-interference of politicians in religious issues. However, the fact that all the sub-groups support the view that politicians should not interfere in religious matters is remarkable, and especially that Muslim students agree with this item more than the other sub-groups.

Freedom of Religion (Prayer in Public Schools) and Religious Belonging

Similarly, there are no significant differences between the four sub-groups in their attitudes to prayer in public schools. The sub-groups rate *'the right'* to have prayer in public schools highly (cf. Table 8.10). The sub-group 'others' evaluates this *'right'* the lowest with a mean value of 4.17. Next to these are the Muslims (mean = 4.34), followed by the Protestants (mean = 4.36). Catholic respondents evaluate this item the highest, with 4.38 (mean). Prayer is a practice that is found in all religions in Nigeria, the support probably derives from that fact.

Table 8.10 Variance analyses for prayer in public schools (FR 2) and religious belonging

Religious belonging	N	1
Others	63	4.17
Muslims	403	4.34
Protestants	289	4.36
Catholics	436	4.38
Sig.		.254

Scheffé's test F-value: .925; sig. <.428

Freedom of Religion (Wearing the Hijab) and Religious Belonging

Table 8.11 shows a slight difference in the students' evaluation of this item. The 'others', Catholics and Muslims do not differ significantly in their attitudes towards the hijab. Nor are there any differences between Catholics, Muslims and Protestants. However, Protestants do differ significantly from the sub-group 'others'.

Table 8.11 Variance analyses for the wearing of the hijab (FR 3) and religious belonging

Religious belonging	N	1	2
Others	63	3.68	
Catholics	436	3.94	3.94
Muslims	403	3.97	3.97
Protestants	289		4.07
Sig.		.174	.784

Scheffé's test F-value: 2.125; sig. < .095

Protestant respondents evaluate the item the highest (mean = 4.07), followed by Muslims (mean = 3.97). Catholics are third in their evaluation of the same item with the mean value of 3.94, while the 'others' are the lowest among the four sub-groups, with 3.68 (mean).

All in all, we can observe that the right to freedom of religion is supported by all the sub-groups. However, the Muslims are more convinced than the others. They are followed by the Protestants, the Catholics and the 'others', in that order.

Freedom of Religion and Sex

For sex, we conducted a T-test because we are comparing only two groups – men and women. Sex is highly significant, as can be seen in Table 8.12. It has a significant negative influence on the dimension of political non-interference, with the male students showing more support (mean = 3.88) than the females (mean = 3.63). As mentioned earlier, the traditional role patterns in Nigeria enable men to be more politically active than women. This could be the reason for differences in attitude between men and women.

According to the table above, female respondents support (mean = 4.44) prayer in public schools more than males (mean = 4.24), perhaps because women tend to

Table 8.12 T-test for freedom of religion and sex

Items	T-value	Significance	Mean
Political non-interference	−3.92	***	Female 3.63
			Male 3.88
Prayers in public schools	3.62	***	Female 4.44
			Male 4.24
Wearing the hijab	2.51	*	Female 4.04
			Male 3.87

be more religious than their male counterparts. They are also more in favour of the wearing of the hijab (mean = 4.04) than males (mean = 3.87).

Correlation Analyses

We conducted correlation analyses to figure out whether there are any connections between the concepts tested. Note that a non-correlation means that the concepts are independent of each other.

From Table 8.13, we can see that the concept 'individual belief' has a strong positive correlation with prayer in public schools (.25**) and wearing of the hijab (.22**). With regard to political non-interference, 'individual belief' is also significant and positive (.09**), but not relevant. Nevertheless, the individual beliefs of the respondents correlate strongly with their attitudes towards freedom of religion via the above two dimensions. In other words, the stronger their individual beliefs are, the more students support the right to freedom of religion.

The trust concept shows a different picture. It correlates positively with prayer in public schools and the hijab, but is not significant with political non-interference. Concerning the hijab, the trust concept is significant (.06*) but not relevant because the value is lower than required. The trust concept correlates strongly and positively (.10**) only regarding prayer in public schools. That is to say, the more a student trusts religion, the more he or she supports prayer in public schools. However, since it is only in one out of the three dimensions that trust in religion correlates strongly with freedom of religion, we cannot conclude that trust in religion is strongly related to the support for this right.

Table 8.13 Correlations between the independent and dependent variables

	FR 1	FR 2	FR 3
Individual belief			
Importance of religion	.09**	.25**	.22**
Trust in religion	.03	.10**	.06*
Perception of religion			
Religion unfit for society	−.02	.05	.07*
Religion good for morality	.12**	.24**	.20**
Conflicts in society			
Perceived conflicts			
Between rich and poor	.07*	.09**	.02
Between religions	.06*	.11**	.07*
Between ethnic groups	.05	.10**	.08**
Perceived maltreatments			
Because rich or poor	−.01	.05	−.03
Because of religion	.05	.02	−.02
Because of race/ethnicity	−.07*	−.02	−.04

All correlations are significant at $p < .01$ level (**) or $p < .05$ level (*)

The table shows that the item 'religion is good for morality' is significant. It has strong positive correlations with our three dimensions of religious freedom. Thus, we can conclude that the more religion is seen as good for the morality of the society, the more students reject the interference of politicians in the affairs of religions, and the more religious practices such as prayer in schools and the hijab, are supported. The respondents consider religion as beneficial for morality and thus, good for society. Therefore, religious practices should be accepted.

The parallel item, 'religion is unfit for modern society' has also a positive correlation with attitudes towards religious freedom. The item correlates positively with wearing the hijab (.07*) and is not significant with the other two dimensions. The value (.07*) is though below the requirement and, therefore, not relevant.

The perceived conflicts in society between the rich and the poor are significant and relate positively with political non-interference (.07*) and prayer in public schools (.09**). However, these are weak correlations. In reference to the hijab, the perceived conflicts in society between the rich and the poor' are not significant. The perception of conflicts and tensions between religions is significantly positive (.06*, .11**, .07* respectively). As we can see, this item has a strong correlation with prayer in public schools, and weak correlations with the other dimensions, meaning that, increasing religious conflicts actually result in a rising approval of freedom of religion in terms of prayer at public schools.

The perception of conflicts in society between ethnic groups correlates positively with prayer in public schools (.10*) and the hijab (.08**), but it is not significant with political non-interference. Besides, the correlation with the item on the hijab is a weak correlation, as the value indicates. Therefore, the perception of conflicts between ethnic groups has a strong correlation only with prayer in public schools, that is, the more conflicts between ethnic groups are perceived, the more the students support the practice of prayer in public schools.

Furthermore, the perceived maltreatments in society show weak correlations with freedom of religion via the three dimensions. The personal experience of maltreatments because of ethnic origins correlates negatively with political non-interference (.07*). However, the value is not relevant.

When we consider our independent variables, individual belief and perception of religion in society relate strongly with attitudes towards freedom of religion. Perception of conflicts and trust in religion, on the other hand, show weak correlations with attitudes towards this right. However, correlation does not imply causality. So, in order to discover the concepts that predict the respondents' attitudes towards religious freedom, we will conduct regression analyses.

Regression Analyses

We now investigate the concepts which can explain students' attitudes towards religious freedom. In order to do this, we have computed three regression models – one for each dimension of religious freedom (cf. Table 8.14).

Table 8.14 Regression analyses for freedom of religion with individual belief, trust in religion, perception of religion, perception of conflicts, sex, age and religious belonging

	Beta (FR 1)	Beta (FR 2)	Beta (FR 3)
Individual belief			
Importance of religion	.040	.165***	.166***
Trust in religion			
Low-low (ref. high-low)	−.021	−.089**	−.044
Low-high (ref. high-low)	.012	−.087**	.008
High-high (ref. high-low)	−.003	−.027	−.005
Perception of religion			
Religion unfit for society	.018	.073**	.081**
Religion good for morality	.099***	.159***	.146***
Conflicts in society			
-Perceived conflicts-			
Between rich and poor	.065*	.027	−.017
Between religions	−.002	.041	.024
Between ethnic groups	.066*	.065*	.068*
-Perceived maltreatments-			
Because rich or poor	−.029	.045	−.002
Because of religion	.061	.004	.001
Because of race/ethnicity	−.116***	−.044	−.048
Sex			
Female (ref. male)	−.106***	.089**	.030
Age			
Age of respondents	.007	−.015	−.116***
Religious belonging			
Protestants (ref. Catholics)	−.007	−.011	.049
Muslims	.084*	.001	.043
Others	.002	−.034	−.034
adj. R^2	.04	.13	.09
F =	4.170***	11.058***	8.033***

N = 1191
*p ≤. 05; **p ≤ .01; ***p ≤ 001
Reference: trust in religion = high-low, sex = male, religious belonging = Catholics

With our predictor-concepts, we can explain 4.3% of the variance of religious freedom in terms of political non-interference, 12.6% of prayer in public schools and 9.1% of wearing the hijab.

The beta values give us a picture of the strength of the impact of the different predictor-concepts on the dependent variable. We shall, therefore, examine the impacts of these concepts separately on the three dimensions of religious freedom.

The results of the regression models indicate that individual belief is highly significant. Individual belief has a positive influence on prayer in public schools and the hijab (Beta = .165*** and Beta = .166*** respectively), but is not significant with political non-interference. Nevertheless, these two beta values are quite strong.

This means that the individual beliefs of the students have a strong impact on their attitudes towards religious freedom. Thus, we conclude that the students approve more of freedom of religion in terms of prayer in public schools and the hijab when their individual belief is high.

Next, we come to the four dummy-variables of trust in religion. The reference category is 'high-low'. In the first and third regression models, there are no significant differences between the trust-in-religion sub-groups and the reference category, high-low. Students of all three trust sub-categories do not differ significantly from the reference category in their evaluation of religious freedom in terms of political non-interference and the hijab. However, in the second regression model, there are significant sub-group differences: students with a low trust attitude in both their own religion and other religions (low-low trust) and those who have an attitude of low trust in their own religion with a high trust in other religions (low-high trust) evaluate prayer in public schools differently from the reference category (Beta = −.089** and Beta = −.087**, respectively). Both groups support this dimension of religious freedom less than students in the high-low trust sub-group – our reference category. Generally, trust in religion has little impact on attitudes towards freedom of religion.

The perception of religion in society has a strong predictive value. The two items of the concept are significant. The item 'religion is unfit for modern society' is significantly positive with reference to prayer in public schools (Beta = .073**) and the wearing the hijab (Beta = .081**), but is not significant with political non-interference. The alternative item 'religion is good for morality' is also significant and positive with these three dimensions (Beta = .099***, Beta = .159*** and Beta = .146***, respectively). Thus, both items have positive beta values. But they are contradictory items. We consider the item 'religion is unfit for modern society' to be of less importance because the beta values are low. The item 'religion is good for morality', on the other hand, has a strong influence on attitudes towards freedom of religion via the three dimensions. Thus, we conclude that the more students perceive that religion helps their personal morality as well as that of the society, the more they support freedom of religion.

Conversely, the perception of conflicts in society has a very small effect on attitudes towards freedom of religion. The perception of conflicts between the rich and the poor is significantly positive with reference to political non-interference (Beta = .065*). It is not significant with the other two dimensions. The perception of conflicts between religions has no significant effect at all. Perceived tensions between ethnic groups are significant, but they also have low beta values (Beta = .066*, Beta = .065* and Beta = .068*, respectively). Perceived maltreatments because of social status (rich or poor) or religion are not statistically significant. On the other hand, perceived maltreatments because of ethnic origin have a strong negative impact on respondents' attitudes towards freedom of religion in terms of political non-interference (Beta = −.116***), but they are not significant in relation to the other dimensions. This simply means that, the more students believe that they are maltreated because of their origin, the less likely they are to support freedom of religion in terms of political non-interference in religious issues.

Generally, the 'perception of conflicts in society' has low beta values, except in connection with the item on 'perceived maltreatments because of one's ethnicity'. It is, therefore, not a strong predictor.

Now, we turn to the socio-demographic factors. Sex has a slight, but significant impact on attitudes towards freedom of religion. It has a strong negative impact on political non-interference (Beta = −.106***), and a slight positive effect on prayer in public schools (Beta = .089**). Considering the hijab, sex is not significant. Female students support the dimension of political non-interference less than males. But they are more supportive of the other two dimensions.

Age has a lower predictive value than sex. It has a negative influence on the hijab (Beta = −.116***), and is not statistically significant with reference to the other two dimensions. According to these findings, the older respondents do not support freedom of religion in terms of the hijab etc. as much as the younger ones.

Lastly, religious belonging has very little influence on respondents' attitudes towards freedom of religion. There are no significant differences between the four religious sub-groups in their evaluation of this right, except in the first regression model. Here, Protestants and the sub-group 'others' do not differ from the reference category (Catholics) in their evaluation of political non-interference. But Muslim respondents differ with the reference category (Beta = .084*). However, the beta value is low, which means in general terms that religious belonging is a weak predictor (Table 8.14).

Discussion

We now attempt a general evaluation of our findings. This will enable us to answer the questions and to figure out whether or not our hypotheses are confirmed.

The Predictors of the Concepts of Religious Freedom

This research showed that the strongest predictor of respondents' attitudes towards freedom of religion is individual belief. This conclusion is confirmed by our findings. Although the concept is not significant with reference to political non-interference, it has quite a strong influence on the other two dimensions of freedom of religion. Thus, students' attitudes towards religious freedom are strongly influenced by their beliefs.

Next to the beliefs of the students is their perception of religion in society. The item 'religion is good for morality' that was used to measure the students' perception of the function of religion in society, has a strong positive influence on their attitudes towards freedom of religion.

The concept 'perception of conflicts in society' has little effect on students' attitudes towards this right. Of the three dimensions, perceived conflicts in society between rich and poor are significant only when referring to political non-interference. The perception of conflicts between ethnic groups has a small effect on the three dimensions. Perceived conflicts between religions are not significant at all. The personal experience of maltreatments because of ethnicity has a strong negative influence on political non-interference. But it is not significant in relation to the other dimensions. In general terms, the perception of conflicts in society is a weak predictor.

The results of this research show that trust in religion is an equally weak predictor as far as respondents' attitudes towards religious freedom is concerned. Trust in religion is only significant in the second regression model. It has a negative influence on the dimension of prayer in public schools. But the influence is negligible owing to a low beta value.

Sex, age and religious belonging were included in the analyses as possible predictors of respondents' attitudes towards freedom of religion. The results show that sex has a strong influence only in terms of the dimension of political non-interference. According to our research, female students support freedom of religion more than male students. However, the males agree more with this dimension than females. This finding confirms our earlier comments on gender roles and behavioural patterns in Nigeria. Age has a strong negative influence on the dimension of the hijab. But it is not significant with the other two dimensions. Age is, therefore, a weak predictor. Religious belonging is not a strong predictor of respondents' attitudes towards freedom of religion. It is only significant in the first regression model, and Muslim respondents support this dimension of freedom of religion more than the other sub-groups.

Research Questions and Hypotheses

In the following paragraphs, we return to the research questions and review the hypotheses with reference to the research findings. The first question is: what are the attitudes of secondary school students in Nigeria towards the three dimensions of freedom of religion, namely political non-interference in religious affairs, prayer in public schools and the hijab? The findings show that all three dimensions are positively evaluated by the students.

In reference to this question, we have the expectation (H 1) that:

(a) the students support the dimension of freedom of religion of prayer in public schools;
(b) they do not support the dimension of political non-interference, and
(c) they are ambivalent to the dimension of the hijab.

Our findings partly confirm this hypothesis.

The second question reads: how far are individual belief, trust in religion, perception of religion and conflicts in society related to the different dimensions of freedom of religion? Whereas individual belief and the perception of religion in society have strong positive correlations with the dimensions of freedom of religion, trust in religion and perception of conflicts in society relate weakly with these. We have attached five hypotheses to this second question:

H 2.1: Individual beliefs of the students show a strong positive correlation with attitudes towards freedom of religion. Indeed the beliefs of the student respondents correlate positively with freedom of religion via the three dimensions. In relation to political non-interference, it is also significantly positive, but has a low value. Nevertheless, individual belief has a strong positive correlation with freedom of religion, thus confirming our expectation.

H 2.2: Trust in religion has a strong negative correlation with attitudes towards freedom of religion. On the contrary, trust in religion has positive but weak correlations with attitudes towards freedom of religion, in this paper. Therefore, we do not confirm this hypothesis.

H 2.3: The perception of religion as good for morality correlates positively with freedom of religion. We confirm this hypothesis.

H 2.4: The attitude towards religion as unfit for modern society shows negative correlations with freedom of religion. This hypothesis does not agree with empirical facts and will not be confirmed, because the item is significantly positive with reference to the dimension of the hijab.

H 2.5: The perception of conflicts in society has a strong positive correlation with attitudes towards religious freedom. On the contrary, the concept 'perception of conflicts' showed both positive and negative correlations with different dimensions of freedom of religion. Besides, these are generally weak correlations. Therefore, we do not confirm this hypothesis.

Then, the third question: are demographic characteristics, religious belonging, individual belief, trust in religion, perception of religion and conflicts in society predictors of attitudes of Nigerian students to the three aspects of the right to freedom of religion? All these concepts contributed to explaining attitudes towards the three aspects of this right. But the strong predictors of the respondents' attitudes here are individual belief and the perception of religion. Perception of conflicts, age and sex have only slight effects on attitudes towards freedom of religion. Trust in religion and religious belonging are also weak predictors. The following hypotheses are attached to this question:

H 3.1: Individual belief has a strong positive impact on attitudes towards freedom of religion. This expectation is confirmed.

Next, H 3.2: An attitude of high trust in one's own religion with a low trust in other religions has a strong negative impact on freedom of religion (a), while a high trust in one's own religion and in other religions as well, has a strong positive influence on religious freedom (b). We do not confirm this hypothesis. Trust in religion has an insignificant influence on the dimensions of freedom of religion.

H 3.3: the more religion is perceived as beneficial for morality, the more freedom of religion is supported (a), but freedom of religion will not be supported when religion is considered to be unfit for modern society. The findings corroborate only the first part of this hypothesis.

The next hypothesis reads: perception of conflicts in society has a strong positive influence on freedom of religion (H 3.4). The concept ‘perception of conflicts’ is a weak predictor in this paper. Again, the expectation that the perception of conflicts in society between religions has a more positive influence on attitudes towards freedom of religion than the perception of conflicts between ethnic groups (H 3.5), has no base on the findings, because the item on conflicts between religions is not significant at all. Therefore, we do not confirm both hypotheses.

With reference to the control variables, we have the following hypotheses: age has no significant impact on students’ attitudes towards freedom of religion (H 3.6). On the contrary, age is significant with reference to the dimension of the hijab. Therefore, this hypothesis cannot be confirmed. By contrast, the hypothesis (H 3.7) that women support the right to freedom of religion more than men, is confirmed.

Lastly, H 3.8: Muslim students support the freedom of religion in terms of political non-interference less than the other sub-groups. This hypothesis cannot be confirmed, because Muslim students support this dimension of freedom of religion more than the other sub-groups.

Conclusion

In a conclusion, it is obligatory to highlight some of the striking findings of the research. First of all, we observed that 78.9% of the respondents confirm the occurrence of conflicts between religions in Nigeria (see Table 8.5). Partly for this reason, we expected (more or less) respondents to demonstrate a negative attitude towards freedom of religion. We also mentioned that this dreadful situation could be traced back to the evangelical strategies of certain religious groups in Nigeria. Be that as it may, the lack of a precise constitutional model of freedom of religion in Nigeria, hinders a sustainable management of the conflicts. Instead, the country needs to embrace true secularism that is nowadays a widely-accepted model for harmonious co-existence in a religiously pluralistic society.

It is also remarkable that more than half of our respondents (58.4%) belong to the high-low trust sub-category, that is to say, they have a high trust in their own religions and a low trust in other religions. This finding supports recent studies that claim there really is a climate of mutual distrust among the adherents of the various religions in Nigeria. This seems to be an alarming trend with enormous implications for the future. The government, therefore, has to evolve pro-active bridge-building measures such as a genuine culture of dialogue, etc. that could help to reduce the ‘gaps’ between the diverse religious identities in Nigeria.

In the preamble to the UDHR, the General Assembly stressed the vital role of education in the service of rights and freedoms (Streich 2008). In this paper, we have raised alarm earlier on about the overbearing influence of religion on the institutions of learning in Nigeria. However the respondents’ massive support for freedom of religion, an attitude we believe to be influenced by the school system, shows that the Nigerian schools can still be relied upon as far as the future of human rights in Nigeria is concerned, especially freedom of religion. Schools are established to perform a social function. A country plagued with religious crisis requires that religion be taught appropriately. The Council of Europe recently reiterated the need for appropriate teaching about religion as part of the measures needed to check the religious renaissance of the last few decades. Such a teaching about religion should reflect global and local issues, and should be based on sound scholarship (Jackson 2014, 24). In order to guarantee the effective delivery of such appropriate Religious Education, Heil and Ziebertz (2010, 577–585) make a strong case for the professionalization of the teaching of religion.

Such international programmes are worthy of emulation. Indeed, according to the comments of our respondents on the prevalence of religious conflicts in the country, Nigeria might need to make a paradigmatic shift in its teaching of Religious Education to enhance the understanding of religious diversity "as a feature of education for all" (Jackson 2014, 2) but not as a replacement of the usual religious socialization by religious organizations and at home. In a 'Distinguished Management Lecture' held in Lagos, Nigeria in 2012, the former Foreign Affairs Minister of Nigeria, Prof. Bolaji Akinyemi declared, while commenting on the country's challenges: "I believe in revolution. I have come to the conclusion that it is a revolution that will solve the problems of this country."[11] We are of the opinion that appropriate teaching about religion has to be part of such a revolution.

References

Achebe, C. (1958). *Things fall apart*. Dunfermline: Heinemann Ltd..

Adegbite, K. (2012). Is Nigeria a secular or non-secular state? *The Newjurist* @: http://www.newjurist.com/. Retrieved on October 1, 2014.

Atado, J. C. (1988). *African marriage customs and church law: A case-study of the Igbos*. Kano: Modern Printers.

Ayandele, E. A. (1966). The missionary factor in northern Nigeria, 1870–1914. *Journal of Historical Society of Nigeria, III*(3), 22.

Beyers J. (2010). What is religion? An African understanding. *HTS Theological Studies, 66*(1), Art.341.

Botvar, P. K., & Sjöborg, A. (2012). Views on human rights among Christian, Muslim and non-religious youth in Norway and Sweden. *Nordic Journal of Religion and Society, 25*(1), 67–81.

Coleman, J. S. (1958). Nigeria: Background to nationalism. In: E. Osaghae, & T. Suberu (Eds.), *A history of identities, violence, and stability in Nigeria* (Working Paper 6). Oxford: Centre for Research on Inequality, Human Security and Ethnicity (CRISE).

Colquitt, J. A., et al. (2007). Trust, trustworthiness, and trust propensity: A meta-analytic test of their unique relationships with risk taking and job performance. *Journal of Applied Psychology, 92*(4), 909–927.

Dada J. A. (2012). Impediments to human rights protection in Nigeria. Annual Survey of International and Comparative Law XVIII. p. 68.

[11] See http://justiceforakwaibom.wordpress.com/2012/07/20/nigeria-needs-a-revolution-now-professor-bolaji-akinyemi/ Retrieved on 01.10.2012.

Duniya, F. (1993). The challenge of religious intolerance in the third republic. The Nigerian Journal of Theology I (I). p. 45.
Ekwunife, A. N. O. (1992). *Politics and religious intolerance: The Nigerian experience*. Nsukka: Spiritan Publications.
Eno-Abasi, S. (2014) Curbing violent extremism with curriculum modification. *The Guardian Newspaper* @: http://www.ngrguardiannews.com/. Retrieved on 28 Oct 2014.
Etuk, U. (2002). *Religion and cultural identity*. Ibadan: Hope Publications.
Ezeh, M. N. E., & Okonkwo, U. U. (2010). Place of religion in national building and security in Nigeria: A historical survey of Aro expedition of 1901. *African Journal of History and Culture, 2*(2), 26–30.
Figl, J. (Ed.). (2003). Handbuch religionswissenschaft: Religionen und ihre zentrale themen. In Beyers, J. (2010). *What is religion? An African understanding. HTS Theological Studies, 66*(1), Art. 341.
Gandonu, A. (1978). Nigeria's 250 ethnic groups: Realities and assumptions. In E. Osaghae, & T. Suberu (Ed.), (2005) *A history of identities, violence, and stability in Nigeria.* Oxford: Centre for Research on Inequality, Human Security and Ethnicity (CRISE), Working Paper 6.
Folarin, B. (1998). *Theories of mass communication: An introductory text*. Ibadan: Stirling Horden Publishers.
Heil, S., & Ziebertz, H. G. (2010). Professionalisierung von religionslehrerinnen und religionslehrer. In G. Hilger et al. (Eds.), *Religionsdidaktik, ein leitfaden für studium, ausbildung und beruf* (pp. 577–585). Kösel-Verlag: München.
Ibrahim, J. (1989). The politics of religion in Nigeria: The parameters of the 1987 crisis in Kaduna state. *Review of African Political Economy, 45*(6), 65–82.
Igwe, L. (2008). Nigeria's educational system needs free thought. http://www.secularhumanism.org/library/shb/igwe_19_2.htm. Retrieved on 25 Sep 2014.
Jackson, R. (2014). The European dimension: Perspectives on religious education from European institutions, professional organization and research networks. In M. Rothgangel et al. (Eds.), *Religious education at schools in Europe 2. Western Europe* (pp. 19–41). Göttingen: Verlag V & R Unipress.
Lemu, B. A. (2014). Religious education in Nigeria – A case study. http://folk.uio.no/leirvik/OsloCoalition/AishaLemu.htm. Retrieved on 3 Oct 2014.
Lewis, P. (2007). Identity, institutions and democracy in Nigeria. In Okpanachi, E. (2012). *Ethno-religious identity and conflict in northern Nigeria.* http://www.cetri.be/spip.php?article2470&lang=fr. Retrieved on 1 Oct 2014.
Lewis, P., & Bratton, M. (2000). Attitudes towards democracy and markets in Nigeria. In Osaghae, E., & Suberu, T. (2005). *A history of identities, violence, and stability in Nigeria,* (Working Paper 6). Oxford: Centre for Research on Inequality, Human Security and Ethnicity ((CRISE).
Lewis, J. D., & Weigert, A. (1985). Trust as a social reality. *Social Forces, 63*, 967–985.
Luhmann, N. (1979). *Trust and power*. New York: John Wiley.
Magesa, L. (2002). *African religion: The moral traditions of abundant life*. Maryknoll: Orbis Books.
Maluleke, T. S. (2001). Identity and integrity in African theology: A critical analysis. In Beyers, J. (2010). *What is religion? An African understanding. HTS Theological Studies, 66*(1), Art. 341.
Mbiti, J. S. (1969/1989/1999). *African religions and philosophy*. Oxford: Heinemann Educational Publishers.
McKnight, D. H., & Chervany, N. L. (2001). Trust and distrust definitions: One bite at a time. In R. Falcone et al. (Eds.), *Trust in cyber-societies*. Heidelberg: Springer.
Murdock, G. P. (1975). Outline of world cultures. In: E. Osaghae, & T. Suberu (Ed.), (2005) *A history of identities, violence, and stability in Nigeria.* Oxford: Centre for Research on Inequality, Human Security and Ethnicity (CRISE), Working Paper 6.
Nnoli, O. (1978). *Ethnic politics in Nigeria*. Enugu: Fourth Dimension.

Odetola, T. O. (1978). Military politics in Nigeria: Economic development and political stability. In E. Osaghae, & T. Suberu (Ed.), (2005) *A history of identities, violence, and stability in Nigeria*. Oxford: Centre for Research on Inequality, Human Security and Ethnicity (CRISE), Working Paper 6.

Odoeme, P. C. (2011). *Human rights and the mission of the church in Nigeria*. Tübingen: Lit-verlag.

Okeke, G. N. (2013). The ambivalence of the 1999 Nigerian Constitution in matters relating to secularism: A case for a constitutional review. *International Journal of Humanities and Social Science Invention, 2*(3), 65–69.

Onwubiko, K. B. C. (1967). *School certificate history of West Africa 1 (AD.1000 – 1800)*. Onitsha: Africana-Fep Educational Publishers.

Onwubiko, K. B. C. (1973). *School certificate history of West Africa: 2 (1800 – Present day)*. Onitsha: Africana-Fep Educational Publishers.

Otite, O. (1990). Ethnic pluralism and ethnicity in Nigeria. In E. Osaghae, & T. Suberu (Ed.), (2005) *A history of identities, violence, and stability in Nigeria*. Oxford: Centre for Research on Inequality, Human Security and Ethnicity (CRISE), Working Paper 6.

Ozigboh, I. R. A. (1993). Religious co-existence in Nigeria: An inquiry and suggestions. *The Nigerian Journal of Theology, 7*(I).

Paden, J. (2007). Comments at the symposium on religious conflict in Nigeria: Contemporary religious dynamics in Nigeria. In Okpanachi, E. (2012) *Ethno-religious identity and conflict in northern Nigeria*. @: http://www.cetri.be/spip.php?article2470&lang=fr. Retrieved on 1 Oct 2014.

Paul, V. I. (1965). Dignitatis humanae. In A. Flannery (Ed.), (1975) Vatican council II. *The conciliar and post conciliar documents*. Northport: Pauline Publishers.

PEFS. (2001). Ethnic Map of Nigeria, 7 vols. In E. Osaghae, & T. Suberu (Eds.), (2005) *A history of identities, violence, and stability in Nigeria*. Oxford: Centre for Research on Inequality, Human Security and Ethnicity (CRISE), Working Paper 6.

Ruby, R., & Shah, T. (2007). Nigeria's presidential election: The Christian-Muslim divide. In Okpanachi, E. (2012). *Ethno-religious identity and conflict in northern Nigeria*. @: http://www.cetri.be/spip.php?article2470&lang=fr. Retrieved on 1 Oct 2014.

Sjöborg, A. (2012). The impact of religion on freedom of religion and freedom of speech among young Swedes. In J. A. Van der Ven & H. G. Ziebertz (Eds.), *Tensions within and between religions and human rights*. Brill: Leiden.

Streich, M. (Ed.). (2008). *Allgemeine Erklärung der Menschenrechte*. München: Knaus Verlag.

Sundermeier, T. (1999). Was ist religion? Religionswissenschaft in theologischen kontext. In Beyers, J. (2010). *What is religion? An African understanding. HTS Theological Studies, 66*(1), Art. 341.

Tapasyananda, S. (1984). *The philosophical and religious lectures of swami Vivekananda*. Kolkata: Advaita Ashrama.

Turaki, Y. (1999). Christianity and African gods: A method in theology. In Beyers J. (2010). *What is religion? An African understanding. HTS Theological Studies, 66*(1), Art. 341.

Van der Ven, J. A. (2010). *Human rights or religious rules*. Leiden: Brill.

Van der Ven, J. A., & Ziebertz, H. G. (Eds.). (2012). *Tensions within and between religions and human rights*. Leiden: Brill.

Ziebertz, H. G., & Reindl, M. (2012). Religious socialization and values as predictors of human rights attitudes. In J. A. Van der Ven, & H. G. Ziebertz (Eds.), *Tensions within and between religions and human rights*. Brill: Leiden.

Ziebertz, H. G., & Reindl, M. (2013). Religion and attitudes towards euthanasia and abortion. In J. A. Van der Ven & H. G. Ziebertz (Eds.), *Human rights and the impact of religion*. Leiden: Brill.

Internet Sources

www.uscirf.gov/reports-briefs/annual-report/2014-annual-report. Retrieved on 20 Oct 2014.
http://www.democracyweb.org/about/democracyweb.php. Retrieved on 1 Oct 2014.
www.nigeria-law.org/ConstitutionOfTheFederalRepublicOfNigeria.htm
http://www.rhr.theologie.uni-wuerzburg.de/
http://www.irinnews.org/report/45857/nigeria-kano-state-directs-all-school-girls-to-wear-muslim-scarf. Retrieved on 1 Oct 2014.
http://justiceforakwaibom.wordpress.com/2012/07/20/nigeria-needs-a-revolution-now-professor-bolaji-akinyemi/. Retrieved on 1 Oct 2012.

Chapter 9
Advancing Civil Human Rights Culture in Tanzania

Clement Fumbo and Carl Sterkens

Abstract This contribution investigates the traditional difficulties faced in advancing human rights culture in Tanzania. It describes the sorts of problems, causes and deeper reasons that hinder the advancement and application of human rights in Tanzania. What is the nature of these problems? And what are the possible solutions? Despite the fact that in theory, Tanzania fully embraces human rights, the country falls short when it comes to applying them. We will argue that specific cultural traditions and customs are to blame for human rights abuses. Strict and conservative beliefs and practices in Tanzania do not align with human rights. More specifically, traditional family values and gender-role stereotypes; arranged (child) marriages; belief in witchcraft; and extrajudicial killings and unjust law enforcement are all implicated in causing harm to human rights culture.

Introduction

This study researches the nature and causes of human rights violations in Tanzania by describing some widespread cultural traditions. In Tanzania, ethnic groups consist mainly of communities formed by kinship (cf. Mbiti 1970, 3; Fumbo 2011, 8). Human rights in Tanzania are often interpreted from the perspective of the beliefs and traditions of strong collectivist communities, as well as of the particular interests these communities serve. In general, human rights reside under a community-based umbrella, which understandably is problematic for civil human rights which are the focus of this volume.

Despite the fact that human rights are embraced fully in theory, actual compliance is highly problematic in practice. Some specific cultural practices and traditions house direct violations of human rights. Conservative cultural patterns–specifically

C. Fumbo (✉)
Faculty of Social Sciences, The Open University, Dar es Salaam, Tanzania
e-mail: gfumbo@yahoo.co.uk

C. Sterkens
Faculty of Philosophy, Theology and Religious Studies, Radboud University, Nijmegen, The Netherlands

H.-G. Ziebertz, C. Sterkens (eds.), *Religion and Civil Human Rights in Empirical Perspective*, Religion and Human Rights 2, DOI 10.1007/978-3-319-59285-5_9

related to religion, clan traditions, and views on family – contradict human rights culture. This study lists some of these traditions. Therefore, the goal of this contribution is to reveal the nature of human rights violations, and discover the deeper causes that hinder the process of advancing a human rights culture in Tanzania.

We will concentrate on 'first-generation' human rights, which express basic liberties: prohibition of inhumane treatment; protection from discrimination; and the right to privacy. We leave out political[1] and judicial rights such as "the right to defend and assert all one's rights on terms of equality with others and by due process of law – not only to vertical relations between government and the citizen but also to horizontal relations between citizens" (Van der Ven et al. 2004, 100).

Before embarking on the questions raised, we will briefly introduce the political background of Tanzania from a historical perspective, and give definitions of civil rights and liberties, traditions and culture, and ethnicity.

Political Background of Tanzania

Tanzania is a constitutional, secular, united republic with a multi-party political system. During the last 20 years Tanzania has become more democratic.[2] Present-day Tanzania is the result of the unification of two countries, Tanganyika and Zanzibar, in April 1964. Before the union, Tanganyika (now mainland Tanzania) was consecutively a German colony (1880s–1918) and a Trusteeship Territory under Great Britain (1919–1961); while Zanzibar had long been a relatively independent Sultanate before becoming a British protectorate in 1890.

In terms of religious affiliation, during the colonial period Tanganyika had about 30% Christians, 35% Muslims and 35% indigenous believers. Zanzibar's population was virtually entirely Muslim. Three years after unification, religious affiliation had changed somewhat. According to the 1967 National Census, 34% of the population was Christian, 31% Muslim, and 35% belonged to other religious traditions. Official census Statistics on religion have not been available since 1967. In the most recent census (2012), Tanzania mainland had a population of 43,625,354 people, and 1,303,569 people live in Zanzibar. According to PEW statistics (2014, 22), 61% of the population of Tanzania is Christian, 35% Muslim, and 4% belong to other religious traditions. Religious distribution in Zanzibar has remained almost unchanged since 1964, meaning that the population is almost completely Ibadi Muslim.

---

[1] A definition of political rights would be the ability to participate in public affairs, voting rights and the right to equal access to public services. Those include freedom of association, freedom of assembly, freedom of speech, freedom of religion/worship, freedom to participate in political life, and the right to take part in governance (cf. Article 21, 25 of the International Covenant on Civil and Political Rights 1966).

[2] https://freedomhouse.org/report/freedom-world/freedom-world-2015#.VYEywUaRD3Y

The constitution guarantees freedom of religion, thus helping to limit religious conflicts (Article 19 and 20; cf. DIIS Report 2006). Every individual has the right to worship anything and is free to affiliate with any religious group, as long as one does not infringe the freedom of others. The leadership succession in Tanzania can be seen as an indicator that tensions between religious groups are limited. The first president, Julius Kambarage Nyerere (1961–1984), was Catholic; his successor, Ally Hassan Mwinyi (1985–1995), a Muslim from Zanzibar. President Benjamin William Mkapa (1995–2005) was Protestant; and Jakaya Mrisho Kikwete (2005–2015) a Muslim. Current president John Magufuli, who was sworn in on 5 November 2015 after winning the October 2015 presidential election, is Catholic.

Tanzania has some distinctive characteristics in terms of peace and unity, by comparison with other related communities in Africa (cf. Kobia 2003, 35). Despite Tanzania being one of the poorest nations of Africa, and third-poorest country in the world, the government tries to stimulate dialogue between different cultures and religions, and also tries to adapt its policies to the plural context. This dialogue has resulted into peace, unity, tranquillity, and relatively few ethnic and religious conflicts – an achievement that is partially the result of the consistent use of *Swahili* as a unifying language for the country in the last fifty years (cf. LHRC & ZLSC 2012, 3).

The late Mwalimu (teacher), Julius Kambarage Nyerere, the founding father of the nation, made the Swahili language (*Kiswahili) a unifying factor*; not only to Tanzania but to Africa as a whole. As a leader on the eve of independence in Tanzania in the late 1950s and early 1960s, he noted that the country's diversity (about 126 ethnic groups and languages) could potentially jeopardise Tanzanian unity and the struggle for independence. Though there are so many languages, no one language is spoken natively by a majority or even a large proportion of the population. Nyerere introduced *Swahili* as the first language of the prospective new nation.

Swahili is now an official language, next to English, in all official communication. It has been compulsory at every public school and college for more than 50 years. It is the official language in business, for national and international political affairs, and for instruction in primary schools. The country has also influenced the spread of Swahili to other jurisdictions across East Africa and beyond. Swahili is taught in various universities across the world, and is seen as an important language; the African Union recognises Swahili as an official language. In March 2015, President Jakaya Kikwete's administration announced that all formal education at primary and secondary level would be in Swahili, rather than English.

About 80% of the total population of 44,928,923 people (census 2012) speak Swahili (Tanzania National Statistics, population 2013, VI). The use of one common language is vital for Tanzania's state policy, and also helps to maintain social cohesion, stability and peace, essential elements of meaningful political freedom and social and economic change, as well as for the realisation of human rights culture in Tanzania. However, several human rights are still under threat, due to specific and persistent ethnic traditions.

Civil Rights, Tradition and Ethnicity in Tanzania

Although protected by law, and despite the unifying effect of Swahili, several civil rights in Tanzania are threatened by specific cultural patterns and ethnic traditions. Before elaborating on these threats, we briefly describe the protection of civil rights and liberties in Tanzanian law, as well as what we mean by tradition, culture and ethnicity.

Civil Rights and Liberties in Tanzanian Law

Tanzania is one of many countries around the world that accepts instruments of international human rights, which address civil rights and liberties. On the domestic level, the Bill of Rights guarantees civil rights and liberties. The Bill of Rights became part of the 1977 text of the *Constitution of the United Republic of Tanzania* through the Fifth Constitutional Amendment Act, in 1984 (Act No. 15 of 1984), more specifically in articles 12–29. Black's Law Dictionary defines civil liberties as 'freedom from undue governmental interference or restraint'. It refers to freedom of speech, freedom of the press, freedom of religion, freedom of association, and other liberties associated with the Bill of Rights (Black's Law Dictionary 2009, 280).

In Tanzania, civil rights refer to the individual rights of personal liberty, which are guaranteed by the *Constitution of the United Republic of Tanzania (originally 1977), more specifically in* part III, known as the *Bill of Rights [of Tanzania] (LHRC and ZLSC 2013, 14). The Basic Rights and Duties Enforcement Act (Act No. 33, 1994)* was enacted with the aim of providing procedures for the enforcement of the provisions provided under the Bill of Rights. In their essence, civil rights especially include the right to vote, the right to due process, and the right to equal protection under the law (Black's Law Dictionary 2009, 281).

Both civil rights and civil liberties fall under the category of negative rights (cf. LHRC and ZLSC 2013, 14). Negative rights entitle a person to refrain from doing an act that might harm the person that is entitled to these rights (Black's Law Dictionary 2009, 1437). The simple distinction between the two is that civil liberties are a protection against governmental actions and seek to restrict the government from abusing its powers, while civil rights refer to basic human rights to which every citizen should be entitled, as their birthright. Nevertheless, they also need support and protection from the government, which some stakeholders say they must still be granted.

Civil rights ensure a citizen's ability to participate in the civil and political life of the country. While civil liberties are protective in nature, civil rights on the other hand are a broader concept. The founding documents, such as the constitution, grant both of these. They are both basic legal rights that each citizen possesses, and which any person should possess. However, this distinction between civil liberties and civil rights may not be very clear, and can at times create confusion to stakeholders.

The newly proposed constitution draft of 2014 has preserved the provision for civil rights and liberties as well (Constitution Draft 2015, Part 4.1, Article 23–48). The constitutional referendum intended to take place in 2015 has been postponed several times. Tanzania has also signed the following treaties: *International Covenant on Civil and Political Rights (1966)*; the *African Charter on Peoples' and Human Rights (1981);* and the *UN Convention on the Rights of Persons with Disabilities (2006),* to mention a few (cf. LHRC and ZLSC 2013, 14). However, Tanzania faces a number of challenges when it comes to the implementation of these civil rights and liberties. In the next section, we briefly define other keywords, such as 'tradition', 'culture' and 'ethnicity'.

Tradition and Culture

There is a close relationship between tradition and culture. Tradition can be described as a long-established action or pattern of behaviour in a community or group of people, handed down from generation to generation (Fumbo 2013, 94). In another interpretation, Vanhoozer (1993, 9) defines tradition as an ongoing cultural interpretation of certain foundational works of the past. These foundational works can take the form of written texts or oral traditions that contain certain values and norms; or they may refer to symbols or rituals that express ideas and convictions that are very much alive in a certain community.

Culture, then, is considered the world of human meaning, and the total sum of people's works that express their beliefs, values and hopes, in an objective form. Culture refers to the vision constructed in a community of what it is to be fully human. Furthermore, Vanhoozer considers culture a way of sharing what people consider valuable ways of thought and of living. There is a relationship between current culture and tradition, insofar as culture interacts with the traditions of the past. Culture interacts with traditions by means of assimilation and accommodation. Vanhoozer's main idea is that in order to minimise gaps between (interpretations of) the past and the present, and in order to avoid alienation from the past, one should not only interpret the foundational works of the past in reference to their original meaning; one should also relate them to current experiences (Vanhoozer 1993, 9).

Considering the many definitions of culture and the scope of this study, we opt for a working definition, which interprets culture as a system of beliefs, practices, institutions and relationships that a community of people uses to identify themselves and distinguish themselves from other communities. It is exactly the strong social embedding of beliefs and practices that makes them widely acceptable, and therefore more problematic for human rights issues. In what follows, we will point to some threats to human rights in Tanzania related to (ethnic) traditions. However, this is not to present a pessimistic view on the human rights culture in Tanzania.

Traditions can change, by being interpreted from the point of view of human rights culture, and by relating foundational works and the current situation.

Ethnicity

Ethnicity, in this discourse, is defined as 'a sense of community' that can be described as the feeling of 'who and what we are'. This means that the commonalities between the individuals in a group are stressed, while the inter-individual differences are minimised (Schilder 1994, 3 and 9). Van der Ven et al. (2004, 340) define ethnicity by using a combination of primordialist and circumstantialist views, in which "[…] *the primordial rootedness in distinctive ethnic groups with myths, rites and customs from bygone times is reconstructed anew each time in accordance with changing circumstances, including the tension between individuality and collectivity and between collectivity and universality – both of which are likewise subject to constant change"*. Tajfel (1982, 2 and 21) defined a group on the basis of both internal and external criteria. Internal criteria refer to an individual's identification with the group, while external criteria refer to the fact that others perceive individuals as members of a common group, on the basis of characteristics they do not possess themselves. Both internal and external criteria are necessary for group identification. More specifically, Tajfel's social identity theory accounts for discourses of difference in social categorisation, patterns of (contra-)identification, and social comparison (cf. Sterkens 2007).

Social categorisation occurs when information about social groups is organised in such a way that similarities in categories and differences between categories are emphasized. In addition, similarities between individual out-group members are considered more important than in-group similarities; while inter-individual differences between out-group members are considered peripheral, and those of the in-group are emphasized. The out-group(s) are attributed uniformly shared conceptions, feelings and values, while the in-group is seen as more diversified (Tajfel 1982; Duckitt 1992). For what Hiebert (1992) calls 'shared values and traits', he shows that individuals within a group share certain distinctive cultural values and traits that symbolise their identity. In this kind of identity, several ethnic groups in a single society may share many traits; while in other cases, the cultural patterns of members of one ethnic group may differ greatly (Schilder 1994, 12). Another characteristic of ethnic groups, as described by Hiebert, is '*consciousness of kind'*, in which people may both identify with and differentiate themselves from 'others'. He says that these variations comprise a map of the society that helps everyone to organise his or her interpersonal relationships (Hiebert 1992, 276ff).

Identification points to the fact that every individual derives his or her self-image from "knowledge of his[/her] membership of a social group (or groups) together with the value and emotional significance attached to that membership" (Tajfel 1982, 255). Individuals strive for a positive self-image by attempting to join groups they evaluate positively, and reduce identification with negatively evaluated group(s), even when they belong to such group(s). Positive stereotypes are applied to oneself, while contra-identification refers to the resistance against generalised negative characteristics of both the out-groups and in-group (Brown 1995).

Social comparison contributes to positive self-esteem by evaluating the characteristics of the in-group favourably vis-à-vis relevant out-groups, as 'better', or 'of higher moral value'. Prejudice, therefore, is an attitude within the relative positioning of two or more groups, rather than related to specific characteristics of groups. This process of identification based on internal and external criteria explains why social groups also have *'ascribed status', as Hiebert (*1992*) calls it. Although* people often become members of ethnic groups and are anchored in a core of the local culture primarily by birth, they receive incentives for ongoing identification with the group. Often they also share myths of a common ancestry, particularly regarding place of origin or residence, paternal or maternal descent, clan ancestors, and historical heritage. These myths lead to an experience of a shared wide range of understanding and lifestyles in the wider society (Hiebert 1992, 276–278). Nevertheless, it is sometimes possible to shift between different cultural spheres, e.g. under political pressure (Schilder 1994, 3ff).

Despite free interaction between members of one ethnic group and those of another, roles and relationships are mainly coloured by ethnicity (Hiebert 1992, 279). C*onsciousness of kind* may result in *limited interaction between and among groups, exactly because of the differences, but also* because of conquests, migration, trade and assimilation by a dominant society (Hiebert 1992, 279; cf. Schilder 1994, 8). The possible trend is that ethnic consciousness either excludes outsiders from the group, or includes the group in society through ethnic assertion. This means that in order to claim autonomy from the wider society, while at the same time claiming incorporation into that wider society, it is necessary to employ the local culture (Schilder 1994, 12).

Threats to Human Rights in Present-day Tanzania

So far, we have shown that Tanzania does recognise international human rights as stipulated in the *Constitution of the United Republic of Tanzani*a (1977), as well as in other founding documents. But if so, what is it that hinders human rights culture in Tanzania? We will answer this question by looking at different instances of human rights abuse, in which we will opt for 'violence' as an indicator. 'Violence' is a complex word, and its meaning is strongly dependent on local culture. For instance, in some parts of Tanzania, beating your partner would not be considered illegitimate violence, but a way of disciplining a spouse, or even an indirect sign of love (Kassimoto 2008, 13). Yet, violence in essence is any act or attitude that is likely to result in physical, sexual, cultural, or psychological harm or suffering, or even death.

Ballard (1979, 13) distinguishes between structural, revolutionary, institutional, ideological, pathological and criminal violence. All these (interrelated) forms can be found in Tanzanian society to different degrees. In what follows, we focus on culture-related forms of violence that are highly problematic for human rights in Tanzania. More specifically, we focus on traditional family values and gender-role stereotypes; arranged (child) marriages; beliefs in witchcraft; extrajudicial killings and unjust law enforcement; and mob violence. These culture-related forms of violence are serious threats to civil human rights in Tanzania.

Traditional Family Values and Gender-Role Stereotypes

Many scholars have described similarities in African cultures with regard to family values, gender roles and marriage traditions. Most values in African culture arise from traditional religions, which have deep roots in people's lives. However, two issues are important threats to human rights: traditional family values, and gender-role stereotypes.

Mbiti (1991, 174–178) describes how traditional family values, and especially the expected role of women, have defined the hierarchical and patriarchal system in many African families. The hierarchy always follows duties and obligations on one hand, and rights and privileges on the other, and is dictated by the moral sense of the community. Essentially, the family's interests trump the interests of the individual; one's family is more important than one's own needs. Because individual family members are representatives of the family, inappropriate behaviour of an individual brings shame on the whole family; and indirectly, the wider clan.

Avoidance of family shame encourages group values and is a catalyst for family harmony. When family conflicts arise, help from outside the family is usually not considered necessary. Traditionally, families settle their quarrels internally or through the aid of informal communities related to the family. The fear of shame is also an important factor in parents forcing their daughters into marriage (see section "Arranged (child) marriages" below). The argument goes that having unmarried girls attending school increases the risk of extramarital pregnancies, which would bring shame on the family (Human Rights Watch 2014, 42).

In African culture, there is a tendency to minimise conflicts (Mbiti 1991, 178). Open displays of anger or conflict within the family are considered shameful. This is especially the case in a closed society in which people belong to related ethnic groups, such as that of the Ndali. These cultural values support the maintenance of family harmony, especially in the public sphere. In the privacy of one's home, physical violence towards children or one's spouse may be considered acceptable in order to maintain family harmony. In some instances, a man may even feel it is his right to 'discipline' his wife when he thinks she is not behaving or performing as he expects her to do. Human Rights Watch (2014, 35) reports that: "The 2010 Tanzania Demographic and Health Survey (TDHS) found that almost half (45%) of women aged 15–49 had experienced either physical or sexual violence. According to the study, 1 in 2 ever-married women aged 15–49 reported having experienced either one or a combination of emotional, physical, and sexual violence at the hands of their current or former husbands. Four in ten men agreed that wife beating is justified".

Acts of domestic violence are likely to be hidden, in order to protect the family's honour and prevent loss of face. Traditionally, children are expected to show respect to parents and elders by obeying them without question. This obligation refers to the concept of filial piety (Mbiti 1991, 174–178). It helps to establish a clear hierarchy in the family, where elders receive the greatest respect, wives respect their husbands, and children show respect to all those older than them.

The hierarchical structure of African families can reinforce the secrecy of domestic abuses. When marital conflicts arise, it is common for older relatives to work as mediators to resolve issues. Sometimes, it is considered a battered woman's obligation to endure abuse for the sake of the family. If she tries to leave her husband, she may even encounter abuse from other family members, or be denied the support of the wider family. Human Rights Watch reported that all the girls they had spoken to in this regard were told by their families to return to their husbands and tolerate the abuse. When girls do decide to leave, they become more vulnerable to both sexual and commercial exploitation (HRW 2014, 10.40).

A lot of field studies point to the fact that apart from bearing children and caring for them, women also take care of their families through different activities, both at home and at other places. In some cases in which polygamy is customary, the arrangement is that many wives are working tools of their husbands, on farms and at home. Women can also be inherited when the husband dies. Often, marital rape is not an offence in customary law (HRW 2014, 69). That these customary rules can have judicial consequences is clear from Human Rights Watch's report: "The Judicature and Application of Laws Act and the Local Customary Law (Declaration) (No. 4), Order of 1963 allow for the application of customary and Islamic laws in matters of marriage, divorce, guardianship, inheritance, and similar matters in Tanzania. The Marriage Act also allows courts to give regard to the customs of the community to which the parties belong when deciding matters of division of matrimonial property" (HRW 2014, 70).

A variety of activities not shared on an equal basis tend to create a gap between men and women, often resulting in the wife becoming (almost) entirely dependent on her husband. Eventually, this is where abuses arise. As mentioned, African families tend to be patriarchal in structure. This is abundantly clear in the initiation (*unyago*) teachings, in which we find three forms of obedience for a women: before marriage she obeys her father, after marriage she obeys her husband, and as a widow she obeys her oldest son (Mbiti 1973). The expectation is that women are the nurturers – those who care for their children, husbands and parents. Therefore, women are always appropriated at the mercy of men, to achieve men's goals. So when a man considers only his own self-interest important, this undoubtedly affects the well-being of his wife.

Men are given greater educational and occupational privileges in most African communities, as well as more freedom. Women, on the other hand, remain in a disadvantaged position. If a family lacks the financial means to send all their children to school, girls are likely to be the first to be withdrawn by their parents. Often the community will consider education and motherhood to be incompatible (HRW 2014, 46–50).

One of many consequences of a lack of education is the fantasies surrounding contraception that are told to girls by their boyfriends, or even by those in their environment as a whole, resulting in numerous early pregnancies (HRW 2014, 42–43). But by routinely conducting pregnancy tests, many schools violate girls' right to equality, privacy and autonomy. When a girl appears to be pregnant, there is a good chance that she will be expelled from school (HRW 2014, 3 and 46). The Ministry of Education and Vocational Tool Kit of 2013 even recommend these tests, in order to decrease the number of pregnant girls in schools. In 2012, 2433 girls left primary school due to pregnancy, and 4705 girls dropped out of secondary school (HRW 2014, 49).

Men, on the other hand, are expected to be providers for and protectors of their families. They are also obliged to keep the family honour and pass on the family name. This preference for men is inevitable in a place where custom-related law gives the male child the right to the family inheritance after his father's death. As Sengo puts it, the logic used in this kind of arrangement is that the son is always the next father to all his sisters, on the father's behalf (Fumbo 2013). In practice, this may result in a women or girl ending up penniless when she is abandoned by the men who ought to be responsible for her wellbeing.

In the end, the shame of divorce and the potential loss of one's family support are often barriers to leaving an abusive husband. Women also fall victim when they fail to produce sons. Unfortunately, infertility is a common problem, and as should be clear by now, this is an enormous threat to women (cf. Mbiti 1973).

Traditional views on gender roles and the family tend to increase the stigma associated with divorce and domestic abuse, and therefore make it harder for victims to seek help or even to admit there is a problem. It should be clear by now that these forms of traditional and cultural compliances are severe violations of human rights. They may be considered responsible for the acceptance of some kinds of abusive behaviour, and are the cause of double standards in Tanzanian society.

Arranged (Child) Marriages

Arranged marriages are another form of human rights violation. Article 16(2) of the UDHR is very clear in this respect: "Marriage shall be entered into only with the free and full consent of the intending spouses". Sadly, social and financial pressure are the order of the day. Katapa (1994, 76-95) reports that in the *Wakurya* tradition, the bride's 'worth' in arranged marriages ranges from 15 to 25 cows, which are paid to the parents of these teenage girls by the groom (or his family). In the *Wasukuma* tradition, the number of cows paid varies according to the colour of the girl; the lighter her colour, the higher her worth. A girl's worth may also be dependent on whether or not she underwent genital mutilation. The dowry is paid to the bride's family in the form of money, cattle or other livestock, or a combination of both.

Arranged marriages do not necessarily require the agreement of the (teenage) girls themselves; rather, they are informed by their parents, or by their future husband. Therefore, the arrangements are usually made between the girl's parents and her husband-to-be. In fact, the dowry payment creates the impression that a wife is owned by her husband, which strongly increases the likelihood of domestic violence.

Most of these girls simply cannot leave, because they lack the financial means to repay the dowry. However, for some women such a marriage is an escape from an abusive workplace. Others enter a relationship because they are pregnant, or in need of food. According to the Human Rights Watch (2014, 34): "In Tanzania, 4 out of 10 girls are married before their 18th birthday. A study by the United Nations Population Fund (UNFPA) estimated that 37% of Tanzanian women aged 20–24 years were first married or in union before the age of 18, between 2000 and 2011." The Human Rights Watch have even documented cases in which girls as young as seven were married off.

These facts become all the more serious when one takes into account that some of these women even face female genital mutilation at the age of 10 to 15, as a rite before marriage. This happens even though the Sexual Offences Special Provisions Act (SOSPA) of 1998 prohibits female genital mutilation for girls under 18 (Human Rights Watch 2014, 36). UNICEF (2014, 2–3) estimates the number of girls and women in Tanzania who have undergone female genital mutilation to be 7.9 million. The report adds that 92% of Tanzanian women want these practices to end.

The young age at which these girls marry makes them probable victims of child labour, which is sometimes even considered a proper preparation for married life. Furthermore, married women are often denied education, giving them very low wage prospects. These factors contribute to their vulnerability in Tanzanian society. In their relationships, women face violence, and even marital rape. If they leave, they receive very little support, if any. In addition, many of them are too young to be pregnant; in general, these women are forced into adulthood before they are mentally and physically ready. As a consequence, some girls even contemplate suicide. It is clear that by allowing these practices, the national government violates international law, which recognises human rights (Human Rights Watch 2014, 62; Nour 2008, 12).

Belief in Witchcraft in Relation to Civil Rights Violations

Witchcraft is widely practiced in African societies, and precedes colonial times, although it varies in different countries (Mesaki 2010, 132–138). The belief in and practice of witchcraft is usually a source of justification for why bad things happen to certain people, leading to accusations against individuals. These accusations usually lead to abuse, and a violation of human rights – more particularly, the right to life, liberty and security; the right to property; and the prohibition against torture – and has led to social and economic marginalization. The members of society most affected are women, elderly people, children, and the poor.

In recent years there has been an increase in violations of the right to life, due to witchcraft-related murders and tortures, including people being buried alive, as a result of unfounded allegations (LHRC and ZLSC 2012, 34). The persecution of people who are suspected to perform witchcraft is brutal and degrading. People accused of such practices are usually punished by mob 'justice'. According to LHRC statistics, a survey from the Police Force indicates that in 2012, 630 people were killed due to witchcraft beliefs, whereas in 2013, witchcraft-related killings claimed the lives of 765 people, of whom 505 were women (LHRC and ZLSC 2013, 36). These killings have increasingly targeted older women (Human Rights Watch 2014, 35f; UNFPA 2012, 95 and 111).

There are also reports of the killing of people with albinism, or the removal of some of their limbs to be sold. Since 2000, 72 killings of persons with albinism have been reported (LHRC and ZSLC 2013, 46). Amputated limbs are held to possess magical powers, making the non-albino rich. A mother who gives birth to an albino child is believed to be cursed, through sorcery, having had an affair, or touching another albino (Southern Africa's Children, African Witchcraft). This despite the fact that Tanzania has legislation that is meant to prevent these kinds of abuses and violations of rights resulting from witchcraft. The *Witchcraft Act (1928)* (Cap. 18 [R.E. 2002]) is an example. However, the Witchcraft Act has not been able to solve the challenges posed by the practice of witchcraft. In 1992, the Nyalali Commission even went as far as to recommend abandoning the Witchcraft Act, and argued that "*…the law dates back to colonial rule and it has remained to date. The law is useless; it should be repealed*" (Nyalali Report, 1994; Cimpric 2010).

This study shows that in Tanzania, witchcraft is a social phenomenon that has led to a violation of human rights, thereby causing the death of a large number of people. The legal system has itself failed to halt the lethal consequences of witchcraft. Moreover, the *Witchcraft Act (1928)* seems to be too out of date to cope with the current situation, and even appears to promote the existence of witchcraft (LHRC and ZLSC 2013, 36). Therefore, a need for new efforts is inevitable, if there is to be any hope of remedying the current situation – including proper education on the unacceptability of some forms of witchcraft, and the bringing to justice of people who are suspected of these practices.

Extrajudicial Killings and Unjust Law Enforcement

In recent years, there has allegedly been an increase in the number of extrajudicial killings by law enforcement bodies of the country, in disregard of the legal processes. The country's political leadership has been accused of doing very little to combat these unlawful acts (LHRC and ZLSC 2013, 20–21). By extrajudicial killings, we mean murders that are supported or committed by the staff of state departments, such as the police, the army, prison warders and paramilitary forces. Police, Sungusungu – a justice organization established by the Sukuma and Nyamwezi ethnic groups that regularly uses excessive violence - and the Tanzania Peoples Defence Force (TPDF) killed 23 people in the first half of 2013 alone (LHRC and ZLCS 2013, 23). Sadly, some traditional community councils from several parts of the country – mostly the *Sukumaland,* in the Shinyanga, Mwanza, Geita and Bariadi districts – are responsible for unjust and sometimes brutal law enforcement, without any form of proper trial. In *Sukumaland*, the ruling council is known as the *Dagashida,* and is composed of only male members of the community. The *Dagashida* has been operating in the *Sukumaland* for many years. Originally, the *Dagashida* council handled only issues to do with pasture and agriculture (Suleyman 2013). Its task is to set customary rules, including sanctions. Some see it as an important and respected assembly.

Since the Dagashida is responsible for natural resources, it deals with violations to do with these issues. It is no secret that punishments can be severe (Nkonya 2008, 11,134–138). The local police report that the *Dagashida* has been responsible for several deaths, resulting from disputes over inheritances and land, belief in witchcraft, and mob violence. On the other hand, some NGOs oppose the Dagashida on issues such as access to natural resources, sanctions on the blocking of cattle tracks, and tree tenure. Mlenge (1994) notes further that some NGOs have succeeded in having women included in the Dagashida, and they therefore praise the Dagashida institution for the emancipation of women and local ethnic groups.

In some cases, politicians are accused of condoning the actions of the *Dagashida* councils for political gain. However, the report states that the Regional Police Commander (RPC) of Simiyu, ACP (name withheld), denies these allegations and accuses the Dagashida councils of being criminals who exploit the traditions of the Wasukuma in the region for personal gain, whether political or economic (LHRC and ZLSC 2013). Nevertheless, this does not change the facts. Furthermore, statistics reveal that 117 people lost their lives in this way in the Simiyu Region from June 2012 to June 2013 (Matandiko 2013).

Mob Violence

In 2013, a severe inter-religious conflict occurred in the Geita region. The conflict arose from differences between Christians and Muslims, with each group claiming the right to slaughter animals such as cows and goats for public consumption. Tanzania has witnessed an increase in incidences of mob violence over the past decade. In 2013 alone, 1669 people were killed through mob violence in Tanzania (LHRC and ZLSC 2013, 28–29). Different explanations are given for the rise of mob violence: a poor criminal justice system, a lack of proper evidence, the non-appearance of witnesses in courts of law, ignorance of the law by the public, lack of trust towards the police, and insufficient funding to conduct the investigation properly. The most important reason is believed to be the failure and collapse of the country's criminal justice system, which in turn has resulted in mistrust of this institution (cf. LHRC and ZLSC 2013, 23).

Conclusion

From what has been said, it is clear that Tanzania is far from the full realisation of the civil human rights it otherwise fully (legally) recognises. The founding documents of the republic have been under discussion and revision ever since Tanzania's independence, contributing to confusion about though little awareness of human rights. A genuine commitment from local leaders and political will in the national government, as well as from civil society, could make a difference in Tanzania on the delicate issue of human rights. It is encouraging that Tanzanian society remains open for dialogue, with both local groups and international bodies, for a better understanding of civil human rights.

But the bumpy road to more human rights awareness is explained by more than just economic deprivation and political hitches. Culture-related forms of violence are a real threat to human rights as well. More specifically, we referred to traditional family values and gender-role stereotypes; arranged (child) marriages; belief in witchcraft; extrajudicial killings and unjust law enforcement; and mob violence, as important cultural phenomena that threaten human rights in Tanzania. Those who suffer most from human rights abuse (i.e. women, children, the disabled and the poor) often lack a voice to protest against it.

It is often suggested that the unifying language of Swahili could contribute to democracy, and could make a difference to human rights awareness. Such a unifying language could help to overcome intergroup differences and shed new light on locally embedded traditions and customs that are harmful to human rights. A shared language could overcome cultural diversities and result in more legitimacy for human rights in Tanzania. Through Swahili, an open dialogue between different groups, as well as with surrounding countries, is more possible. Recently, the government has made much effort to stimulate the spread of Swahili throughout the country, as well as in East Africa and beyond (though often at the cost of English). Whether this will contribute significantly to human rights remains to be seen.

References

Ballard, P. H. (1979). *A Christian perspective on violence*. London: British Council of Churches.
Brown, R. (1995). *Prejudice. Its social psychology*. Oxford: Blackwell.
Cimpric, A. (2010). *Children accused of witchcraft. An anthropological study of contemporary practices in Africa*. Dakar: Unicef.
Constitution of the United Republic of Tanzania. (1977).
DIIS Report. (2006).
Duckitt, J. (1992). The social psychology of prejudice New York/London.

Fumbo, C. D. (2011). The interface between human rights and the African concept of community, with special reference to the Ndali people of Tanzania. *Teofilo Kisanji University Journal, 2*(1), 1–15.
Fumbo, C. D. (2013). The Moravian church response to domestic abuses among couples in Tanzania: A case study of Mbeya municipality, with special reference to (Wa-)Ndali and (Wa-) Nyakyusa traditions (comparison and contrast), PhD dissertation, The Open University, Tanzania.
Garner, B. A. (Ed.). (2009). In *Black's law Dictionary* (9th ed). West: Thomson Reuters.
Hiebert, P. G. (1992). *Cultural anthropology* (2nd ed.). Grand Rapids: Baker Book House.
Human Rights Watch. (2014). No way out. Child marriage and human rights abuses in Tanzania. New York [etc.]: HRW.
Kassimoto, T. (2008). *A Handbook on Gender Studies in Education: Gender equality, Development and Peace* (n.p.)
Katapa, R. S. (1994). Arranged marriage. In Z. Tumbo-Masabo & R. Liljestrom (Eds.), *Chelewa, Chelewa the dilemma of teenage girls* (pp. 76–95). Stockholm: The Scandinavian Institute of African Studies.
Kobia, S. (2003). The courage to hope. World Council of Churches: The roots for a new vision and the calling of the Church in Africa.
Legal and Human Rights Center [LHRC], & Zanzibar Legal Services Center [ZLSC]. (2012). Tanzania human Rights report 2012. Dar es Salaam/Zanzibar: LHRC& ZlSC.
Legal and Human Rights Center [LHRC] & Zanzibar Legal Services Center [ZLSC]. (2013). Tanzania Human Rights Report 2013. Dar es Salaam/Zanzibar: LHRC& ZlSC.
Matandiko, K. (2013). *Mauaji ya kutisha mkoani Simiyu* Mwananchi Newspaper 10 Sept 2013.
Mbiti, J. S. (1970). *Concepts of God in Africa*. London: S.P.C.K.
Mbiti, J. S. (1973). *Love and marriage*. London: Longman.
Mbiti, J. S. (1991). *African religion and philosophy* (2 nd Ed ed.). Oxford: Heinemann.
Mesaki, S. (2010). Review of witchcraft and the law in Tanzania. *International Journal of Sociology and Anthropology, 1*(8), 132–138.
Mlenge, W. (1994). Revival of Customary Landcare. *Ileia Newsletter, 10*(2), 9.
Nkonya, L. K. (2008). *Rural water Management in Africa, the impact of customary institutions in Tanzania*. New York: Cambria Press.
Nour, N. (2008). An Introduction to Maternal Mortality. *Journal of Obstetrics and Gynecology, 1*(2), 12.
Pew Research Center [PEW]. (2014). *Global religious diversity*. Washington, DC: Pew.
Schilder, K. (1994). Quest for self-esteem. State, Islam, and Mundang ethnicity in northern Cameroon: African studies centre research series.
Sterkens, C. (2007). Reflection on the limits of 'religious' explanations of violence. A social psychological perspective. In: Timmerman, C. & Hutsebaut, D. et. al. (eds.). Faith-based radicalism. Christianity, Islam and Judaism between constructive activism and destructive fanaticism (Gods, Humans and Religions 10) (pp. 181–190). Brussels/Oxford [etc.]: Peter Lang.
Suleyman, M. (2013). Are they the law unto themselves? The Citizen newspaper, 8th Feb 2013.
Tajfel, H. (1982). *Human groups and social categories*. Cambridge: Cambridge University Press.
UNFPA [United Nations Population Fund]. (2012). *Ageing in the twenty-first century*. London/ New York: UNFPA: A celebration and a challenge.
United Republic of Tanzania, Population Distribution by Age and Sex. (2013).
Van der Ven, J. A., Dreyer, J. S., & Pieterse, H. J. C. (2004). Is there a god of human rights? The complex relationship between human rights and religion. In *A south African case*. Leiden: Brill.
Vanhoozer, K. J. (1993). The world well staged? Theology, culture, and hermeneutics. In D. A. Carson & J. D. Woodbridge (Eds.), *God and culture* (pp. 1–30). Grand Rapids: William B. Eerdmans Publishing Company.

Index

A
African Traditional Religion (ATR), 179, 180, 191
Age, 28, 35, 44, 46, 49, 51, 54, 56, 70, 71, 78, 81–83, 102, 104, 105, 128, 146, 151, 164, 167, 168, 171, 172, 184, 186, 188, 191, 193, 200, 205, 207–210, 225
Albinism, 226
Anglican, 162, 164, 165, 167, 172
Assembly, freedom of, 92, 101, 102, 107, 111, 113, 115, 116
Authoritarian, authoritarianism, 7, 11, 62, 69, 77, 85, 96
Authoritarian, authoritarianism, right-wing authoritarianism, 8, 63, 68, 69, 77–81, 84, 86, 102, 105, 111, 115
Autonomy, 6, 9, 19, 20, 23, 25, 63, 65, 67, 221, 224

B
Basileia [kingdom] of God, 99, 100
Belief, 3, 7, 9, 10, 18, 22–25, 28, 30, 32, 34–36, 38, 39, 42–52, 54, 55, 70, 71, 73, 78, 80, 84, 85, 102, 110, 111, 125, 142, 145, 150, 154, 157, 158, 160, 172, 180, 181, 187–189, 192, 193, 195, 199, 203–205, 207–209, 225, 227, 228
Benedict XVI, 8, 96
Bill of Rights, 218
Boko Haram, 178, 182

C
Catechism of the Catholic Church, 23, 117
Categorisation, social, 220
Catholic, 3–7, 10, 23, 24, 71, 92–99, 101, 102, 104, 107–109, 112, 113, 115, 117, 123–129, 132–138, 162, 164, 165, 167, 172, 186, 187, 191, 200–202, 205, 207, 217
Catholic, catholic positions, 94
Catholic, Catholicism, 5, 8, 25, 92, 94, 123–125, 137, 180
Child labour, 225
Chile, 122–127, 129–136, 138
Christianity, 19, 22, 57, 122–124, 179–181, 183, 188, 189
Church of Norway, 142
Civil human rights, 127, 129–133, 135, 138, 215–217, 219–228
Civil liberties, 216, 218
Civil rights, comparison, social, 221
Civil society, 68, 97, 116, 124, 143, 154, 228
Clergy, 6, 93, 124, 125
Cognition, 183
Colonial, 10, 11, 123, 182, 216, 225, 226
Colonial times, 182, 225
Colonialism, 13, 14, 181
Communication, 97, 123, 217
Community, 4, 6, 7, 9, 10, 12, 14, 21, 22, 39, 58, 65, 68, 69, 86, 124, 146, 150, 158, 162, 163, 173, 178, 179, 215, 219, 220, 222–224, 227

H.-G. Ziebertz, C. Sterkens (eds.), *Religion and Civil Human Rights in Empirical Perspective*, Religion and Human Rights 2, DOI 10.1007/978-3-319-59285-5

Concepts, theological, 99
Concordat, between Italy and Holy See, 97
Consciousness of kind, 220, 221
Consensus
cultural, 5, 14
moral, 1
political, 2
Cosmological exclusivism, 181
Cultural conformity, 105, 111, 113, 116, 128

D
Dagashida, 227
De-institutionalisation, 125
Democracy, 11, 22, 64, 97, 98, 124–126, 149, 182, 228
Dignity
concepts of, 62
dignity, human, 9, 10, 18–25, 27–33, 35, 37–46, 48–52, 54–56, 58, 62–71, 73–86, 95
inherent dignity, 19–21, 24, 25, 31, 36, 37, 49–56, 66–68, 71, 73–75, 78, 80–86, 178
of identity, 66, 67
of merit, 66, 67, 70, 71, 73, 74, 77, 78, 83–86
models of, 63–69
in philosophy of health-care ethics, 64–67
of social stature, 31, 37, 44
religious arguments for, 64, 67, 68
in Russian Orthodox Church, 25, 64, 66–68, 85
Divine law, 24, 94, 95, 98
Dowry, 24, 225

E
Education in religion, 145, 147, 148
Emotions, 18, 25, 26
Empathy, 2, 13, 25, 26, 32, 36, 39, 40, 44, 46, 47, 49, 51, 52, 54, 55, 57, 62, 63, 70, 71, 73, 76–78, 83, 84, 86, 102, 105, 111–113, 117
England, 92, 161–163, 165, 170, 173
Ethnicity, 182, 183, 197, 203, 205, 207, 208, 216, 218–221
Ethnicity, in Tanzania, 216, 218–221
Ethno-religious identity, 182, 183
Evangelical, 6, 7, 183, 184, 196, 210

F
Faith, 4–7, 42, 43, 46, 49, 57, 105, 111, 112, 122, 145, 150, 152–154, 159, 163, 184, 186, 188
Faith schools, 163
Family socialisation
education of the parents, 71, 77–79, 81, 82
religiosity of the parents, 71, 77–79, 81, 82
Foundational, 1, 2, 4, 5, 7, 8, 10, 12, 13, 21, 23, 24, 219, 220
Francis, Pope, 5, 8, 96
Fraternity, 3, 122
Freedom of religion, 5, 7, 76, 77, 79, 92, 94, 101, 102, 105, 107–109, 111–113, 115–117, 132, 136–138, 142, 147, 157, 158, 160, 162, 170, 171, 177, 178, 185–196, 198–200, 202–210, 216–218
public role of religion in society, 68, 73, 75–80, 84, 132
religion and change, 76–79, 84
religion and spirituality, 76–79
Functional differentiation, 122, 123

G
Gender, 28, 35, 47, 51, 52, 54, 56, 102, 105, 112, 113, 115, 128, 144, 145, 149, 151, 154, 160, 186, 208, 222–224, 228
God, 2, 4–6, 8, 9, 19, 21–24, 32, 36, 38, 42, 45, 46, 48–54, 57, 64–66, 85, 86, 94, 95, 99–102, 105, 111, 125, 144, 145, 150–154, 181
Gregory XVI, 93

H
Habermas, Jürgen, 96, 99, 116, 122
High school, 104, 146
Hijab, 159, 182, 186–189, 192–195, 199, 200, 202–210
Homosexuals, 92, 102, 105, 107, 115, 117, 130–138
Human dignity
concepts of, 36, 37, 52, 55, 68, 74
in philosophy of health-care ethics, 64–67
in Russian Orthodox Church teaching, 25, 63–67, 85
models of, 63–69
of identity, 66, 67

of merit, 66, 67, 70, 71, 73, 74, 77–79, 84, 86
of social stature, 31, 37, 44
religious arguments for, 64, 67, 68
Human rights
cultural, 215–228
first generation, 3, 4, 11–14, 92, 98
foundation, 1, 2, 10, 96
political, 3
secular/religious approaches toward human rights, 116, 117, 134–137
Human rights, declarations
The African Charter on Human and People's Rights (1981), 3, 178
The Declaration on the Rights of Persons Belonging to National or Ethnic, Religious, and Linguistic Minorities (1992), 3
European Convention for the Protection of Human Rights and Fundamental Freedoms (1950), 3
European Union Charter of Fundamental Rights, 22, 158
International Covenant on Civil and Political Rights (UN, 1966), 93, 158, 178, 184, 219
International Covenant on Economic, Social, and Cultural Rights (UN, 1966), 3, 178
United Nations Declaration on the Elimination of All Forms of Intolerance and Discrimination Based on Religion or Belief (UN, 1981), 3
Universal Declaration, 93, 95, 98
Universal Declaration of Human Rights (UDHR, 1948), 2, 3, 21, 92, 157, 178
Humanist, humanitarian, 3, 5, 7, 10, 11, 13

I
Image of God, 6, 23, 64, 66, 99–101
Immigrants, 57, 92, 96, 144, 150
Incarnation, 23, 66
Indigenous African religion, 180, 181
Individual
belief, 187–189, 191–193, 195, 203–205, 207–209
identity, 179
Individualism, 14, 124, 125
Individualistic, 96
Influence over public opinion, 128
International Covenant on Civil and Political, 3, 20, 21, 93, 158, 184, 219
Islam, 8–10, 13, 14, 53, 125, 179–181, 183, 187, 189
Italian Constitution, 95, 101, 102

J
John Paul II, 96
John XXIII, 4, 95
Justification, 1, 23, 24, 98–101, 116, 225

K
Killings, extrajudicial, 222, 226, 227

L
Laicite, 159
Latin American, 123, 125, 137
Law, 1, 3–5, 11–13, 19, 22, 24, 56, 57, 94, 96–98, 101, 117, 142, 158–160, 162, 183, 184, 216, 218, 222–228
Law, divine, 24, 94, 95, 98
Leo XIII, 4, 94
LGBT rights, 99
Liberal
democracies, 64, 94, 122
societies, 99, 122
Likeness of God, 23
Limitations placed on the public manifestation of religion or belief, 158
Lutheran church, 150

M
Magna Carta, 92
Marriage, arranged, 222, 224, 225, 228
Marzano, Marco, 97, 98, 116
Migration, background, 33, 36, 41, 45–51, 55
Military government, 124
Model of personality, 164
Moral consensus, 1
Morality, 3, 4, 8, 19, 25, 26, 32, 124, 190, 192, 193, 196, 197, 203–207, 209
Multicultural, 144, 150, 154
Multiculturalism
attitudes towards, 62, 70
openness towards, 63, 83
Muslim, 3, 9, 10, 28, 29, 45, 48, 50, 71, 159–161, 166, 171, 178, 180–183, 186, 187, 191, 193, 194, 200–202, 205, 207, 208, 210, 216, 217, 227

N
National bans in place on some religious dress and symbols, 159
National culture, 75, 128
Natural law, natural rights, 1–4, 13, 24, 94, 96, 117
Naturalism, 20
Ndali, 222
Neo-liberalism, 125
Nigeria, 178–186, 192–194, 196, 198, 201, 202, 208, 210, 211
Non-foundationalist, 2
Norway, 141, 144, 146, 149–153, 155, 159, 161

O
Orthodox, Christian, 13

P
Paul VI, 95
Pentecostal, 6, 126, 180
Perception of conflicts in society, 188, 190, 191, 193, 197, 198, 204–210
Perception of religion in society, 187, 188, 190–192, 196, 197, 204–209
Personality, 63, 64, 69, 102, 164, 165, 171, 172
Pius IX, 93, 94
Pius VI, 93
Pius VII, 93
Pius XI, 94
Pius XII, 95
Pluralisation, pluralism, 9, 98, 105, 111, 113, 142, 160, 179, 180
Political
  political consensus, 2
  political non-interference, 186–188, 192–195, 198, 200–208, 210
Politics, 94, 122–124, 180, 182, 194
Prayer
  prayer rooms in public schools, 141
  in public schools, 186–188, 194, 195, 199–203, 205–208
Prejudice, 143, 150, 162, 164, 183, 221
Privatisation, 97, 124–126, 136
Pronouncements of the Roman Catholic Curia
  dialogue and proclamation, 100
  Dignitatis Humanae, 23, 95
  Evangelium Vitae, 96
  Gaudium et spes, 4, 95
  Libertas, 6, 94
  Mirari Vos, 93, 96
  Non abbiamo bisogno, 94
  Pacem in Terris, 4, 95
  Quanta Cura, 94
  Quod aliquantum, 93
  Rerum Novarum, 94
  Syllabus Errorum, 94
Protestant, Protestantism, 3, 5–7, 10, 24, 97, 126–129, 132–136, 138, 180, 186, 187, 191, 200–202, 205, 207, 217
Public
  public prophetic voice, 128
  public sphere, 5, 96, 99, 122–126, 137, 141–155, 222

R
Reformation, 6, 24, 181
Religion
  distance, 122
  function of, 62, 75–77, 81, 82, 102, 105, 111, 113, 130–134, 136, 137, 187, 190, 207
  public rule, 108
  as a purely private matter, 122
  religions promote more involvement, 122
  roles of, 127–129, 131–136, 138
  and society, 71, 73, 75–82, 84, 86, 87, 93, 102, 105, 116, 137
Religion, freedom of, 142, 157–168, 171–173, 178–211
Religiosity, 28, 62, 63, 68–71, 73, 76–87, 144, 145, 150, 152–155, 164, 168, 171, 172, 183, 193
Religious
  affiliation, 29, 32, 44–46, 48–51, 55, 68, 108, 116, 125–127, 129, 132–136, 138, 159, 164–166, 168–172, 180, 216
  belonging, 32, 69–71, 73, 77, 78, 81, 84, 85, 102, 104, 186–188, 191, 192, 197, 200–202, 205, 207–209
  clothing, 141, 158–168, 170–173
  diversity, 158–168, 170–173, 180–182
  education, 70, 78, 86, 145–148, 151, 153, 154, 165, 173, 211
  expressions, 94, 95, 109, 130, 142, 143, 147, 152, 154, 160, 179
  freedom, 5, 102, 105, 107, 109, 111–113, 116, 117, 137, 142, 158–168, 170–173, 178–200, 202–211
  practice, 97, 102, 105, 108, 116, 122, 123, 125–138, 142, 143, 147, 172, 193, 204
  rights, 6, 130, 131, 133–138, 142
  symbols, 141–144, 147, 148, 154, 155, 158–168, 170–173, 194

Religious affiliation, 104, 117, 127, 129, 132–136, 160, 164, 169, 172, 216
Rights, 1, 18, 64, 92, 122, 141, 157, 178, 215, 216
Rights of
to freedom of religion, 5, 94, 105, 117, 157, 158, 178, 185, 186, 199, 202, 203
of homosexuals, including the protection from discrimination, 102, 105, 107, 117, 130
of women, 9, 105, 107, 108, 110, 111, 113, 117, 130–135, 137, 138
Rights, gay and sexual rights, 107, 108, 111–113, 115–117
Right-wing authoritarianism, 69–71, 76, 77
Russian Orthodox Church, 7, 8, 25, 64, 66, 67, 71, 79, 81, 82, 85

S
Sect, 178, 180, 181
Secular, 5, 6, 8, 10, 62, 64, 65, 67, 68, 76, 97–99, 101, 116, 123, 144, 155, 182, 184, 216
Secular state, 184
Secularism, 8, 13, 109, 210
Secularization, 96, 122, 136, 137, 150
Sex, 9, 28, 35, 36, 44, 46, 47, 49, 51, 52, 54, 56, 58, 70, 71, 78, 79, 81, 101, 164–166, 168–171, 186–188, 191, 200, 202, 203, 205, 207, 209
Sexual abuse, 125
Signs of the times, 95
Sin, 19, 23, 24, 64–67
Social capital
bonding, 143
bridging, 143, 144, 149
Religion as social capital, 143
Social trust, 143–145, 149, 152–155
Socialisation, 27–30, 34–36, 42–51, 53–55, 69, 71, 73, 77, 78, 80, 81, 83–86, 88, 102, 103, 105, 112, 113, 115, 193, 211
Sovereignty, 123
Spiritual service, 105, 111, 113, 115, 116
Status, ascribed, 221
Stereotypes, gender-role, 222–224, 228
Subsystems, 123

T
Tolerance, 141, 143, 144, 151, 155, 160
Transcendence, 20, 179, 181
Trust
in religion, 32, 36, 39, 44–46, 48–52, 54, 102, 105, 111, 113, 116, 188–190, 192, 196, 198–200, 203–206, 208, 209

U
United Nations (UN), 2, 3, 11, 20, 21, 95, 96, 157, 178, 225
Urbinati, Nadia, 97, 98, 116

V
Values, family, 222–224
Violence
domestic, 223, 225
mob, 222, 227, 228
physical, 222
sexual, 222

W
Wales, 162, 163, 165, 170, 173
Wearing and displaying religious clothing and symbols, 158
Witchcraft, 222, 225–228
Women's rights, 14, 107, 110–113, 115–117, 137
Worldview, 21, 29, 38, 42, 53, 70, 123, 124, 157, 161, 170, 181, 189

Y
Youth, 17–19, 21–34, 36–39, 41–50, 52–57, 62–86, 123, 125–129, 131–133, 137, 138, 142, 151, 177, 180, 185, 186

Z
Zanzibar, 216

MIX
Papier aus verantwortungsvollen Quellen
Paper from responsible sources
FSC® C105338

If you have any concerns about our products,
you can contact us on
ProductSafety@springernature.com

In case Publisher is established outside the EU,
the EU authorized representative is:
Springer Nature Customer Service Center GmbH
Europaplatz 3, 69115 Heidelberg, Germany

Printed by Libri Plureos GmbH
in Hamburg, Germany